D1744087

Electric Trains in Britain

Below: In 1974 completion of the Euston-Glasgow electrification transformed rail travel between London, the Midlands and Scotland. Class 86/2 No 86.245 hums in casual style with the 13.45 Euston-Glasgow in June 1975 through the Lune Gorge, once the scene of much impressive effort by steam locomotives and thudding of diesel engines.
/Peter J. Robinson

Previous page: Class 310 emu No 047 leaves Watford Tunnel on a Rugby-Euston stopping service.
/Brian Morrison

Electric Trains
in Britain

B.K.Cooper

LONDON

IAN ALLAN LTD

Contents

First published 1979

ISBN 0 7110 0972 4

All rights reserved. No part of this book may be
reproduced or transmitted in any form or by any
means, electronic or mechanical, including photo-
copying, recording or by any information storage
and retrieval system, without permission from the
Publisher in writing.

© Ian Allan Ltd 1979

Published by Ian Allan Ltd, Shepperton, Surrey,
and printed in the United Kingdom by
Ian Allan Printing Ltd.

Preface

The journalist who admits to knowledge of a specialised subject, however slight, is likely to be thankfully hailed as an expert by his colleagues whose interests are different. In this way I was called upon soon after World War II to edit the electric traction section of a technical journal, and soon became aware of the dearth of books on the subject. Fortunately a good library was at hand and I remember first reading explanations of series/parallel control and automatic acceleration in a book from an American publisher. Often the treatment of electrical equipment in descriptions of rolling stock published in this country were perfunctory. Relegated to the final paragraphs, between notes on the upholstery and the list of principal contractors, this essential apparatus tended to be sketched in a series of stereotyped phrases which were by no means self-explanatory. What on earth was bridge transition, or field diversion, or a camshaft controller? Sometimes one came across that obnoxious phrase 'the well known figure-of-eight circuit'. Well known to whom? Probably, one suspected, not to the writer who used the term. Later I was employed in the electrical industry where these things were explained to me by patient experts to whom I have been grateful ever since. It became apparent that electric traction offered an unexpectedly wide field of interest, some of which I hope to have communicated in this book. It is also a fast-expanding field, broadening in directions that could not have been foreseen 25 years ago. Not only can the traction engineer today improve on what he has done in the past, but he can do things previously beyond his reach.

Classic control systems and new electronic circuitry will exist side by side for a long time to come. One needs to know something of both. In the early days of semiconductors my colleagues on an engineering paper used to say 'if it's transistorised it must be good', a sceptical comment on the effusive publicity handouts of the period. Today the words 'thyristor control' or 'chopper control' fall upon the ears with equal persistence and it is time to find out what they involve. 'If it's thyristorised it may be good' but not simply because of notchless acceleration. Control engineering has become an art in itself with widening ramifications. This is a formidable subject. I have before me a book containing the circuit for phase-angle control of a simple industrial thyristor equipment, and it is a double page spread. In practice, no doubt, the whole thing will go into a 'package' about two inches long and an inch and a half wide with nothing to show its complexity, but it should always be at the back of one's mind when thyristor systems are under discussion that there is much more to them than the power-handling devices themselves.

I must admit to a certain nostalgia for contactors. The driver of a Swiss electric locomotive once invited me into his cab and, putting his machine into neutral as it were, swept his controller hand-wheel round through all its 40 notches. From the machine room there was the sound as of mighty castanets as contacts clattered open and shut in elaborate sequences like the figures of a dance. Setting a potentiometer and sitting back seems a poor substitute, but that is what we shall become accustomed to. The years from the 1950s to the 1970s were years of transition and in this book I have tried to show the evolutionary process at work.

I am greatly indebted to the Public Relations Officers of the London Midland, Southern and Eastern Regions of British Railways for the facilities they made available and to the many technical officers of the Regions with whom they put me in contact, all of whom were generous with their time and information.

Stoneleigh, Surrey

B. K. Cooper
November 1978

1
The Direct Current Era

At the end of World War II the future of railway electrification in Great Britain seemed firmly committed to direct current systems. The only remaining alternating current section in 1945 was on the former Midland Railway lines linking Morecambe, Heysham and Lancaster, totalling 9½ route-miles, which had been electrified with 25Hz single-phase alternating current at 6,600V in 1908.

Two committees had pronounced in favour of dc for British electrification. The first was appointed in 1920 under the chairmanship of Sir Alexander Kennedy to consider the subject and report to the Minister of Transport. Its interim report published on 29 September 1920 recommended a standard pressure at substation busbars of 1,500V dc but agreed that existing 600V and 1,200V systems should be continued. Where it could be shown to be advantageous, 750V could be adopted. The need for interrunning between high- and low-voltage systems was recognised and locomotives and motorcoaches should be able to run when necessary on either 600/750V or 1,500V. Higher voltages should be limited to multiples of the standard 1,500V.

The Committee had before it a submission from the London, Brighton & South Coast Railway giving comprehensive details of a scheme for extending its suburban electrification over the main line to Brighton. The LBSCR had electrified with single-phase ac at 6,600V and proposed to continue with that system. But the Grouping of railways was impending and the Kennedy Committee had its reservations. Its final report acknowledged the heavy cost of changing the LBSCR system but recommended further consideration of the company's proposal in the light of requirements for through running and interchangeability of rolling stock with other sections of the proposed Southern Railway Group.

Left: An ex-North Eastern Railway Bo-Bo shunting locomotive No 26501, in BR livery, shunts in Newcastle Quayside Yard. Electric working on the Quayside branch ended on 29 February 1964. Sister loco No 26500 is preserved in the National Railway Museum at York./*J. D. Smith*

The London & South Western Railway had electrified a considerable London suburban mileage at 660V dc, and after formation of the Southern Railway the same system was used on surburban lines of the former South Eastern & Chatham. The 'Brighton' continued as odd man out, but not for long. The Southern Railway decided that electrification must be uniform throughout its system and in 1926 announced an electrification programme which included laying a 660V third rail on all the lines which had been equipped with the LB&SC overhead system for ac supply. The year 1929 saw the last of the Brighton section ac electric services.

A further committee was appointed in 1927 under the chairmanship of Sir John Pringle to review the recommendations of its pre-Grouping predecessor. Its report endorsed the choice of direct current but slightly expanded the recommendations on voltage and method of collection. The higher voltage remained at 1,500 but 750V became the recommended lower voltage rather than a permissible alternative. The Southern Railway representative on the committee, however, dissented from the proposal to make 750V the lower-voltage standard and the SR continued to use 660V in extending its suburban electrification and its first main line schemes.

With regard to method of current collection, the Committee further provided that third-rail collection at the higher voltage might be specially approved in cases where 'technical, structural or economic conditions, having due regard to safety, justify its adoption.' A railway could also apply to use 3,000V dc in special conditions. The idea of third-rail collection at 1,500V seems surprising today but it had actually been used in the USA while in this country the Manchester-Bury line had been operating at 1,200V with a protected third rail since 1913. It has also been suggested that third-rail had been considered for the North Eastern Railway's proposed 1,500V dc electrification from York to Newcastle although concrete evidence is lacking.

Between publication of these two reports a committee under Lord Weir had been set up in 1925 to review the national problem of the supply of electrical energy. Its findings led to the Electricity (Supply) Act of 1926 and the establishment of the Central Electricity Board with powers to construct a nationwide 'Grid' distribution system. The availability of power from the Grid transformed the outlook for railway electrification.

In the earliest days of electrification railways had generated their own supplies as dc at the voltage used by the trains. Later, they generated high-voltage ac at a low frequency, such as 25Hz, which was changed into dc at substations equipped with rotary-converters. There were design problems at first in building machines to convert ac at higher frequencies, particularly in heavy-current and fault conditions on the dc side, but by the 1920s these had been overcome and protection had been improved by the development of high-speed dc circuit-breakers which ensured very rapid disconnection of the machines from the track feeders when a fault occurred. By the Electricity (Supply) Act of 1919, however, new power stations could only be built or extended with the consent of the Electricity Commissioners. A railway had to show that it could not obtain an adequate supply at no greater cost from an electricity undertaking before permission to build would be granted. In 1922 the South Eastern & Chatham Construction Company sought to build a power station at Angerstein Wharf, between Woolwich and Deptford, to supply the SE&CR suburban electrification. The application was refused, and the supply was taken instead from the London Electricity Supply Corporation. No railway power station has been built subsequently. At the end of World War II the only survivors were at Stonebridge Park, LMS and Durnsford Road (Wimbledon), SR. Stonebridge Park, originally a 25Hz station, had been converted to 50Hz early in the war and was running interconnected with the National Grid. It continued in operation until 30 July 1967, after which current for all BR services was taken from the National Grid. Durnsford Road generated at 25Hz until closure in the 1950s.

In 1929 Lord Weir was invited to head yet another committee, this time with the following terms of reference: 'In view of the progress which is being made towards the widespread availability of electrical energy, to examine into the economic and other aspects of the electrification of the railway system in Great Britain with particular reference to main line working.'

The Weir Committee studied the cost of electrifying the whole of the railway system on the 1,500V dc system recommended by the Pringle Committee and envisaged a programme spread over 15 – 20 years at a capital cost of about £261 million. It urged that for the fullest economic advantage to be derived from railway electrification in this country any scheme adopted should be comprehensive, preferably comprising all the non-electrified lines, less such branches as could be worked more economically by other means. The size of the sum involved, said the committee, should not be a deterrent and it pointed to the huge sums being spent on road improvement at the time. A railway electrification programme should be given 'most earnest and careful consideration' on its economic and social merits.

Economic depression and gathering war clouds in the 1930s were not a favourable environment for putting the Weir proposals into practice. The Southern Railway schemes that brought the live rail to Brighton, Eastbourne, Hastings, Portsmouth, Gillingham and Maidstone between 1932 and 1939 were logical extensions of existing schemes and only affected passenger traffic, freight being still steam-hauled. After publication of the Pringle report, the only electrification at the recommended 1,500V dc up to the war had been the Manchester South Junction & Altrincham line in 1931 (8.7 route-miles). Electrification of 10.7 miles of the LMS lines in the Wirral peninsula in 1938 was at 650V for inter-running with the Mersey Railway, and in the preceding year the LNER electrified its South Tyneside line at 630V to complete a unified electrified network based on Newcastle and totalling 42.1 route-miles. Meanwhile the Railway (Standardisation of Electrification) Order of 1932 had officially endorsed the Pringle Committee's findings, while conceding that the Southern could continue with 660V rather than 750V for the extensions it already had in hand. But at that time the prospect of new work at 1,500V seemed remote. In 1935, however, the Government announced plans for making credits available to assist electrification in the London area and elsewhere. Around London, some inner suburban routes and branches of the main line railways were electrified at 600V so that Underground services could be extended over them. Some of these works were held up by the war, and not all came to fruition afterwards, but on 14 April 1940 London Transport Northern Line trains took over the service on the LNER branch to High Barnet. Under the same Government-aided schemes the LNER embarked on the electrification at 1,500V dc of its main line out of Liverpool Street as far as Shenfield; and of the former Great Central route between Manchester and Sheffield via the Woodhead Tunnel, together with its branch from Penistone to the marshalling yards at Wath. These two schemes, both completed after the formation of British Railways, were to dominate the main line electrification scene in the immediate postwar years.

The Liverpool Street-Shenfield electrification – the first 1,500V dc electrification in the London area – was

opened on 26 September 1949. In the following year the British Transport Commission held an International Convention on Electric Traction at the Institution of Electrical Engineers in London. In his opening address (*Proc IEE Vol XCVII, Part 1A*; the Institution of Electrical Engineers) the Chairman of the BTC, Sir Cyril (later Lord) Hurcomb, expressed the view that outside south-east England 'haphazard' electrification of many types had retarded progress and the Railway (Standardisation of Electrification) order had been made far too late in the day. He looked forward to an extensive programme of suburban and main line electrification providing it was prudent on economic grounds, and although it might be necessary to retain the conductor rail system in south-east

Top: Eastleigh-built parcels van No 68000 leaves Pelaw for South Shields, South Tyneside line, on 24 December 1962. /*I. S. Carr*

Above: A South Shields to Newcastle emu enters Tyne Dock station on 16 September 1962. The service was taken over by dmus in January 1963./*I. S. Carr*

England, elsewhere they would adopt the 1,500V overhead system. He had been advised that no serious difficulties need arise in inter-running between the overhead and the conductor rail systems and that electric vehicles could be fitted, if necessary, with equipment suitable for running on either. This comment on inter-running echoes Kennedy and Pringle. At that time inter-running was being considered only in relation to 1,500V lines and the Southern Region system. There was a prospect of extending the Manchester-Sheffield electrification, then in progress, to Liverpool, and it was noted that round both Manchester and Liverpool there were obvious opportunities for linking up and extending the existing 'bits and pieces' of electrified lines. From such beginnings Sir Cyril Hurcomb envisaged the gradual spread of electrification all over the Lancashire rail network. As events turned out, however, there was to be no inter-running between different systems on British Railways until the end of 1976 when Eastern Region suburban trains began running to and from Moorgate via Finsbury Park, the systems then involved being 25kV ac and 750V dc.

In forecasting the general use of 1,500V dc Sir Cyril Hurcomb was anticipating the findings of a committee which had been appointed by the Railway Executive and the London Transport Executive in 1948, under the chairmanship of Mr C. M. Cock, to 'review the methods of electrical operation now under their control and the system or systems to be adopted in future electrification schemes'. At that time Britain was supplying several important railways overseas with 3,000V dc equipment and so this higher voltage was taken into account in the committee's studies. Costs for electrifying selected lines were estimated and it was shown that 3,000V had a material advantage over 1,500V only on routes where the traffic was relatively light. The committee considered that electrification in this country was likely to be confined to lines with high traffic density, where the 1,500V system was at little disadvantage; moreover, the construction and maintenance of equipment to work on 1,500V and the existing 750V conductor rail system would be less costly than for 3,000V/750V operation. Once again the decision was influenced by the thought of inter-running, and was in favour of 1,500V dc.*

The electrified lines of British Railways in 1950 totalled 924 route-miles. Power was generally taken as three-phase ac at high voltage from the national network and distributed by railway feeder cables to the substations where it was transformed and rectified to provide dc for the trains. By that time mercury-arc rectifiers predominated, and had in fact been used throughout the Southern Railway main line electrification extensions of the 1930s. Earlier practice remained, however, in the Southern's inner suburban area for which power supplies were generated in the railway generating station at Durnsford Road, Wimbledon, and in a power station at Deptford built for the railway supply by the electricity authority. Conversion to dc took place in 49 rotary-converter substations. In 1954 all were replaced by rectifiers and the whole of the Southern Region electrified network was connected to the Grid.

At rotary-converter substations staff normally had to be on hand to supervise the running of the machines but by the middle 1920s remote control systems were coming into use on a limited scale. In the Southern Railway's Dorking North/Guildford electrification of 1925 the rotary-converters at Leatherhead and Clandon were controlled from Effingham Junction substation, and the machine at Oxshott from Hampton Court Junction. The full development of remote supervisory control of groups of substations, however, came with the arrival of the static mercury-arc rectifier in the 1930s. These rectifiers could be in the form of glass bulbs or steel tanks. The glass bulbs had the advantage at first that it was easier to make them proof against loss of the internal vacuum necessary for the rectifying action and they had simple air-cooling with fans. The early steel tank types, which allowed more rectifying capacity in a given space, needed water cooling and this in turn could lead to loss of vacuum. Both water and vacuum pumps had therefore to be provided. In later years an improved sealing process maintained the vacuum without pumping, and air-cooling dispensed with the water pumps. The pumpless air-cooled steel tank rectifier in conjunction with remote supervisory control was widely believed to have made dc traction secure against challenge in the countries where it was already established. This was an area in which the railways drew upon experience and progress in other branches of industry. Indeed, one of the characteristics of the period was the flow of new ideas and technology into what had once seemed a somewhat inward looking and self-sufficient undertaking.

There was less sense of innovation at first in the traction equipment itself. Resistance control systems with series/parallel switching of motors were found throughout the range of multiple-unit stock and met the requirements of the day, which normally required rapid progression through the control steps to put the motors on full operating voltage as soon as possible. Provision was made for running at half-voltage if speeds on full volts were too high for the operating conditions, and there was usually a weak-field step so that after attaining full volts higher balancing speeds could be achieved. Control switching was mainly by means of individual contactors, generally with electro-pneumatic operation although much stock with electro-magnetic contactors was still in operation.

London Transport showed two departures from the

*Electrification of Railways. Report of a committee appointed by the Railway Executive and the London Transport Executive. British Transport Commission, 1951.

Top: A North Tyneside motor parcels van of 1904, withdrawn and de-motored in 1938, survived as conductor rail de-icing van No DE 900730 until the end of the North Tyneside electrics in 1967. The van, now part of the National Railway Museum collection, was photographed in May 1977 while on loan to the Monkwearmouth Station Museum. /I. S. Carr

Left: The 08.24 North Tyneside electric express from Monkseaton to Newcastle via the Benton South-East Curve disgorges passengers on to the up main line platform at Manors East on 1 March 1967./I. S. Carr

Below: A six-car unit from the South Tyneside line passes Castle Junction and approaches Newcastle Central on 27 July 1948./BR

above pattern. It had been an early user of camshaft controllers, and had a number of surface line train units equipped with an alternative to resistance control called a 'Metadyne'. The contactors in a control scheme must operate in a fixed sequence. In individual contactor systems the sequence is controlled by circuits switched through auxiliary contacts by the mechanisms which open and close the main contactor contacts. In camshaft control the sequence is fixed by the angular setting of the cams on the shaft, similarly to the opening and closing of the inlet and exhaust valves in an internal combustion engine. The camshaft may be driven electrically or by some other form of power under electric control.

The Metadyne is a rotary machine which provides a constant current at increasing voltage while the traction motors are accelerating. This is similar to the effect of resistance control, but without the loss of energy as heat inevitable in resistance systems. London Transport installed Metadynes in a number of prewar surface line motorcoaches and also in three battery locomotives used for maintenance trains, although these were later converted to resistance control. The Metadyne system was not continued in surface line stock built after the war.

There was an important development in traction motor practice in 1947 when the Southern Railway introduced lightweight motors weighing only about half as much as previous machines of similar power. The earlier motors had been totally enclosed, relying for cooling on the flow of air over the exterior of their frames caused by the motion of the train. To dissipate the heat the frames were of massive construction and usually finned. Protection of the rotating parts against brake dust, water, snow and foreign matter from the track in general was obtained at the expense of weight. The new lightweight motors were cooled by air flowing through them internally. It was drawn in from protected openings high in the sides of the motor-coach by means of a fan on the armature shaft and conveyed to the motor through ducts and flexible bellows. A motor cooled in this way is called 'self-ventilated' and the practice soon became universal in motorcoach stock because of the lighter motor construction which it allowed. Motors for locomotives, however, are normally forced-ventilated by the airflow from separate motor-driven blowers.

The electric traction motor is not an impressive machine to look at. Indeed, it is rarely seen at all except in maintenance depots and when removed from its normal habitat in a bogie has a singularly inert appearance. The dc machine is often commended for its 'ruggedness' but this description scarcely conveys the precision of manufacture and assembly necessary to achieve the smooth flow of heavy currents through the sliding contact between commutator and brushes which is fundamental to its operation. This process must not be disturbed by heavy vertical and lateral shocks transmitted from the track, particularly when traversing points and crossings, or the oscillation of the bogie even in the best conditions. The axle-hung motor was universal in the 1950s, even in the small number of electric locomotives then in operation. Motors fully suspended in the bogie frames with flexible drives to the axles were not seen on British Railways until 1959.

Plain sleeve bearings were in general use for supporting a motor on the axle but there was a trend towards roller bearings for this purpose since lubrication is easier and they need less frequent attention. Where traction return current flows via the wheels to the running rails, however, it may pass through the bearings and sparking can occur, with consequent pitting of the rollers. It is therefore usual to provide a by-pass in the form of a lead from the motor frame which conducts the current from the motor directly to the axle via an earthing brush.

In 1950 only five electric locomotives were operating on British Railways. Two were ex-NER units dating from 1905 employed on the Tyneside freight lines in Newcastle (one is preserved in the National Railway Museum at York) and the other three were the so-called 'booster' locomotives on the Southern (Fig 1), the first of which had entered service in 1942. The first of the mixed-traffic locomotives for the Manchester-Sheffield electrification was still on loan to the Netherlands Railways. London Transport had 18 locomotives in service on the Metropolitan Line for hauling Chesham and Aylesbury trains between the City and Rickmansworth, where steam locomotives took over, and nine battery locomotives for maintenance trains.

Since 15 May 1949 the Southern locomotives had been working Victoria-Newhaven boat trains, making this the first main line passenger service in the country with regular electric locomotive haulage. These duties were combined with freight workings and seasonal inter-Regional passenger trains which had previously been steam-hauled over the Southern electric tracks.

The three Southern locomotives were a landmark in the history of electrification on the railways of this country and had their influence on later design for the region. 'Boosting', or adding the voltage of a motor-driven generator to that of the supply, is associated with 'bucking', when the generator opposes the supply volts and the difference between the two voltages is applied to the load. Buck-and-boost schemes were used in industry to provide control of votage without resistances in the power circuit, and this was a useful characteristic of the circuit adopted for the Southern locomotives. It was a bonus from a system designed

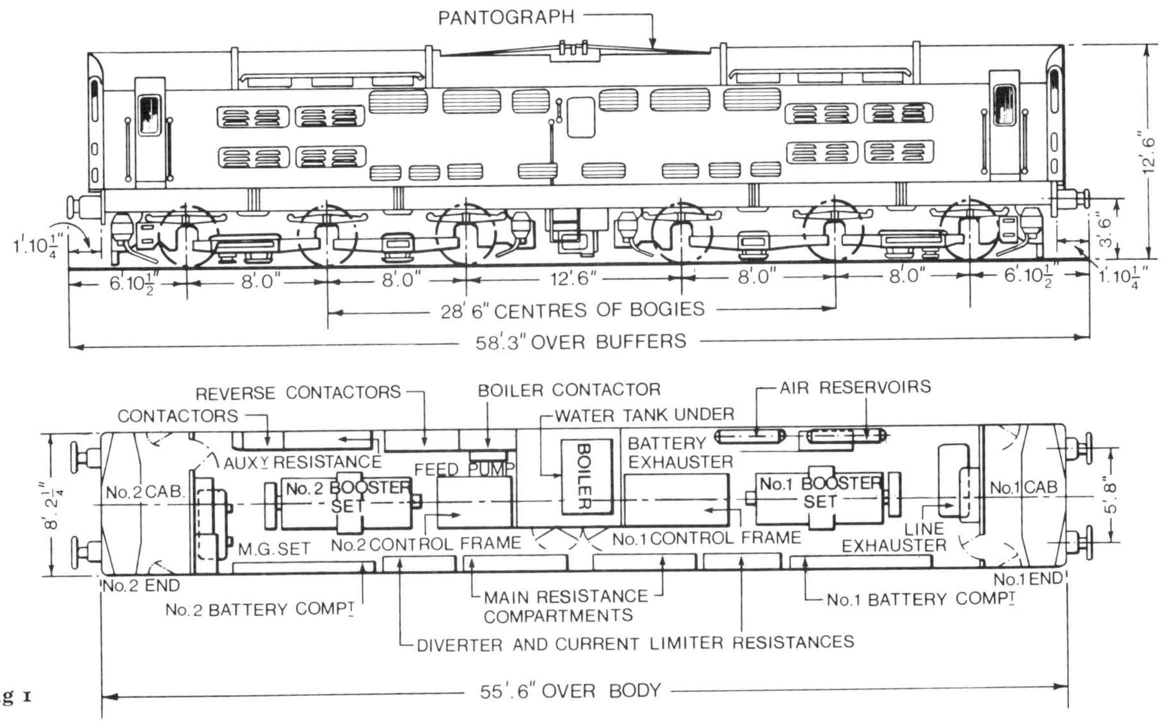

PANTOGRAPH

12'.6"

3'.6"

1'.10¼"

6'.10½"   8'.0"   8'.0"   12'.6"   8'.0"   8'.0"   6'.10½"   1'.10¼"

28'.6" CENTRES OF BOGIES

58'.3" OVER BUFFERS

REVERSE CONTACTORS   BOILER CONTACTOR   AIR RESERVOIRS

CONTACTORS   WATER TANK UNDER

AUX^Y RESISTANCE   FEED PUMP   BATTERY
                                                                      EXHAUSTER

No.2 CAB.   No.2 BOOSTER   BOILER   No.1 BOOSTER   No.1 CAB.
                          SET   SET

8'.2¼"   5'.8"

M.G. SET   No.2 CONTROL FRAME   No.1 CONTROL FRAME   LINE
                                                                                                      EXHAUSTER

No.2 END   No.1 END

No.2 BATTERY COMP^T   MAIN RESISTANCE   No.1 BATTERY COMP^T
                                            COMPARTMENTS

DIVERTER AND CURRENT LIMITER RESISTANCES

55'.6" OVER BODY

Fig 1

Fig 1 (*top*) The Southern 'booster' locomotive. This was the only main line electric locomotive design in service in Great Britain from 1942 to 1959.

Above: A parcels train formed of a motor parcels van and trailer pulls away from Tynemouth station.
/W. Hubert Foster

13

primarily to overcome the difficulty of operating electric locomotives on a conductor rail system of supply.

Unless the stock it is hauling is specially equipped, an electric locomotive can only be supplied with current from its own collector shoes. When traversing the gaps in conductor rail at points and crossings it is possible for all its shoes to be out of contact with the supply, and at low speeds there is the risk of stalling before the train can coast over the gap to the next section of conductor rail. The solution in the Southern locomotives was to connect the traction motors in series with the generator of a motor-generator set driven from the live rail and to mount a flywheel on the shaft of the set so that it kept running while the supply to its motor was briefly interrupted. Stored mechanical energy in the flywheel was converted into electrical energy and supplied to the motors while passing over the gap.

The booster system was associated with a long-standing preoccupation of the Southern Railway and its nationalised successor. Trains which began their journeys on the electrified system sometimes ran to destinations beyond the limits of the live rail, and at certain times they might have to pass over electrified sections where power was cut off for maintenance. When the booster system was first studied the possibility of using batteries to power the set in these circumstances was considered, but the size and weight of the cells made it impracticable. In the first loco-motive, however, a battery was fitted large enough to

Above: Manchester-Bury with its 1,200V dc system remains an odd man out. Note the protected third rail in this view of Class 504 two-car units introduced in 1959. /*P. J. Sharpe*

drive it if it stalled on a gap in the complicated point and crossing work at a terminal station. After three years this was removed, never having been used. The electro-diesel idea was born at this early period (see Chapter 10).

The first of the Southern booster locomotives was numbered CC1 in the alphanumeric style favoured by O. V. S. Bulleid, Chief Mechanical Engineer of the Southern Railway, who designed the mechanical parts. The electrical equipment was supplied by The English Electric Co Ltd to the design of Alfred Raworth, the railway's Electrical Engineer. As in-dicated by the number, the wheel arrangement was Co-Co (two three-axle bogies, all axles motored). There were two booster sets, each supplying the three traction motors in one bogie, and the three motors of each group were connected in series. At standstill the generator voltage opposed the live rail voltage, 'blocking' it fully so that no current flowed through the traction motors. As the driver notched up, the generator voltage was reduced. The difference between the live rail and generator voltages was now applied across the motors, which took current and developed power for starting the train. With the generator volts reduced to zero, the motors received the full live-rail voltage. On the next controller notch the output from the generator was reversed and its voltage added to that from the live rail. This was the 'boosting' phase and continued until the generator was delivering its full 600V, which added to 600V from the live rail gave 1,200V across each motor circuit, or 400V per motor. The motors were rated at 245hp.

Generator output was controlled by small resistances in its field circuit, involving negligible loss of power so that every notch on the controller could be used for continuous running. There were 26 of them, including three weak-field notches. One early problem occurred while the locomotive was running in the notches with the booster set opposing the live rail. If there was a nearby fault, causing a sudden collapse of live rail voltage, there could be an abrupt reversal of current flow in the booster circuit which might lead to a flashover. This tendency become more pronounced as drivers grew familiar with the locomotives and made greater use of the early notches. At first they had tended to alternate between full power and coasting in the manner to which they had become accustomed in driving multiple-unit sets. The problem was overcome, but memories seem to have lingered among some drivers, for as late as 1954 when I had a run on one of the locomotives at the head of the Newhaven boat train speed through the suburban area was controlled almost entirely by alternating between full power and coasting. There is no doubt, however, that the multi-notch characteristic was valuable in working freight and parcels trains. In some conventional resistance-controlled locomotives at this period the driver could run on certain resistance notches for a limited time but a red light warned him not to stay on them too long and risk burning the resistances out.

The second Southern booster locomotive appeared in 1945. CC2 had a few electrical modifications introduced by C. M. Cock who succeeded Raworth as Electrical Engineer of the Southern. In 1949 the third and last locomotive of the class came out, numbered 20003. CC1 and CC2 were renumbered 20001/2 at the same time. By this time S. B. Warder was the Southern's Electrical Engineer.

The interior arrangement of all three locomotives was similar. There was a booster set at each end with a traction motor blower on its shaft. A flywheel weighing one ton was mounted on the shaft between the two armatures. Electrically the armatures were interchangeable, each acting as a motor in one phase of acceleration and as a generator in the other. Originally a pantograph was fitted for current collection from overhead wiring in yards and depots where the live rail would be a hazard to staff. If depot wiring was unserviceable, a locomotive would sometimes be brought out by plugging into a fixed supply and running up the boosters. When the supply was unplugged the flywheels would keep the sets running long enough to power the locomotive for a distance about equivalent to the length of an eight-car train – sufficient to bring it out of the shed and on to a live rail.

The plate frame bogies were unusual in that there was no secondary suspension. Each was pivoted directly from the main frame in segmental bearings spaced 9ft apart along the centre line. This arrangement prevented tilting of the bogies relative to the frame so that weight transfer at high tractive efforts was very small. As a mixed traffic design with heavy wartime freight traffic in view, the class was first rated for a tractive effort of 40,000lb at 21mile/h, increased to 45,000lb in No 20003. Maximum speed was 75mile/h to allow the working of 450 ton passenger trains to 65 mile/h schedules. It was claimed that hunting was eliminated by the long bogie wheelbase of 16ft and side control by springs. Having ridden in No 20002 on the Newhaven boat train, I recall good stability but a perceptible grinding sensation from under the floor at intervals, in strong contrast to the buoyant suspension of a French National Railways Bo-Bo on which I rode on the following day. The bogies were designed by Bulleid and the same arrangement lived on in the Southern main line diesel-electrics, the English Electric Class 40s and the various versions of the 'Peak' class. In these diesel-electric designs there was an additional carrying axle in the bogie.

In the first locomotive the controller power handle worked in a notched quadrant. This arrangement was replaced by a handwheel in CC2. Both locomotives had a separate lever to select the weak-field notches. No 20003 retained the handwheel type of controller but used it for selecting all notches. Before the driver could move it into the weak-field sector, however, he had to shift the reverser handle into a second 'forward' position – 'forward weak-field'. When he returned the handwheel to Notch 23 (maximum volts, full field) the reverser handle sprang back automatically to the normal 'forward' position.

Weighing 99 tons 14cwt for a rating of 1,470hp (No 20003 was 5 tons heavier), the Southern boosters would win no prizes today for power/weight ratio but they were very much a 'special case'. Each was said to do the work of three steam locomotives, but as freight traffic declined in the postwar years there was little opportunity to keep them economically employed on a section of the Southern Region where passenger operation was overwhelmingly by means of multiple-unit trains. By the time of the Eastern Section electrification to the Kent coast more modern and powerful electric locomotives had been designed, but still based on Raworth's booster principle. The Co-Co class was withdrawn in 1969.

Outwardly there has been little change in traction

motors over the period covered by this book, whether for dc or ac, but in fact there have been important developments. New insulating materials have enabled the rating of a motor of given size to be doubled over the span of 20 years. The TIG (tungsten inert gas) method of welding armature coils to the commutator connections ('risers') has drastically reduced troubles from failures at these joints and prolonged the life of the machines. Previously motors had been rewound at intervals of about 10 years. Thanks to new materials and methods something like 20 years between rewinds can now be expected.

Below: The 16.00 Manchester-Bury accelerates away from Bowker Vale and down the hill to Heaton Park Tunnel on 9 April 1976./*David A. Flitcroft*

2
Elements of dc Traction Control

Today the series motor is all but universal in electric traction and where other types are used they are in most cases made to reproduce the series characteristic as closely as possible. Field and armature windings of the series motor are connected in series so that both carry the same current. The heavy current that flows at starting or low speed creates a strong magnetic field and hence a high torque. The torque, or turning effort, at the motor shaft appears as tractive effort at the drawbar. During the initial phase of acceleration from rest, current and torque are maintained at a high and constant level by the control equipment but thereafter they decrease as speed increases. While the tractive effort exceeds the resistance of the train to movement acceleration continues, but when the two are in balance it stops and the train runs at a steady 'balancing speed'. Clearly, train resistance depends upon gradient and curvature among other factors, and when a figure for balancing speed is quoted straight and level track is assumed.

The balancing speed when the motors are supplied at their designed operating voltage may be higher than is appropriate to the circumstances. The train may be in a speed-restricted area, for example. To run at lower speed the voltage must be reduced, and since the supply is fixed the change must be made by equipment on the train. In any case, a low voltage must be applied to the motors at starting because their resistance to the flow of current when stationary is negligible and full volts would be equivalent to a short-circuit of the supply. Additional resistance which can be brought into circuit when starting the train and switched out in steps as it gathers speed, is therefore one essential of a dc control system.

Resistances, however, are not a satisfactory method of controlling voltage and speed during normal running. While they are in circuit, power is converted into heat in the same way as in an electric fire, which is a waste of energy and would also burn the resistances out if the process went on too long. Resistances, therefore, have a necessary function at starting but they must be by-passed as soon as possible. Fortunately

there is another way of reducing the voltage between the terminals of a traction motor. Fig 2a shows two motors connected across a 750V dc traction supply (as on the Southern Region of British Railways, for example). Between the collector shoes and the running rail return there is a drop in voltage from 750V to zero (theoretically). Motors 1 and 2 are identical, and so the voltage drop across each is 375V. But these motors are designed for 750V and so when connected as shown (in series) they run at half speed.

The voltage drop across each motor is accounted for by the fact that when the motor is running it develops an electromotive force opposing the supply (known as the 'back emf'). There is therefore a drop in the supply volts between the motor terminals just as there is when current flows through a resistance, but this time the result is useful work at the motor shaft instead of unwanted heat. The back emf is proportional to the speed of rotation, increasing as speed rises, so that current and tractive effort fall away correspondingly.

A starting resistance (R_1, R_2) is connected in the motor circuit. It is cut out in steps by contactors C as the back emf rises and eventually short-circuited completely.

For further acceleration the motors are reconnected in parallel (Fig 2b), when there is a separate circuit from collector shoes to running rails through each motor; resistance is restored, to be cut out in steps as before until the full 750V of the supply is applied to each motor. The machines continue to accelerate until balancing speed is reached when the back emf only allows enough current to flow to maintain speed constant. If back emf is now reduced, more current will flow and the motors will accelerate to a new and higher balancing speed.

Back emf is produced by the generator effect of the armature conductors cutting the magnetic field within the motor. It can therefore be reduced by weakening the field. The field is set up by electromagnets, and so it can be weakened by diverting current from the magnet windings F. This is a valuable method of in-

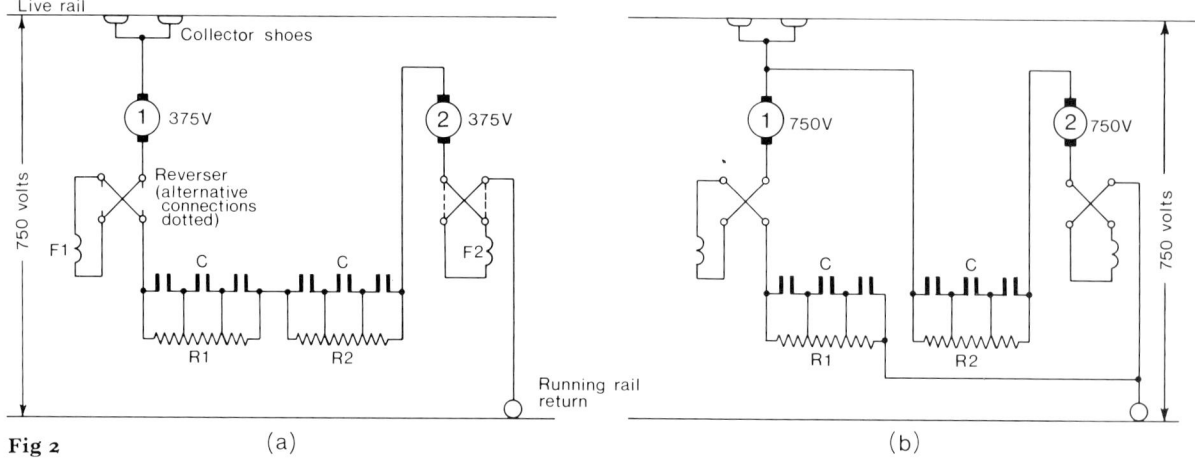

Fig 2   (a)   (b)

creasing the driver's choice of speed. One weak-field step is usual in emu control systems but the practice is carried much further in locomotives. Fields can be weakened by tapping or by diverting current through a resistance in parallel.

Only two motors are shown in the series/parallel switching diagrams of Fig 2. In some older motorcoaches with four motors the two motors in each bogie are controlled as shown there, each pair having its own set of control gear. In low-voltage motorcoaches today, however, it is more usual for the two motors in a bogie to be connected permanently in parallel and to be controlled by series/parallel switching of the two pairs. This is sometimes called 'simplex' control in contrast with the older 'duplex' method and only needs one set of control equipment.

Throughout the process of bringing the motors up to full operating voltage and weakening the fields the current swings above and below an average value and the tractive effort is nearly constant. Changes in current as each step of resistance is switched out are shown graphically in Fig 3. Here the fall in current as the train begins to move can be seen. When it reaches a value called the 'notching current' (in this example 250A) a section of resistance is switched out, automatically in emu equipments but in locomotives sometimes by the driver moving his controller handle one notch. The accelerating procedure is often called 'notching up'.

On the reduction of resistance in switching from one notch to the next, the current rises sharply, but with increasing speed it again falls to the notching value and the process is repeated. The change of grouping is called 'transition' and is also automatic in emu equipments. Usually the switching is arranged so that there is no interruption of tractive effort ('bridge transition'). Notches 15 and 16 are additional resistance notches to give a smooth entry into weak-field.

Fig 2 (*above*) Traction motors in series (a) and parallel (b).

Fig 3 (*below*) The effect of notching up on traction motor current during rheostatic acceleration. Each notch is taken when current falls to 250A. Note the rise in current towards 300A as each step of resistance is cut out.

Fig 3

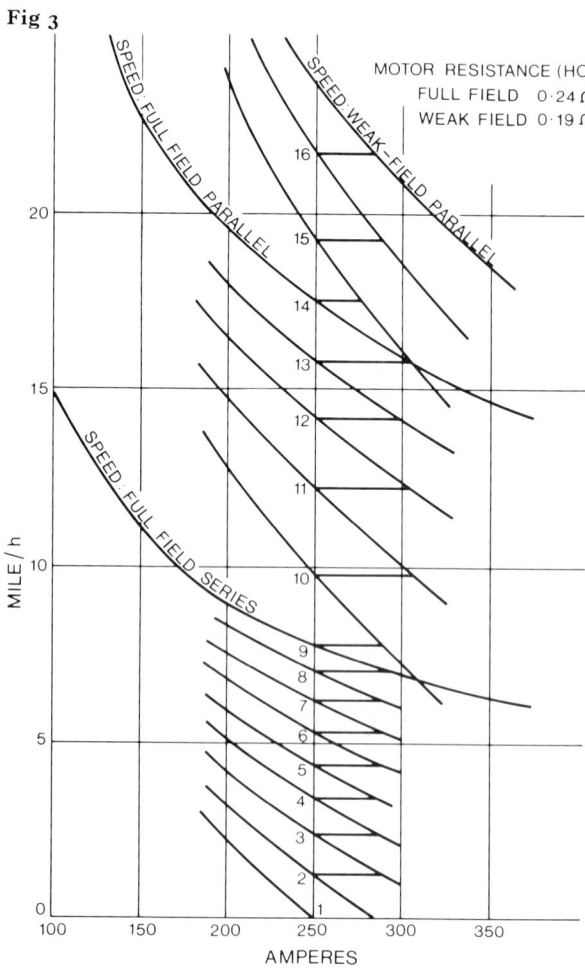

After the notching period is completed and the motors are running at full voltage in parallel weak-field, acceleration continues up to balancing speed at a rate depending on the inbuilt characteristics of the machines. This phase is called 'speed-curve acceleration' (see Fig 4). On a short run between stations the driver will probably cut off power before balancing speed is reached, allowing the train to coast for a time before braking to a standstill. Traction equipments for suburban service are designed specifically for the average conditions of the route and schedule. Allowance is made for regaining lost time by keeping power on longer. One of the speed/time curves in Fig 4 shows how the run time between stations can be reduced by this method, but it is at the cost of increased energy consumption. It will be noted that the whole notching process is completed in under half a minute. The diagram also shows the steady current maintained during notching and the way in which current falls thereafter with increasing speed.

The controller in an emu cab is properly called a 'master controller' because it controls not only the equipment in its own unit but those in other units coupled to it to form the train. For this purpose control cables run through each unit and are interconnected by flexible 'jumper' cables plugged in between the end coaches. An emu master controller usually has four positions to select the following conditions of running:

1 Shunting notch for slow movements in depots, coupling-up etc. All resistance is in circuit and automatic acceleration does not operate (Notch 1 in Fig 3).
2 Series. Automatic acceleration to full series (ie motors in series and no resistance in circuit).
3 Parallel. Automatic acceleration to full parallel.
4 Parallel weak-field.

Position 1 must be used only for short periods, about four minutes being the maximum. In one emu class the driver was instructed that if he remained in the shunting notch for two minutes continuously he must not return to it for 10 minutes to allow time for the resistances to cool. Where a train must be driven at 'crawling' speed, perhaps in fog or through engineering speed restrictions, the usual practice is to alternate between the series notch and coasting. The shunting notch has other uses. If the wheels slip on starting under automatic acceleration, the driver may return the controller to 'off' and then hold the handle briefly in the shunting notch, waiting for the wheels to regain their grip before resuming automatic acceleration. It can be used to 'ease' a train over gaps in the live rail. When power is interrupted by a gap, the equipment returns automatically to the 'off' condition. If the handle has been left in one of the running notches, the rapid automatic notching up when power comes on again at the other side of the gap can cause the train to surge forward. Momentary use of the shunting notch before automatic acceleration is resumed will cushion the effect. It may be noted here that the driver of an emu cannot reduce power by 'notching back' direct from weak-field or parallel to series. The handle must be returned to off and then moved forward to the position required.

With the handle in positions 2, 3 or 4 the equipment is normally allowed to run up automatically to the condition selected. In some emu equipments, however, a driver can go through the series notches step by step by moving the handle to and fro between the 'Series' and 'Shunt' positions – in exceptionally slippery rail conditions, for example. Provision may be made for less extreme conditions of slippery rail by two rates of automatic acceleration. Often the lower rate is selected automatically if the handle is placed at 'Series' or 'Parallel' and the higher rate if it is moved straight to 'Weak Field'. Alternatively the reverser handle may have two 'forward' positions selecting low and normal rates of acceleration. The 57 three-coach

Fig 4 (below) Speed and current in relation to time over a typical suburban station to station run, showing normal driving with early coasting and 'all-out' running with power kept on longer to make up time:
a Series grouping in full-field,
b Parallel grouping in full-field,
c Parallel grouping in intermediate field,
d Parallel grouping in weak-field.

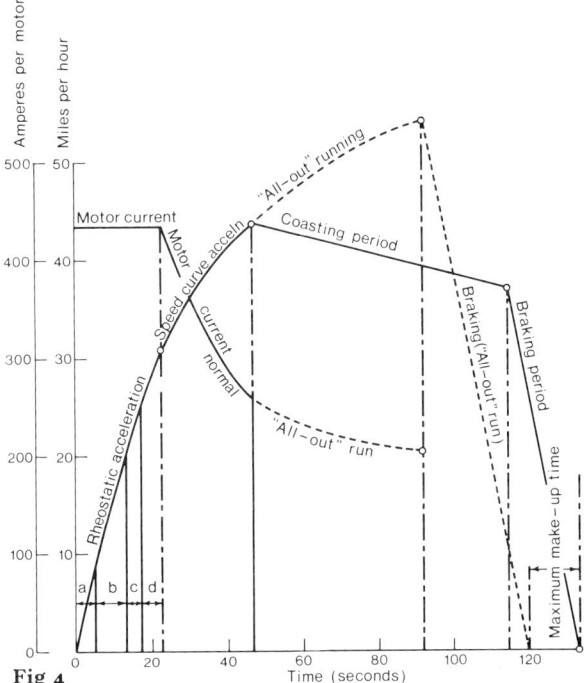

Fig 4

sets of Class 501 introduced in 1957 on the 630V third-rail Euston-Watford and Broad Street-Richmond routes actually had three rates – two (0.92 and 1.25 mile/h/sec) selected by the reverser, and a third obtained by putting the reverser at 'forward normal' and pressing a button. This was a special rate used if the unit had to start on the 1 in 37 gradient in the Primrose Hill flyunder near Euston with one pair of motors out of action. The name of the pessimist who conceived this unlikely combination of circumstances is unknown,

but one assumes he did so from bitter experience. The control engineer met his requirement by arranging for the button to short-circuit part of a resistor in the shunt coil circuit of the accelerating relay.

In very adverse conditions a train might not accelerate fast enough in parallel for the current to fall to the notching level before the resistances overheated. Main line stock on the Southern Region is therefore provided with a two-position switch in the cab labelled 'Normal/Series Only'. This must be set at 'Series

20

Top left: No 20003, the third of the Southern 'booster' locomotives, draws on the energy in its flywheels as it picks its way through the crossings on leaving Victoria with the Newhaven boat express in 1950./*BR*

Left: Armatures and flywheel of one of the two booster sets in a Southern Co-Co booster locomotive. /*GEC Traction Ltd*

Above: Booster set of a Class 71 locomotive. In this class one set served the four traction motors./*GEC Traction Ltd*

Only' when climbing the 1 in 36 gradient on the Folkestone Harbour branch to prevent the equipments in the train from notching up into parallel.

Resistance switching, transitions, and connection and disconnection of power are effected by contactors – remotely-controlled switches operated over low-voltage circuits switched by the driver's controller. Electro-pneumatic contactors are all but universal today for power control although some contactors used for lighter duties in auxiliary circuits are electro-magnetic. In the older classes of dc rolling stock all the contactors are individual switches. More recent practice has been to use heavy-duty individual contactors in parts of the circuit where they have to break full load or fault currents, but to short-circuit the accelerating resistances with groups of contactors operated mechanically by a camshaft, often driven by a combination of air and oil pressure.

The contactors between the supply and the power circuits are known as 'line switches' and they open automatically if the overload or 'no-volts' relays detect excessive current or an interruption of power supply. In locomotives there may be two or more line switches in series and they are sometimes arranged to open in sequence when clearing a fault, the first to act switching in resistance so that the current is reduced before being finally broken. Sometimes fault protection is given by a high-speed circuit-breaker but this was unusual in British dc practice although it is normal in ac locomotives.

An electro-pneumatic contactor closes its contacts when air is admitted to the operating cylinder by a magnet valve. The control system has to energise the magnet valves in the correct sequence, and this is ensured by taking the operating circuits through auxiliary interlock contacts linked with the main contactor mechanisms. While a contactor is open, its operating coil is connected to an 'actuating' wire in the control circuit. Control current flows in the wire when the accelerating relay contacts close, which they do when the traction current passing through the relay coil has fallen to the 'notching' value, at which point the pull of the relay spring overcomes the magnetic attraction of the coil on the relay contacts. The magnet valve on the contactor is now energised and opened, and air pressure closes the contactor contacts so that a section of resistance is short-circuited. Simultaneously the interlock contacts linked with the contactor mechanism move as well. In so doing they break the supply to the magnet valve via the actuating wire but they connect the valve to a permanently energised 'holding' wire. Consequently the valve is held open and the contactor stays closed.

The increase in traction current when the resistance section is short-circuited strengthens the pull of the accelerating relay coil so that it overcomes the spring and the relay contacts reopen. The movement of the interlock contacts when the contactor closed also connected the magnet valve of the next contactor in the sequence to the actuating wire. When the relay contacts close again, therefore, the next contactor is operated, and this process is repeated until all the resistance is short-circuited. At this stage further contactors come into action to change the motor grouping, the resistance contactors are opened to restore resistance in the traction circuit, and then they reclose again in turn as before.

To reverse the motors the connections to the field coils are changed over so that current flows in the opposite direction through the field windings, although in the armature coils it remains unchanged. Reverser contacts are usually grouped together in a single switching unit and operated by movement of a drum or camshaft with electro-pneumatic drive. In drum and camshaft systems the sequence in which the contacts operate is mechanically fixed.

In multiple-unit working the ratio of power to weight does not change with the length of train, since the addition of coaches brings a corresponding increase of horsepower from the extra motors. Conditions are different with locomotive haulage, and as load is increased the time spent on resistances during acceleration will be longer. Locomotive resistances must therefore be dimensioned to withstand heavier duty without overheating than those of a motorcoach. In a dc locomotive they occupy a considerable part of the space inside the body. Motorcoach resistors are carried below the underframe, where they are often easily visible, and their exposed position helps cooling by natural air flow.

An electric locomotive must be able to work different types of passenger and freight trains over a broad pattern of schedules. The driver therefore needs more running positions on his controller than the three normally provided for an emu if he is to observe the timetable accurately and economically. Hitherto there has been less 'automation' in dc locomotive control, and manual control of acceleration has been preferred, while to provide a wider selection of running notches on the controller greater use has been made of different motor groupings and weak-field steps. The Southern booster locomotives, with their motors connected permanently in one grouping, were a special case. In Britain the only dc main line locomotives with resistance control have been the two classes for the Manchester-Sheffield 1,500V dc

electrification and the Southern Region's Class 73 electro-diesels. Of the former, the Bo-Bo series (BR Class 76) has two motor groupings with four weak-field steps in each, giving 10 continuous running notches. The Co-Co series, which went to the Netherlands Railways when passenger services over this route ended in 1967, had three motor groupings with three weak-field steps in each, or 12 running notches in all. To obtain three groupings the six traction motors were connected at first all in series (250V per motor), then changed to two parallel groups of three in series (500V per motor), and were finally connected as three parallel groups of two in series (750V per motor). The choice of 750 as the operating voltage for the motors of both these 1,500V dc classes was made because certain dimensional features of a motor are governed by the voltage for which it is designed, and at 750V the machines could be smaller and lighter than if they had operated at full line voltage.

A low-voltage supply for control circuits in dc emu stock is normally taken from a motor-generator set. The motor runs off the traction supply, while the generator provides an output somewhere in the range between 50 and 110V according to the power requirements. A battery 'floats' across the generator so that certain auxiliary services can be supplied when the generator is not running, and the battery is kept charged. A motor-driven compressor running on the traction supply provides air for braking and the electro-pneumatic control system. Heating is also fed from the traction supply but lighting is usually connected to the low-voltage system so that it can be maintained by the battery in the event of a supply failure. A dc locomotive is equipped similarly but also carries blowers for traction motor cooling. In some installations there are two motor-generator sets, each with a traction motor blower coupled to it, or the blowers may be driven by their own motors.

Both dc and ac control systems incorporate a so-called 'dead man' arrangement to bring the train to a stand if the driver relaxes his hold on the controller handle. Sometimes the handle is biassed upwards by a spring and a slight downward pressure must be maintained while running, or a knob may have to be held down similarly. In either case, if the handle or knob is released and allowed to lift, air is admitted to the train brake pipe and at the same time air-controlled electrical contacts are opened and power to the traction motors is cut off. The same contacts provide a safeguard against the train being driven with insufficient air pressure for braking since they will not close until the correct pressure is available.

Every control system includes a number of protective relays. A description of their functions in a typical installation will be found in Chapter 10.

3
Shenfield and its Forerunners

The working life of the Southern locomotives (Chapter 1) extended from the time when an electric locomotive was a rarity in this country to the full tide of the London Midland Region high-voltage ac electrification between Euston and the north-west. In the meantime two of the prewar 1,500V dc undertakings had come to fruition. The first to be completed was electrification of the 20¼ route-miles from Liverpool Street to Shenfield on the Eastern Region main line to East Anglia via Colchester. Overhead contact wires had already been seen in London on the LBSCR ac electrification, but Liverpool Street-Shenfield was the first 1,500V dc scheme in the South.

For some years there was a reminder at Ilford car sheds on the Shenfield line of the earliest days of 1,500V dc electrification in this country. One of the Bo+Bo electric locomotives built for the NER's Shildon-Newport electrification of 1915 had been rebuilt as a shunter and served at Ilford until it was withdrawn in 1964. Electric traction had been chosen for the Shildon-Newport line as an economical method of conveying coal from the Bishop Auckland area to the Erimus marshalling yard at Newport, later to become the nucleus of Tees yard, one of the great automated marshalling yards of the north-east.

The Shildon-Newport electrification was more successful operationally than financially. Coal traffic began to decline and the coal strike of 1921 hit its results badly. Electric working ceased in 1935. As far as technical performance was concerned, however, the Shildon-Newport venture encouraged plans for the North Eastern Railway to electrify the main line from York to Newcastle. Provisional approval was given to the project in 1919 and on the strength of this the company's Chief Mechanical Engineer, Vincent Raven (later Sir Vincent), had the celebrated express electric locomotive No 13 built at Darlington. No 13 was finished in 1922 but by that time the North Eastern was on the eve of absorption into the LNER. The electrification project was shelved, and soon Gresley's Pacifics where thundering over the metals which in other circumstances might have borne a

fleet of smoothly gliding 2-Co-2 electrics conceived by Raven, an enthusiastic pioneer in railway electrification.

No 13 went into store. At one time there was some prospect of its return to work on the Manchester-Sheffield electrification but nothing came of it. Even in the early postwar years the power bogie electric locomotive was seen as the formula for the future and this type was chosen for the Manchester-Sheffield express passenger Co-Cos. Renumbering of No 13 as BR No 26600 was a mere formality for the erstwhile No 13 was towed to a breaker's yard for scrapping in 1950. Nonetheless, No 13 had descendants. Metropolitan-Vickers, who supplied the electrical equipment, profited from the trials and produced a similar scheme for the locomotives it supplied for the Bombay-Poona electrification of the Great Indian Peninsula Railway in 1925-29.

The next venture with 1,500V dc was of a more mundane sort, but again a pioneer in British practice in certain respects. The Manchester South Junction & Altrincham line (8¾ miles) was converted to electric traction on 11 May 1931. This was the first use in Britain of the 1,500V overhead system for passenger traffic, and the MSJ&A was the first line to adopt it after recommendation of the system in the Pringle report. Compound catenary was used with a contact wire of 0.375sq in cross-section. Substations at Timperley and Old Trafford were connected to the public 11kV supply. At Old Trafford a mercury-arc rectifier worked alongside two rotary-converters in providing the supply to the contact wire, and equipment was installed for remote control of the rotary-converters at Timperley. The machines could be started and stopped, their output controlled and the whole operation monitored from the Old Trafford control panel. The 1,500kW mercury-arc rectifier at Trafford Park was the first of its kind to be used for traction supplies in this country. The first glass bulb installations for railway traction were made on the LMS Liverpool-Southport line in 1932.

Trains on the MSJ&A were formed of three-car

units of compartment stock comprising motorcoach, trailer and driving trailer with first and third class accommodation. All axles of the motorcoach were motored and the control equipment was housed inside the coach behind the driving compartment. The two motors in each bogie were connected permanently in series. All four machines were in series at starting and were reconnected as two series pairs in parallel (750V per motor) for full-speed running. Maximum speed was 70mile/h. Acceleration was automatic and this caused some problems at first, drivers being unaccustomed to the liveliness with which the trains gathered speed. They tended to stay too long in the first controller notch provided for slow shunting movements, with the result that there was a crop of burned-out resistances. An engineer associated with the installation used to relate how on the first day of running trains came into the stations with drivers leaning out of the cab windows to escape smoke billowing out of the equipment compartment behind them.

The MSJ&A was the last 1,500V electrification completed in this country before World War II, but by 1939 work was already in hand on much larger schemes. One of these was the electrification of the slow tracks of the LNER main line from Liverpool Street as far as Shenfield, together with the branch from Stratford to Fenchurch Street, 23 route-miles in all.

Liverpool Street-Shenfield was one of the schemes embraced by the London Passenger Transport (Agreement) Act of 1935 under which the Treasury was empowered to guarantee facilities to London Transport, the GWR and the LNER for new works to improve transport in the London area. In LNER territory the Shenfield electrification was bracketed with extension of the LT Central Line from Liverpool Street through Stratford to connect with the LNER branch to Loughton. From the point of junction the branch was electrified on the LT third – and fourth-rail system for through running by tube trains and its operation was taken over by London Transport.

Below: The booster system was used again in the Class 71 Bo-Bo locomotives for the Kent Coast electrification. Here No E5012 passes Shortlands with the up 'Golden Arrow' on 21 June 1968./*J. H. Cooper-Smith*

Above right: The North Eastern's prototype 1,500V dc electric locomotive No 13 was in store from Grouping until withdrawn as BR No 26600 in 1950. Here it makes a brief appearance, propelled by a steam locomotive, at the Railway Centenary celebrations in 1925./*F. R. Hebron*

Below right: Ex-NER Newport-Shildon Bo-Bo No 26510 emerged from store to work as a shunter at Ilford car sheds after the Shenfield electrification of 1949. It was withdrawn in 1964./*F. W. Day*

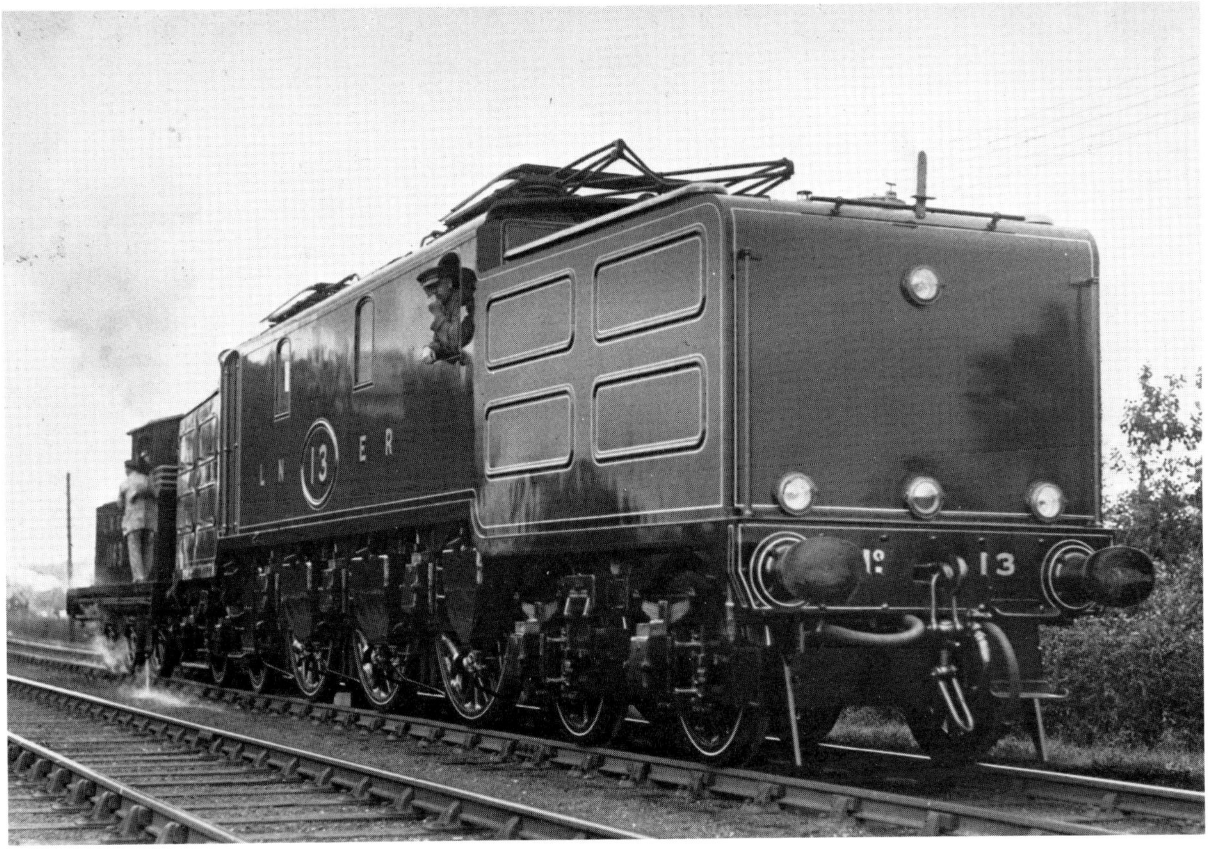
L N E R
13
No 13

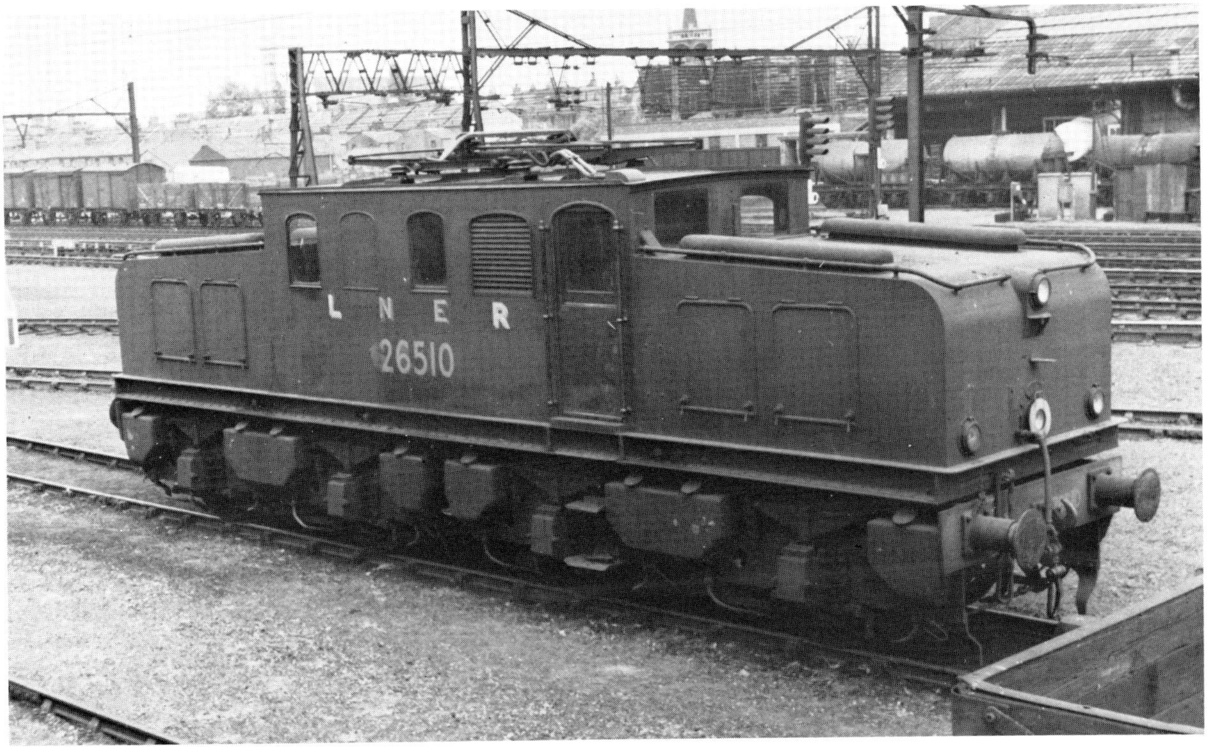
L N E R
26510

The 1,500V overhead system was chosen for the main line for two reasons: safety of pw maintenance on this busy section, and the likelihood of electrification being extended to Southend and Colchester. At 1,500V, substations could be further apart, and if future operations required locomotives it would be unnecessary to adopt special measures for overcoming the problem of gaps in the live rail.

Work was begun in 1937 but suspended in 1940. When it was resumed in 1946 the original plans were followed apart from extending electrification to the through lines. Power was taken from the Grid at Crosswall and Chadwell Heath substations, and there were further substations at Bethnal Green, Stratford, Gidea Park and Shenfield. Distances between substations ranged between three miles in the inner area and six miles in the country.

By this time pumpless air-cooled steel tank rectifiers were fully established. Rectifiers for the Shenfield line were installed as 2,000kW units, each unit consisting of two six-anode tanks. The transformers between the high-voltage supply and the rectifiers could be adjusted by remote control from the control room at Chadwell Heath to maintain 1,500V output during variations of up to plus or minus $7\frac{1}{2}\%$ in the input. The rectifier tanks were cooled by fans which could draw air from outside the substation building; from inside; or from both sources together. Circulation was assisted by extractor fans discharging air to the outside. From

the Grid supply points at Crosswall and Chadwell Heath substations, the railway installed its own lineside high-voltage cable route to feed power to the other substations.

The catenary system was of compound construction with stranded copper main and auxiliary cables and a cadmium copper contact wire of 0.26sq in cross-section. All elements of the catenary were 'live', giving a total cross-sectional area used for carrying current equivalent to a single 0.75sq in copper conductor. The auxiliary catenary was suspended from the main catenary by droppers at 35ft spacing and the contact wire from the auxiliary by droppers at 17ft 6in spacing. Supporting structures were normally at intervals of 210ft. The contact wire was held 12in to right or left of the centre line of the track at alternate structures, crossing the centre line in mid-span. This was to avoid undue wear of the collector pan of the pantographs by extending the portion over which sliding contact with the wire was made, and a similar 'stagger' of the contact wire is general practice in overhead systems. Most of the structures were a simple portal design made of broad-flanged beams and spanning four tracks. Lattice girder construction was used for wider spans and for the anchor structures at the mid-points of catenary sections.

The catenary was in sections about a mile in length. Adjacent sections overlapped by about 200ft so that there was no break in continuity of supply to the trains.

Top left: The Manchester South Junction & Altrincham provided the first 1,500V dc passenger services in this country. Three-car unit 28573 is at Altrincham Depot in 1958./*T. K. Widd*

Above: An Altrincham train passes Timperley substation on 4 May 1970. The light 25kV overhead system has been installed in readiness for the changeover in 1971. At this period the original MSJ&A trains were fitted with Faiveley pantographs to suit the characteristics of the catenary, which was energised at 1,500V dc pending conversion. *M. H. Spilsbury*

Sectioning was provided by circuit-breakers in track-sectioning cabins between substations, sited at overlaps. There were also overlaps at substations, and at other points dictated by operational requirements. The sectioning circuit-breakers were controlled remotely from Chadwell Heath, but at some overlaps the adjacent sections were connected through hand-operated isolating switches which could only be opened after permission from the control room had been obtained.

To operate the Liverpool Street-Shenfield services 92 train units were ordered, each consisting of a motorcoach, trailer and driving trailer. The vehicles were open saloons with two pairs of electro-pneumatic sliding doors in each. A nine-coach train seated 528 passengers and provided standing room for 660. The motorcoaches were powered by four 210hp motors, giving an acceleration of 1.25mile/h/sec up to 26mile/h and a balancing speed with all seats occupied and some standing passengers of 64mile/h. In 1960 the units were rebuilt for ac working and eventually became BR Class 306.

The control system provided a shunting notch, nine series notches, five in parallel and a weak-field notch. While in series a shunt coil on the accelerating relay opposed the 'pull' of the main coil holding the contacts open against the tension of a spring. This allowed the spring to close the contacts at a higher current than if it had to overcome the full force of the series coil. In parallel the shunt coil was de-energised and the notch-

ing current value was reduced. A separate relay controlled the entry to weak-field.

The traction control equipment was contained in three cases, below floor level in the motorcoach. Also below the floor were a 1,500/52V motor-generator set for the control circuits, lighting and battery charging; and a 1,500V motor driving a two-cylinder reciprocating compressor to maintain air supplies for braking, operation of electro-pneumatic contactors, and control of the pantograph. The pressure of the collector pan on the overhead contact wire was 16lb/sq in.

During the design of this rolling stock some calculations were made of how emu performance would compare with that of a nine-coach train hauled by a 76 ton steam locomotive. The results are shown graphically in Figs 5 and 6. On the run from Seven

Kings to Goodmayes (Fig 5) the trains are climbing a gradient of 1 in 390. The advantage of the emu in attaining a high speed quickly, is clearly demonstrated. With 12 axles in the train motor-driven, more than a third of the train weight contributes to adhesion, enabling high tractive effort to be developed without wheelspin. Fig 6 compares the two performances over the longer distance from Brentwood to Shenfield, where the first third of the run is up 1 in 85, followed by a third at an average rise of 1 in 200, and the remainder on a falling gradient of 1 in 136. The effect of the steep initial climb is evident in both curves in the time taken to reach maximum speed but the steam locomotive is worse hit.

The Shenfield electrification was formally inaugurated on 25 September 1949 but some steam trains continued running until the full changeover to electric traction on 7 November. The timetable was planned for 21 electric trains an hour out of Liverpool Street.

An essential preliminary to operating this intensive

Above: Control equipment on a SR Class 411 unit. Left to right: line switches, the air-operated switch group controlling series/parallel transitions, and protective relays. /BR

Fig 5 (*below*) Electric and steam train speed/time curves (calculated) between Seven Kings and Goodmayes.

Fig 6 (*below right*) Calculated speed/time comparisons between Brentwood and Shenfield.

service was the construction of a flyover between Manor Park and Ilford to enable up local trains starting from Shenfield and Gidea Park to reach the east side of Liverpool Street station without crossing main lines on the level. This rearrangement also facilitated interchange with London Transport trains at Stratford. In installing new colour-light signalling the former dc track circuits were replaced by ac circuits with impedance bonds, because where both rails were used for the return traction current the track circuits could no longer be separated by insulated rail joints. The impedance bonds had the effect of confining the ac signalling currents to their respective circuits while allowing dc to flow without interruption.

On 11 June 1956 the electrification was extended from Shenfield to Chelmsford, and on 31 December of the same year from Shenfield to Southend Victoria. For the Liverpool Street-Southend service 32 four-car units were built by BR at Eastleigh. Electrical equipment was by GEC. The unit formation was unusual for its time, comprising driving trailer, motorcoach trailer composite and driving trailer. This was the first dc stock on BR in which the motorcoach was an intermediate vehicle in the unit, an arrangement commended at the time for the fact that the leading bogie of the unit in either direction of travel was unmotored and likely to be less severe on the track. On the other hand the motorcoach was not mobile without the driving trailer, but this was soon to become a commonplace. The new Southend stock went into service after the decision to standardise ac traction at 25kV, 50Hz, had been announced and this was to mean a new generation of emus in which some of the auxiliary equipment and machines formerly carried on a motorcoach would be transferred to the adjacent driving trailer in order to make room under the motorcoach for the transformer and rectifier. Thus the 'battery driving trailer' came into being, so-called because the equipment it carried included the battery and battery-charger.

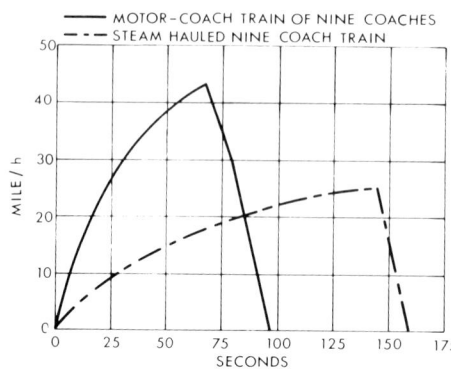

Fig 5

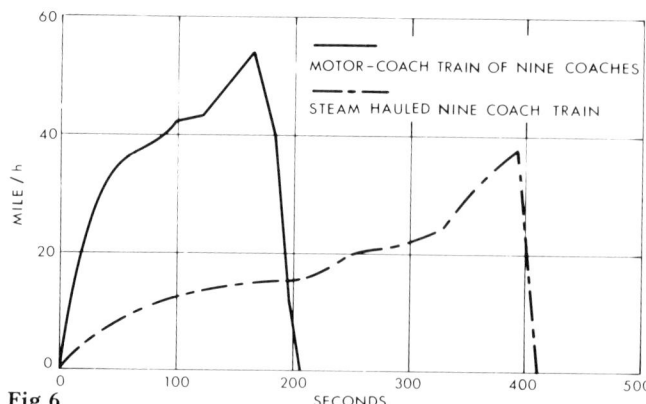

Fig 6

4
Manchester-Sheffield-Wath

'Up we soar, loudly vocal but without apparent effort' wrote Cecil J. Allen in a characteristic phrase describing a 'Director' class 4-4-0 lifting the 3.20pm Marylebone-Manchester from Sheffield towards Woodhead. The line over the Pennines between Manchester and Sheffield that was to become part of the Great Central Railway was the work of Joseph Locke. Near the summit of the route he drove the Woodhead Tunnel through the rock for three miles. It is said that when in later years he took the Lancaster & Carlisle Railway over Shap he contemplated a summit tunnel there as well but decided against it on grounds of economy. Shap was notorious among enginemen for its steep approaches and climax from the south of four miles at 1 in 75 but Woodhead added problems of its own. The Manchester-Sheffield line carried heavy flows of freight, much of it originating in the Yorkshire coalfields and travelling via the marshalling yard at Wath to join the line to Manchester at Barnsley Junction, Penistone. Conditions in the three-mile tunnel when four engines – two at the head and two banking a heavy freight – were working hard sometimes threatened the crews with suffocation. The LNER, which absorbed the GCR at Grouping, studied electrification of the line as early as 1926.

If the gable-shaped profile of Locke's line made steam working arduous, it offered an unique opportunity to electric traction. The motors of a train coasting down the gradients on either side of the summit could be made to generate power and return it to the overhead system – converting the energy given to the train free of cost by gravity into electrical energy for use by an ascending train. This was an attractive proposition even before conservation of energy had become urgent and it had the advantage that the descending train, while regenerating power, would be held at a steady speed without using the brakes.

The studies of 1926 found the prospects for electrification favourable, but the depression of the early 1930s was looming and the plans were shelved. In 1936, however, Government measures to reduce unemployment included finance for railway electrifica-

tion, enabling the first steps in the Woodhead scheme to be undertaken. The system was to be 1,500V dc as recommended by the Kennedy and Pringle Committees and by this time operational on the Manchester South Junction & Altrincham line. By 1939 orders had been authorised for 70 locomotives and eight three-car emus, the latter for local services between Manchester, Hadfield and Glossop. Work on foundations and steelwork for the overhead had been put in hand, but was suspended in 1940. One locomotive was already well advanced and was completed the following year. On 19 February 1941 it was inspected at York by the Chairman and chief officers of the LNER. This was LNER Bo-Bo No 6071, first of the series later known as BR Class 76. After trials on the MSJ&A line, the only 1,500V dc section still available, No 6071 was stored until the end of the war. In 1947 it was loaned to the Netherlands Railways, then suffering from an acute shortage of motive power. While in Holland No 6701 was affectionately nicknamed *Tommy*, a name it later carried on official nameplates after its return to British Railways as No 26000.

Resumption of work on the electrification was authorised in 1946, although priority was given to Liverpool Street-Shenfield. It had been proposed to retain the two single-track bores of the Woodhead Tunnel but it soon became apparent that they were unfit for repair and in 1947 it was decided to replace them with a new double-track tunnel on a parallel alignment. Work on this major project, the first undertaking of its kind on such a scale in Britain in the present century, was begun in February 1949. While it was in progress electric working of freight was inaugurated between Wath and Dunford Bridge, at the eastern end of the tunnel, on 4 February 1952.

The new Woodhead Tunnel was opened by the Minister of Transport, the Rt Hon Lennox-Boyd, on 3 June 1954. From that date electric freight trains began working through from Wath to Manchester but electric passenger working was confined for a short time to the Manchester-Penistone section because the line from Penistone to Sheffield was not ready for it.

This section was energised three months later and from 14 September 1954 the full electric service between Manchester and Sheffield operated.

This was the first all-electric main line in Britain and many travellers now experienced for the first time the effortless acceleration and uniform speed of the electrically-hauled express, all the more noticeable in an environment where the steam locomotive had been working near its limit. Some comparative times of the period are tabulated below:

Express passenger	Steam min	Electric min
Sheffield-Manchester	70	56
Manchester-Sheffield	68	56
Mineral		
Wath-Mottram	162	97
Ashburys-Woodburn Junction (Sheffield)	154	101

From Sheffield the summit point of the line is approached by gradients averaging 1 in 127 for 19 miles. From Manchester the gradients average 1 in 147 for 22½ miles and on both sides of the summit the ruling gradients are 1 in 100. There is much curvature throughout. Little more than 10% of the route is straight. The branch from Barnsley Junction, Penistone, to Wath includes the Wentworth Bank of 2.2 miles at 1 in 40. This section was freight only.

On 3 January 1955 the overhead system was extended from Sheffield Victoria to the traction exchange sidings at Rotherwood, bringing the total route-mileage of the scheme up to 68. Ten years later, in June 1965, there was a further extension over a short section of the Sheffield-Rotherham line and round one side of the Darnall triangle to allow electric working to and from Tinsley Yard. It was stated at the time that this new work was suitable for 6.25kV ac 'for possible future integration'.

Power for the electrification was taken from the Grid at Aldam, Gorton and Neepsend and distributed to 11 substations at an average spacing of 6.2 miles. At four substations the rectifiers were water-cooled and pumped, having been partly manufactured before the war. The remainder were air-cooled although still equipped with vacuum pumps. Total cross-section of the catenaries and contact wires over each track was the equivalent in conductivity of 0.75sq in of copper.

It had been proposed originally to work the line with four-axle locomotives, including 10 of the stored Newport-Shildon units. In 1948, however, it was decided to build 27 Co-Cos for fast passenger traffic. An economy drive later reduced this number to seven and the locomotive stock finally provided was 58 Bo+Bo and seven Co-Co. The Newport-Shildon locomotives did not reappear on this electrification; the only one to see service again was No 26510 as a shunter at Ilford car sheds (Chapter 3).

In the new Bo+Bo locomotives the principle of articulated bogies as in the Newport-Shildon design was retained. This arrangement had its origin in some powerful locomotives in the USA of earlier years and was still favoured where heavy traffic on severe gradients was involved. With the drawgear mounted on the bogie headstocks, tractive effort was transmitted at low level and one of the forces tending to unload the leading axles when starting was reduced. One bogie carried at its inner end two triangular projections, one above the other. A single similar projection on the second bogie fitted between them and a pin was inserted through all three to complete the coupling.

Although the articulated bogie was retained from the Newport-Shildon locomotives, the central cab arrangement was not. By this time centre cabs were *démodés*; they were still to be seen on the two quayside branch shunters in Newcastle but the Metropolitan Railway Bo-Bos had been rebuilt years before with end cabs and the space inside the body between them occupied by control equipment and machines. This was the pattern of the MSW Bo+Bos. The four 750V traction motors were axle-hung but a little 'give' was provided in the drive by the use of resilient gearwheels in which the toothed ring was not solid with the centre but attached to it by rubber-bushed driving pins.

Ten continuous running notches were provided by means of four weak-field steps in each motor grouping (series and series-parallel). In terms of speed this meant that the driver of a 750 ton mineral train climbing a gradient of 1 in 100 could set his controls so that the train would settle down to any one of ten balancing speeds between approximately 15 and nearly 35mile/h. Control was fully manual, with separate handles for notching up, changing the motor grouping and controlling the regenerative brake. The accelerating lever moved in a quadrant with 19 notches. By notch 15 all resistance was cut out and the motors were running in full-field. Notches 16 to 19 were weak-field steps. During acceleration and in certain conditions while running the driver had to keep an eye on his two ammeters. Full instructions on how to manipulate the controls were given in a driver's manual:

Right: The Glossop branch and its triangular junction with the main line were electrified at 1,500V dc at the same time as the Manchester-Sheffield main line. A Class 506 unit on a Manchester to Hadfield via Glossop working enters the branch on the curve from Dinting station. */Brian Morrison*

1 **To start and accelerate in motoring connections**

a Ensure Passenger/Goods and double-heading cocks are correctly set.

b Depress deadman's treadle.

c Switch ON weight transfer.

d Select FORWARD or REVERSE.

e Select SERIES.

f Release brakes and notch up accelerating lever until the current is 800A.

g Wait for the current to drop to 700A, then continue notching in this way until FULL FIELD is reached.

2 **If greater speed is required**

a *Go to weak field series*

i Switch OFF weight transfer.

ii Notch up to WF1, WF2, WF3, WF4, when the current drops to 650A.

OR

b *Go into parallel*

i Leave the weight transfer switch ON.

ii Select PARALLEL.

iii When the current on notch 15 series is not more than 700A return the accelerating lever smartly to notch 1.

If the button on the end of the lever is pressed, the lever will stop automatically at notch 1.

iv Notch up again as before, until notch 15 (FULL FIELD) is reached.

v If a further increase of speed is required, switch OFF weight transfer and take weak-field notches at 650A until the desired speed is reached.

These explicit instructions, which seem only to have omitted the fact that at Stage f in Phase 1 the train should have started to move, were followed by various notes. Drivers were told to switch weight transfer OFF when the current fell below 550A, not to use weak-field notches if they brought the steady current to more than 550A, and to observe certain precautions if obliged to use the first five notches to keep the speed down for fog working or slow running. On these notches resistances were in circuit, and although they were specially rated a time limit and a current limit had to be observed in using them.

The weight transfer switch mentioned in the instructions was an anti-slip device. Mechanical design can only go part way towards countering the tendency of a locomotive starting a train to transfer weight from the leading to the rear axle of each bogie. Closing the weight transfer switch weakened the fields of the motors driving the two leading axles and reduced their tractive effort, thereby lessening the likelihood of slip.

In this locomotive an inductive shunt – an iron-cored coil of high inductance – was connected in each field-weakening circuit. It acted as an electrical 'damper' to check a sudden rush of current as each weak-field step was taken, an effect which could cause a flashover in the traction motors. These components were not fitted in the Co-Co locomotives, where the proportion of the field windings remaining in circuit in all weak-field conditions was enough to provide the necessary inductance.

Regenerative braking is based on an effect already noticed – the back emf developed by a motor (Chapter 2). However, if the motor were simply disconnected from the supply and reconnected in a closed circuit,

current would flow only momentarily even if the motor continued turning. This is because the back emf would send a current through the armature in the opposite direction to the current previously drawn from the supply. In flowing round the closed circuit this current would also flow round the field windings in the opposite direction and wipe out the magnetism. With no magnetic field there would be no emf and generation would stop. Motors can be interconnected in a way that makes them self-exciting but the usual practice in locomotives with regenerative braking is to take the excitation for braking purposes from a separate source. In the MSW Bo+Bos and Co-Cos this source was a motor-generator. Locomotives of both classes carried two mg sets, one for battery charging and auxiliary services and the other for traction motor excitation during braking. Both machines were coupled to blowers for traction motor cooling. The motor of the exciter set therefore served a useful purpose even when electric braking was not in use.

A regenerating handle on the master controller set up the connections for regeneration. When it was moved away from the MOTORING position the traction motors were disconnected from the supply and their fields regrouped and connected to the exciter set. The regenerating handle was then advanced slowly notch by notch until the motor armature voltmeter in the cab showed the same reading as the line voltmeter. Movement of the accelerating handle to notch 15 then reconnected the motors to the line and the regenerating handle was notched up further to increase the generated volts until the centre-zero armature ammeter in the cab showed that current was flowing back into the supply. Again the driver's manual gives a step-by-step account of the procedure in one of the Bo+Bo locomotives:

1 **To apply regenerative braking**
   a If the speed is between 16-33mile/h and is unlikely to be greater than 33mile/h select SERIES. If the speed is between 30-55mile/h and is unlikely to be less than 33mile/h select PARALLEL.

   The accelerating lever must be at OFF before setting up regenerative connections, and the train speed controlled by friction brake if necessary.

   b Notch up regeneration lever until the motor voltmeter reads the same as the line voltmeter.
   c Move the accelerating lever quickly to notch 15.
   d Release the friction brake.
   e Notch up the regeneration lever to get the required braking effort.

2 **To increase speed**
   Notch back the regeneration lever towards MOTORING.
3 **To reduce speed**
   Notch up regeneration lever.

If the gradient eases while a train is regenerating, and speed falls, the generated voltage falls as well and if it is reduced below that of the overhead line current will flow back from the supply through the motors, producing more power and raising the speed again. These changes between regeneration and motoring take place automatically, without any action by the driver, and maintain a very constant speed down the steepest gradient. I remember riding in the cab of a freight train from Dunford Bridge to Wath and seeing the driver sitting back with his arms folded after he had set up regeneration and the train was rolling steadily down the 1 in 127 gradients towards Penistone.

It must be admitted that regeneration is not as simple as it looks. There are frequent fluctuations in the line voltage, which would mean corresponding variations in braking effort were it not for a stabilising circuit in the locomotive. This is arranged so that regenerated current, Ir, and excitation current, If, flow through stabilising resistors. If Ir increases because of a drop in line voltage, there is a greater volts drop across the resistors and the excitation current in the field windings is correspondingly reduced.

If the regenerated power is not absorbed there can be a build-up of voltage at the pantograph sufficient to trip the overvoltage relays in the locomotive. This would mean the sudden loss of braking effort. On the MSW scheme, therefore, certain substations were equipped with banks of resistors into which the regenerated current was switched automatically if it was not being absorbed by other trains, and the power was dissipated as heat. The resistances were switched into circuit automatically by a thyratron when a rise in voltage was detected. When the thyratron fired it struck the arc of an ignitron, allowing current to flow through the operating coils of the switching contactors. The closing of the contactors shorted the ignitron out so that it stopped conducting until the next operation. The resistors were rated continuously at 600A, 1,500V and were fan-cooled while carrying current. These arrangements were provided in the substations at Strafford Crossing (near the Wentworth Bank), Barnsley Junction, Gorton and Wharncliff Wood.

In their later years the Class 76 locomotives were equipped with rheostatic braking in addition to the regenerative brake so that electric braking could continue down to about 3-4mile/h. Drivers were recommended to use the rheostatic brake for controlling

Above: Manchester-Sheffield Co-Co No 27004 leaves
Manchester London Road with an express for Marylebone.
/Eric Treacy

train speed on falling gradients below 20mile/h. In
this system the traction motors were separately-
excited as during regeneration but the generated
voltage sent current through the starting resistances in
the locomotive instead of back to the line. The kinetic
energy of the train was converted into heat, as in
ordinary friction braking, but by an electrical process.
In rheostatic braking, the braking effort increases as
the resistance in circuit is reduced. An additional three-
position switch was fitted in the cab to set up the
connections and give three steps of excitation control.
In any position of the switch the braking effort could
be finely controlled by notching up or back with the
accelerating lever, which operated the resistance
contactors in the same way as when the locomotive
was under power.

The Co-Co locomotives made their appearance in
1954. They were a postwar design but similar in
principle to their predecessors, although the bogies
were not articulated and the weight transfer switch
was omitted together with the sanding equipment of
the Bo+Bos. Slipping at starting could be checked by

notching back and pressing an anti-slip brake pedal,
which made a partial brake application on all axles by
admitting air at 10lb/sq in to the brake cylinders.

With six traction motors, three motor groupings
were available:

a   All motors in series
b   Two parallel groups of three motors in series.
c   Three parallel groups of two motors in series.

Three weak-field steps in each grouping gave 12
continuous running notches. They were selected by
means of the regeneration handle, which could be
moved to positions marked WF1, 2 and 3 when the
accelerating handle was in notches 17, 27 or 35 (corresponding to groupings a, b and c above respectively).
Transition between groupings took place automatically
as the accelerating handle was advanced round its
quadrant. During regeneration the regeneration handle
was used in the same way as on the Bo-Bos, its function as a weak-field selector not being required in that
condition. A separate combination lever was used for
selecting the motor grouping for regeneration, which
could only take place in groupings a and b.

The traction motors were axle-hung and drove
through resilient gears as in the Bo+Bos but the nose

33

suspension now took the form of a link with rubber-bushed attachments to the bogie frame and to the motor nose. Lateral movement of the motors was restrained by struts with similar rubber-bushed attachments to the motor and bogie frames, and while vertical and lateral movements of the motors could take place under the control of the rubber, the suspension bearings could not come into contact with the wheel bosses.

The Bo+Bos were the first 1,500V dc locomotives in this country to work both passenger and freight traffic, and the Co-Cos were the first electrics built specifically for express passenger traffic on a British main line and to enjoy a working life. Some details of the two classes are tabulated below:

	Co-Co	Bo+Bo
Weight in working order	102.5 tons	87.3 tons
Length over buffers	59ft	50ft 4in
Wheel diameter	43in	50in
Continuous rating:		
Full field	2,400hp at 44.2mile/h TE 20,100lb	1,240hp at 31.9mile/h TE 14,600lb
Weak field	2,400hp at 57.5mile/h TE 15,600lb	1,360hp at 51.5mile/h TE 8,800lb
One-hour rating:		
Full field	2,700hp at 41.5mile/h TE 24,000lb	1,740hp at 26.3mile/h TE 25,100lb
Weak field	2,760hp at 52.7mile/h TE 19,500lb	1,868hp at 45.3mile/h TE 15,400lb
Maximum TE	45,000lb	45,000lb
Ventilating air per motor	2,200cu ft/min	2,000cu ft/min
Maximum speed	90mile/h	65mile/h

The Co-Co locomotives had a short working life in this country. After the closure of the ex-Great Central main line and withdrawal of through trains to and from Marylebone a regular interval service was maintained between Manchester and Sheffield, but a reappraisal of traffic on the route in 1967 led to the conclusion that it would have a greater potential if confined to freight, and from 1 January 1970 all Manchester-Sheffield passenger traffic was concentrated on the ex-MR Hope Valley line. The Co-Cos thus became redundant and were sold to the Netherlands Railways. Now that naming of electric locomotives has been resumed it may be recalled that the Co-Cos were given names during their service on BR and carried them as follows: 27000 *Electra*; 27001 *Ariadne*; 27002

Aurora; 27003 *Diana*; 27004 *Juno*; 27005 *Minerva*; 27006 *Pandora*.

The Bo+Bo series has soldiered on for nearly a quarter of a century in all, lately in dwindling numbers. Apart from the rheostatic braking modification, which required no change in the original resistance installation, larger compressors were fitted for working air-braked trains and some locomotives were equipped for multiple-unit working in pairs. Certain trains are worked between Wath and Barnsley Junction by four locomotives, a pair at the front and a pair at the rear. An inductive telephone system was installed in the

cabs enabling the two crews to communicate via the 1,500V overhead contact wire. Both when climbing Wentworth bank and when regenerating, certain current limits have to be observed and crews have to co-ordinate their actions if a train is checked on the bank and has to be restarted. The telephone system replaced the code of whistle signals used previously, which could not be heard by the rear crew of a very long train. These veterans were unperturbed by the changes in duties and traffic consequent upon the reorganisation of trans-Pennine freight traffic in 1967 and in their later years the time between shopping for

major maintenance was actually extended from two to four years. This extension was made possible by certain modifications shown to be necessary by experience, the most important being the replacement of brass in the surfaces of the inter-bogie coupling by a material more resistant to wear.

The Manchester-Sheffield-Wath electrification made it necessary to train drivers whose previous experience had been confined to steam locomotives. In the early

Below: Bo-Bo No 76.049 takes a train round the south side of Tinsley Yard./*Eric Bullen*

stages of the scheme I visited the training school at Wath where a course of 78 volunteers from Mexborough mpd was under instruction. Their ages ranged from 42 to 63. A classroom introduction to the locomotives in the first week of the course explained the equipment in simple language, without mathematics, avoiding technical terms where possible but providing a glossary of the essential ones. Some interesting problems of 'communication' came to light. For example, the instructors found that references to 'closing' a circuit were misunderstood at first because 'closing' was associated with shutting off steam or air supplies. During this phase trainees were taken over a locomotive in the sheds. Lectures were also given on the supply and distribution of power, with special emphasis on how sections of the overhead system could be isolated in case of faults.

Instruction in the second week introduced circuit diagrams. The full power circuit of the Bo+Bo was explained but trainees were also shown simplified diagrams of motor groupings, the connections for regeneration and so on. These had been prepared by the instructors themselves. There is much to be said for making circuitry comprehensible by picking out essentials and showing them in isolation. Once the elements of a circuit are understood, they are easily recognised when presented collectively and so the full diagram of the power and braking circuits in a locomotive becomes less daunting.

A technical examination was held at the end of the second week of the course, by which time trainees had had the opportunity to handle a locomotive in the sidings. Successful candidates then spent at least 30 hours working trains on the main line under instruction before being passed as drivers.

In the optimistic 1950s the MSW scheme seemed destined for extension. There was talk of continuing southwards over the GC London main line to Woodford Halse for exchanging traffic with the Western Region, and eastwards to Lincoln and Whitemoor. Provision was made in the power control room at Penistone for supervising 15 more substations. Over the years the traffic over the line changed materially and its prospects dimmed. Mottram marshalling yard was closed in 1972 but six sidings and an engine line were retained for traction exchange on mgr trains bound for Fidlers Ferry power station near Warrington. The sidings at Godley Junction were also reduced in number and used for traction exchange on trains to and from Merseyside. Company block trains largely replaced general freight and the need for marshalling facilities and transfer trips declined.

The story of 1,500V dc traction in Britain virtually began and ended with freight, for the MSJA line was converted to 25kV ac in 1971 and the local service now runs through to and from Crewe. On the far side of Piccadilly station, Manchester, the 1,500V catenary still feeds the Hadfield and Glossop emus but they seem only an afterglow of the days when *Electra* and the other classical ladies passed to and fro under the wires with their main line expresses.

Below: A chemical train at Torside Crossing on 28 June 1976 is double headed by Nos. 76.029 and 76.023. /*Rodney Wildsmith*

5
First Steps in ac Traction

At the end of the first half century of main line electrification the world's electrified railway mileage was divided roughly equally between alternating current and direct current systems. This distinction is to some extent misleading, for all by then received their supply as alternating current, whether from public power networks or their own generating plant. The conventional electric generator with conductors revolving in a magnetic field (or, in power station practice, a revolving magnetic field cutting stationary conductors) is fundamentally an ac machine. A dc generator is in effect an alternator with a commutator on its shaft to reverse alternate half cycles so that the output at the terminals is unidirectional.

The voltage at which power is supplied can be stepped up or down in a transformer. Since electrical power is the product of voltage and current, a high voltage means a low current for a given power, and conductors of smaller cross-section in the distribution system, with consequent economy in material. Power station alternators generate at some 14,000V but long-distance transmission of power takes place at 132,000V and upwards, the usual maxima today being 275,000V and 400,000V.

The supply in the 'Grid' distribution system is three-phase, which means that the individual conductors in the overhead lines carry currents which are 'out of step' with each other, reaching their positive and negative maxima in rotation. Power can be transmitted more efficiently by this method than as single-phase, and a three-phase supply is more convenient for the types of motor most widely used in industry. It is less suitable for railway traction for two reasons: three-phase motors cannot readily be controlled to run over the wide speed range required in railway operation; and two overhead wires are necessary above the tracks. Only limited use has been made of three-phase traction in the past. Nonetheless, the idea has continued to attract railway engineers because of the mechanical simplicity of three-phase motors, and today electronics offers the possibility of converting single-phase ac into three-phase ac of a form which allows continuously variable speed control.

When a three-phase supply is provided, the user can connect his equipment to individual phases and so obtain single-phase power. This is the usual procedure on ac railways. The dc railways accept the power as three-phase and rectify it. In fact, by appropriate interconnection of transformers and rectifiers they can produce the equivalent of a six-phase or even a twelve-phase supply, and when this is rectified there is a minimum of ac 'ripple' in the dc fed to the trains.

Whether a railway feeds alternating current to its trains or converts it to direct current by rectification the motors in the locomotives and motorcoaches are usually similar in principle. It has been shown in Chapter 2 that to reverse a dc series motor the direction of current is reversed in the field but not in the armature coils. If the current in both is reversed simultaneously the motor continues to run in the same direction. This simultaneous reversal occurs many times a second in a motor supplied with alternating current, and so the motor does not simply oscillate to and fro as might be expected but runs continuously in one direction or the other. Reversal is achieved in the same way as before, by changing the *relative* direction of current flow at any moment in the two sets of windings.

Unfortunately the use of alternating current in a series traction motor encounters a difficulty not met with in a similar dc machine. As the commutator spins under the brushes every armature coil is momentarily short-circuited. At this instant the pulsating magnetic flux induces a voltage in the short-circuited coil and a heavy current flows in it. The repeated breaking of these short-circuit currents as the armature revolves can cause heavy sparking and burning of the commutator segments, particularly at starting and speeds up to about 15% of the maximum. Maintenance is then required at shorter intervals, and restoring a commutator to the high degree of accuracy necessary for its proper performance is an exacting task.

This difficulty, known as the 'transformer effect',

does not occur in the dc motor because there the flux is steady. The problem was recognised from the earliest days of ac traction. Since the effect is proportional to frequency, it can be reduced by using a frequency lower than the usual industrial standards of 50 or 60Hz. It can be further alleviated by connecting resistance in the field winding circuits, but this method, developed early in the century by the Swiss engineer Behn-Eschenburg, is only fully effective above a certain speed and does not help the difficult starting situation. Before the motor starts to revolve, the short-circuit currents can overheat the affected coils, brushes and commutator segments. This is one of the reasons for the widespread use on ac railways of flexible couplings between motor and axle. The motor can move slightly before taking up the full load. With a rigid coupling there could be an appreciable standstill period during which the short-circuit current would circulate in some of the armature coils. The committee which produced the 1951 *Electrification of railways* report for the British Transport Commission studied low-frequency ac electrification in practice and watched the traction motor of a locomotive starting a train of 565 tons on a 1 in 70 gradient between Munich and Stuttgart. They noted:

'One of the motors was observed during the start, the commutator cover having been removed. At first the sparking at the brushes was severe; it gradually diminished as the speed increased, but had not completely ceased by the time the train was running at about 10 miles per hour.'

The countries which adopted ac electrification at low frequency did so for the sake of economies in construction of the overhead supply system gained from using a small section contact wire carrying some 15,000V. The current for a given horsepower on a 15,000V single-phase system is not much more than

Below: The Midland Railway's low-frequency ac electrification of its Lancaster-Morecambe-Heysham lines in 1903 was to provide a proving ground for industrial-frequency ac traction in this country 50 years later. Ex-MR motorcoach No 28611 is still at work on the system in LMS days./*W. Hubert Foster*

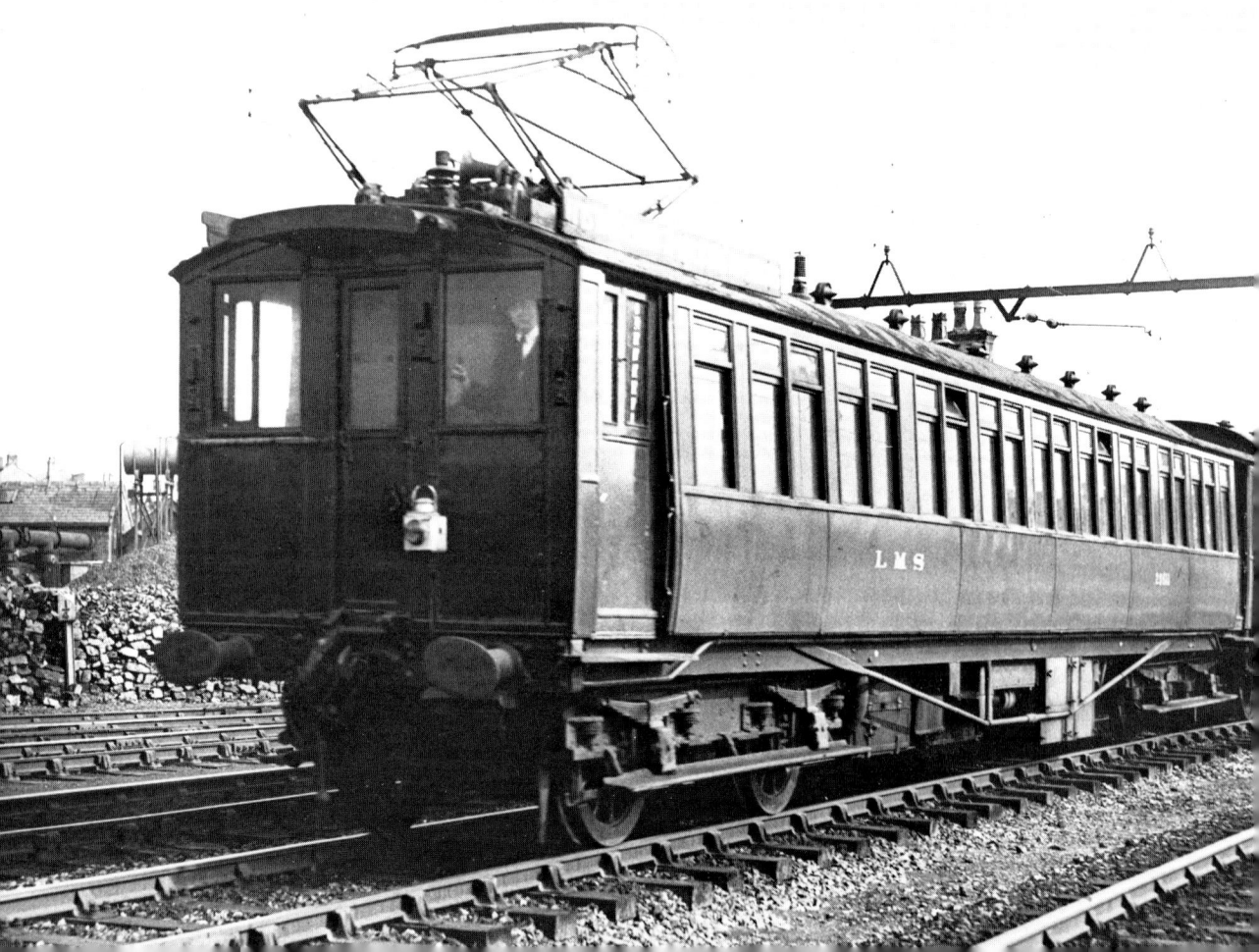

one-tenth of that required on a system operating at 1,500V dc. Often the railways which chose ac electrification had hydro-electric plants for generating their own low-frequency supplies, usually at $16\frac{2}{3}$Hz. Where they had to use an industrial frequency source they installed rotary-converters in substations to provide the low frequency, but these machines are less efficient than the rectifiers in a dc railway substation – about 84% against 95-96% in a typical example.

Various experiments were made in using a standard industrial frequency for traction, but most of them involved the installation of converting machinery in the locomotives. The first major scheme at 50Hz was carried out by the Hungarian State Railways between 1931 and 1934 when the line from Budapest to the Austrian frontier at Hegyeshalom (118 route-miles) was equipped with a single-phase overhead supply at 16,000V taken from the 110kV national power network. Rotary machines in the locomotives converted the supply to three-phase ac for the traction motors. Each locomotive was powered by a single motor driving the axles through side rods and arranged to run at four basic speeds by changing the effective number of poles in the magnetic system. In a motor of this kind the transformer effect is put to good use. The three-phase supply in the stationary field windings sets up a rotary magnetic field which cuts the rotor conductors and induces currents in them. Induction provokes a reverse reaction, ie the rotor conductors tend to move in such a way that the inductive effect is cancelled. The rotor therefore starts to revolve to 'catch up' with the rotating field for if it could do so the 'cutting' would stop and with it the rotor current. In practice the two never revolve in synchronism, for that would bring the process to a halt, but the speed of the rotor lags behind that of the field by an amount sufficient to produce a torque. There is no commutation problem, but the switching necessary to provide a limited number of speeds is complex, and resistance has to be connected in the rotor circuit through sliprings and brushes to limit the induced currents at starting.

Meanwhile the ideal of using conventional series traction motors on an industrial frequency supply was being pursued. The first important steps towards 50Hz traction as understood today were taken in Germany in 1936 when the Reichsbahn electrified the $31\frac{1}{4}$ miles between Freiburg and Seebrugg in the Black Forest (the Höllentalbahn) with a 50Hz supply at 20kV. A single feeder station at Titisee, near the centre point of the line, supplied power for the whole section. Of the four experimental locomotives, two were equipped with mercury-arc rectifiers and dc traction motors, one had motors operating on ac at 50Hz, and the fourth was a version of the type used on the Hungarian State Railways described above. One of the rectifier locomotives used grid control for varying the voltage applied to the motors. The thyristor control systems of the present day are the semiconductor equivalents of this grid-controlled mercury-arc rectifier scheme.

After World War II the Höllentalbahn was in the French Zone of Occupation and the long-standing problem of 50Hz traction was attacked afresh by French, German and Swiss engineers. At that time there was considerable faith in the future of the 50Hz motor. It is interesting that although Brown Boveri had supplied one of the original Höllentalbahn rectifier locomotives, the company published a statement in 1951 in the following terms:

'There is no doubt that by reason of its simple construction the locomotive with motors fed with 50Hz current is the best answer even if in the present state of development it may seem preferable in some circumstances to use locomotives with rectifiers or rotary converters. The problem of the 50Hz motor is not a new problem; it is simply one of adapting the thoroughly proven $16\frac{2}{3}$Hz motor for the new 50Hz frequency. There are still some difficulties to overcome before it can be used in all circumstances, but it is certain that a few years hence the 50Hz single-phase commutator motor, by then fully developed, will enable all traction problems to be resolved.'

French thinking was on similar lines at first. In using the Höllentalbahn as a test bed for their own forthcoming 50Hz electrification, their first trials in 1950 were with a motorcoach and a locomotive both equipped with 50Hz motors, and of the next three units ordered two had 50Hz motors and one a rotary-converter installation.

A traction motor for the 50Hz frequency was at a disadvantage in several respects compared with one for $16\frac{2}{3}$Hz. To reduce the transformer effect it was necessary to reduce the flux per pole and one of the measures taken to this end was to adopt a lower operating voltage for the motor. But this involved higher currents and increased heat losses. Reducing flux per pole also made it necessary to have more poles for a given output, resulting in a larger and heavier motor. Figures for a 750kW (1,000hp) motor published in 1951 showed it to be 60% greater in outside diameter and in weight than a corresponding machine for $16\frac{2}{3}$Hz. There were 28 brush sets at 4in spacing round the commutator compared with 10 sets at 6in spacing, so that both the amount and intricacy of maintenance in this difficult area were increased. Later the differences were narrowed and many 50Hz motors have given satisfactory service, but in the meantime development had swung on to a new course with a revival of interest in rectifier locomotives.

The *Electrification of railways* report for the British Transport Commission was written before the French gave their first demonstration of their work on 50Hz traction at an international conference held in Annecy from 12-15 October 1951. The authors of the report had only the prewar Höllentalbahn locomotives to go on as practical examples of motive power for the system. They estimated that 50Hz locomotives and motorcoaches would be higher in first cost and would cost more to maintain than 1,500V dc equipment, and considered that it would be more complicated to arrange for inter-running with the Southern Region low-voltage dc system. They would have needed a highly sophisticated crystal ball to have seen all that was going to occur in the field of rectification, and how some 25 years later it would enable 50Hz ac trains operating a London commuter service to pass to and from a low-voltage third-rail underground section between Drayton Park and Moorgate. The committee's recommendation that a line should be equipped experimentally for the 50Hz system went no further than recognising that it 'might conceivably have advantages for the conversion of secondary lines provided it were not prejudicial to operation on ad-jacent lines equipped on the standard system.'

The motive power exhibited by the French at Annecy included a motorcoach with dc motors fed through single-anode mercury-arc rectifiers of American design, and a Bo-Bo locomotive which almost as an afterthought had been equipped with multi-anode rectifiers. These two exhibits stole the show. In the years which followed, the rectifier system quickly became dominant in the very rapid development of 50Hz traction on the French National Railways, where the idea of its being a system for secondary lines with light traffic was forgotten almost overnight. The characteristics of the dc series motor are acknowledged to be the most suitable for traction of any electrical machine. The rectifier system allied them with the advantages of a high-voltage ac supply. At the same time the transformer in the locomotive, which was in any case necessary to reduce the voltage to a suitable level for the motors, offered a means of voltage control with a much greater number of steps than is

Below: A Morecambe train at Heysham on 6 November 1965 is formed of a three-car unit of Willesden-Earls Court stock converted for industrial-frequency ac working.
/*John Marshall*

practicable on dc, all of which can be used for continuous running because no resistance losses are involved.

A further advantage is that the motors can be connected permanently in parallel. This is important not only for the fact that switchgear for changing the grouping once or twice during acceleration is eliminated, but also for its effect on starting performance. When a locomotive starts with its motors in series in a conventional dc arrangement, the motor driving an axle which starts to slip accelerates rapidly and builds up a high back emf which reduces the current through the whole circuit so that the other machines cannot compensate for the loss of tractive effort. In parallel, however, the effect is to divert more current through the other motors so that they help to keep the train moving until the slipping axle regains adhesion. Much was made of these facts in the mid-1950s and amid the general acclaim of rectifier motive power the 50Hz motor and its problems receded into the background.

The rectifier system has its problems as well, although on a minor scale. It has been mentioned earlier that in fixed traction substations polyphase rectifier connections are used to minimise ripple in the dc output. The rectifier in a locomotive or motorcoach is handling a single-phase input and the ripple is appreciable. In fact, the French refer to the output from a single-phase rectifier as *courant ondulé* rather than *courant continu* (direct current). The ripple causes the magnetic flux in the motor to pulsate and this can involve losses through heating by eddy currents as well as poor commutation. Fortunately the difficulties are easier to overcome by certain constructional features in the motors or by additional circuit components than in the case of the 50Hz motor.

The proposal that British Railways should experiment with 50Hz traction was quickly taken up. Engineers from the British Transport Commission had witnessed the demonstrations by French Railways at Annecy in 1951 and had followed subsequent developments closely. In the same year the BTC announced that trials had been authorised on the Lancaster-Morecambe-Heysham lines of the London Midland Region. These lines had been electrified by the former Midland Railway in 1908 with single-phase ac at 6.6kV, 25Hz. The original trains were withdrawn in 1951 and plans went ahead for restoring an electric service using the same overhead system and voltage but taking power at 50Hz. Three redundant three-car dc emus which had operated between Willesden High Level and Earls Court until the service was withdrawn in 1940 were made available to the English Electric Co Ltd, which equipped them with transformers, rectifiers and new dc motors. The whole route was fed from a new substation at Lancaster Green Ayre connected to a 6.6kV ring main of the North Western Electricity Board, and the former 25Hz motor-generator plant at Heysham Harbour was closed down. Trial running began in November 1952 and regular passenger services were instituted from August 1953 – the first to be operated at 50Hz on British Railways.

In order to put 50Hz traction to a practical trial with as little delay as possible, considerable use was made of standard components. The four 215hp motors in each motorcoach were, in fact, standard machines and the two six-anode rectifiers were an industrial pattern modified only by the use of anti-vibration mountings. There were two environmental hazards for the mercury-arc rectifier installed in a railway vehicle. One was vibration, causing splashing of the mercury and consequent malfunction; the other was low temperature. Voltage surges may occur if full load is applied to a cold rectifier, and when rolling stock was parked in the open overnight during severe weather this could be a problem when the trains were required for service in the morning. Preheaters were fitted to the Lancaster-Morecambe-Heysham rectifiers to meet this difficulty and provision for preheating in one way or another became standard in later classes of motive power with mercury-arc rectifiers.

The transformer was designed specially for the job, with a tapped secondary winding for control of the output voltage to the rectifier/motor circuits. In common with industrial practice the windings were immersed in oil which served both for additional insulation and for cooling. For this purpose the oil was circulated by pump round an external circuit with a fan-cooled radiator.

The tap-changer was made from a standard camshaft-operated contactor group which the company was then supplying for 3,000V dc motorcoaches on the Polish State Railways. Other switchgear on the dc side of the circuit was of types fitted in Southern Region emus.

In the motorcoaches in which the installations were made the original dc control equipment had been carried in a compartment behind the driver's cab. This space and the adjacent luggage compartment were merged to house the ac apparatus and rectifiers, part of the passenger accommodation in the vehicle being converted into a new luggage compartment. Acceleration was automatic, and there were two steps of resistance control in the sequence as well those provided by tap-changing. The master controller had four positions corresponding to those of dc emus: shunt, half-voltage (dc series), full voltage (dc parallel) and weak-field.

The notching resistors were carried on the underframe together with a field shunt resistor for the weak-field step and its associated contactors, the electro-pneumatic reverser and the battery. As time went on specialised rectifiers designed for underfloor mounting were tested in the stock but continued to be mounted above floor level in the equipment compartment where they were more accessible for observation during trials.

One of the new rectifiers tested in the stock was of special significance for the future. This was a 750kW unit with germanium diodes developed by the British Thomson-Houston Co Ltd. Trials began on the Lancaster-Morecambe-Heysham lines in 1955 and in the following year were continued in the London area between Fenchurch Street and Bow Junction. This section had been equipped for 1,500V dc to connect with the Liverpool Street-Shenfield electrification and was specially energised for the trials with high-voltage ac. Germanium had its problems of liability to breakdown at high temperatures but the promise of the semiconductor rectifier was already good enough for substantial quantities to be ordered when the first contracts for 25kV ac motive power were placed at the end of the year.

Although most of the existing overhead equipment on the Lancaster-Morecambe-Heysham lines was kept in use for the 50Hz electrification, a new installation designed for 20kV (at that time the maximum envisaged) was put in on a section about $2\frac{3}{4}$ miles long between Green Ayre and Morecambe Promenade stations. Here the light poles and cantilevers so familiar on high-voltage ac lines today were seen for the first time together with the slender contact wire of 0.166sq in cross-section. This was of cadmium copper and suspended from a single catenary cable formed of seven stranded hard-drawn copper wires of the same cross-section. Lancaster-Morecambe-Heysham continued to be a proving ground until the first generation of purpose-built ac emus began to appear and the first services in this country at 25kV started to operate on the pilot electrification between Colchester, Clacton-on-Sea and Walton-on-Naze in 1959.

Below: The Class 304 units introduced originally for local services in the Manchester and Liverpool areas of the LMR 50Hz electrification represented the first major use of emu stock on an industrial frequency system and the most widespread application of semiconductor rectifiers at that time. Class 304/3 unit No 039 arrives at Liverpool Lime Street from Crewe on 23 September 1976./*Brian Morrison*

6
Ac in Practice

One of the questions discussed by the International Railway Congress at its meeting in London in 1954 was the choice of electrification system. The Congress, while agreeing that the 50Hz ac system employed the cheapest fixed equipment and was the ideal system where traffic was light or infrequent, was not convinced that the same advantage would be shown for heavily loaded lines or where the cost of obtaining electrical clearance was excessive.

Much of the information before the Congress had been gathered and co-ordinated by S. B. Warder, Chief Electrical Engineer of British Railways, in his capacity as Reporter for the English speaking countries and Special Reporter for all Railway Administrations. Warder's views on the future of the 50Hz system, gained from first-hand observation and discussions during his term as Reporter, were much broader, and some nine months later, in September 1955, he presented a report to the British Transport Commission which was to change the course of electric traction practice in this country. The British Railways modernisation plan had been published in the meantime, and its proposals for further main line electrification included Euston to Crewe, Birmingham, Manchester and Liverpool. Warder's report reviewed the current state of 50Hz traction development in France, compared the technical aspects of the 1,500V dc and 25kV 50Hz systems, and made estimates of the cost of both if applied to the LMR project.

With regard to the overhead contact system, he estimated that at 25kV only about a third of the weight of copper required at 1,500V would have to be suspended above the tracks. The contact wire itself would be only one-third the cross-section of the 1,500V wire, while the current collected per locomotive for equal duty would at 25kV be only one-fifteenth of the value at 1,500V. The pantograph pressure in consequence would be only about one half as great and he foresaw a significant increase in the life of the contact wire and pantographs. Assuming the use of 25kV on all the lines proposed for electrification in the modernisation plan, he reckoned a saving in material for overhead construction of about 27,000 tons of copper and 16,000 tons of steel, adding that 'ultimately this may well be multiplied tenfold, having regard to the trend towards electrification and the probable absence of other sources of power later in the century'. Considering the LMR scheme alone, it was suggested that the total cost of an ac electrification would be 86% of that for 1,500V dc.

Warder's recommendation on motive power was to concentrate on the rectifier principle. His investigations of Continental practice had shown that while railway and contractors' engineers had improved the performance of the 50Hz commutator motor 'out of all knowledge', it remained a 'very complicated motor demanding a high standard of maintenance'. Equipment trials on the Lancaster-Morecambe-Heysham lines suggested that an ac emu could have its transformer, rectifier and control gear mounted underfloor as in its dc counterpart and that the ac system held prospects of extending the sphere of usefulness of this type of motive power.

The most difficult aspect of adopting high-voltage ac on British Railways was likely to be the provision of safe clearances through tunnels and under bridges between the underside of the contact wire and the highest point of the loading gauge profile. With 1,500V the normal requirement was 10in and the minimum 4in, but Warder pointed out that those values had been laid down in 1928 and in the light of subsequent experience 4in had become the accepted norm. He thought the normal clearance for 25kV could be 11in, and that where this could not be provided without unacceptable civil engineering costs and labour, the voltage should be reduced to 6.6kV and the clearance brought down to 4in.

Such was the celebrated 'dual voltage system' which the public relations departments of the day tended to hail as a unique British contribution to 25kV electrification practice. For Warder it was simply an expedient, necessary at the time but eventually applied only on a limited scale. It was, however, an essential ingredient of his original proposals and he referred to it in his report as 'what I already begin to consider as the usual mixture of low-voltage sections where clearances are difficult and high-voltage sections wherever adequate clearances can be obtained at a reasonable cost.' It featured again in his final conclusion:

'In short, my conclusion is that provided our reasonable hopes that the existing 1,500V clearances will prove adequate for a voltage of 6.6kV or some lower voltage of this order, there would be little difficulty in using 25kV as a standard for the whole of the country except the third rail area of the Southern Region and the cost of conversion would, I think, be only a small off-set against the total prospective economy of adopting the ac system as the standard for the country.'

At the end of 1955 Warder's recommendation was accepted. Those who had watched the development of 50Hz traction on the Continent had not expected the decision to be otherwise, although it was not universally welcomed. A certain coolness developed between British Railways and the electric traction industry. British contractors had been asked to comment on a brief specification for ac rectifier locomotives suitable for the LMR scheme, and the weights and prices they quoted in reply did not bear out the French claim that the 50Hz ac locomotive had not only proved to be a better locomotive than its dc counterpart but

also was cheaper in first cost and maintenance. Perhaps one of the reasons for the discrepancy, Warder suggested, was that 'until British contractors have actually built locomotives they have a natural reluctance to accept the possibilities which the French claim for the ac locomotive, coupled perhaps with a natural tendency to desire to continue to make commercial use of the development charges they have incurred in their dc designs.' Warder considered that he and his engineers were in a position to be better informed than the contractors and that the cost of ac locomotives could easily have been overestimated. He did not accept the 'glib suggestion' that 'the present price of French ac locomotives is not one that will be maintained indefinitely or bluntly that it is a cut price to establish the ac system'. Nor did he accept that the success of Continental groups in obtaining orders for 50Hz equipment as in Portugal and Turkey was entirely due to lack of experience on the part of British contractors or to subsidies of the foreign offers.

These comments were made in an internal report, but the sentiments they echoed inevitably spilled over into external relationships with the railway industry at all levels. Up to that time main line electrification in this country barely existed except in a somewhat specialised form in the Southern Region, but British electric locomotives and fixed equipment were being supplied for dc main lines in many parts of the world. At home there was virtually a blank page to write on,

for the motive power of the Manchester-Sheffield-Wath lines was largely of prewar conception. The new opportunities were taken, but the arguments continued.

British Railways supported its decision with the claim that the 50Hz system would offer the best prospects of taking advantage of technical development. Few at that time foresaw how rapid that development would be or how it would branch out into new and unexpected directions.

The Southern Region and other low-voltage dc lines were left undisturbed but the 'one-off' 1,200V dc third-rail electrification from Manchester Victoria to Bury came up for consideration. If it were to be converted in the interests of uniformity it would have to be to 50Hz ac, but its rolling stock urgently called for renewal and priority was given to keeping the service running by building new trains for the existing system. Conversion was shelved, and 26 two-car units (Class 504) were built at Wolverton, going into service in

Below left: Class 81 (originally AL1) was the first of the prototype locomotive classes for the LMR electrification. No 81.001 heads an express at the top of Camden Bank on 16 May 1973./*Brian Morrison*

Below: No 81.017 at Springs Branch on 26 May 1977 has acquired a 'blanked out' train description panel and marker lights – symbols of the reliance now placed on electronic describer systems for train identification by signalmen. /*Eric Bullen*

1959. The coaches gave a foretaste of some of the ac emus to be seen later, the cabs being of a new profile 'providing better vision and improving front end appearance'. This was not difficult to do considering the uncompromisingly dull coachwork of the ac trains for the LT&S line which gave the public its first sight of the new breed in the same year.

The Bury stock was equipped by English Electric. Motorcoaches had four 140hp motors connected in series pairs under 'simplex' series/parallel control (Chapter 2). All equipment was insulated for 1,500V to earth and standard 1,500V items were used as far as possible. Shoegear remained as before, the shoe being a plate pivoted near the top and spring-loaded so that the lower end was held against the side of the conductor rail. The inner face and top of the conductor rail in this system are protected by continuous boarding, and there is similar protection of the outer face, but spaced away from the rail sufficiently to allow passage of the shoes.

Electrification from Euston to the north-west was the showpiece of the electric traction proposals in the modernisation plan but the improvement of suburban services was also a priority. In the London area a beginning had been made with the Liverpool Street-Shenfield-Southend electrification (Chapter 3); the plan added the lines from Liverpool Street to Enfield and Chingford, to Hertford and Bishops Stortford, and the London, Tilbury & Southend line from Fen-

church Street. It also brought electrification to Scotland for the first time by including suburban lines in the Glasgow area. All these projects were now to be carried out at 50Hz ac. Conversion of the Liverpool Street-Shenfield-Southend lines to the same system was inevitable because the electrification proposals also covered the GE main line from Shenfield to Ipswich together with the Clacton, Harwich and Felixstowe branches.

To cover suburban service requirements in the London and Glasgow areas and on the LMR main line 361 traction equipments for new multiple-unit trains were ordered; also 124 equipments for converting existing 1,500V dc emus to ac operation. Work was put in hand without delay on the new electrifications in the London and Glasgow areas and on the Manchester-Crewe section of the LMR main line scheme. The first locomotive orders for the latter totalled 100 units of five different classes. In order to obtain early operating experience it was decided to electrify the branch from Colchester to Clacton-on-Sea and Walton on the Naze and to work services with new emu stock as it became available. This was the first section of

British Railways to carry public traffic at 25kV ac. The first of 112 four-car units intended eventually for the London, Tilbury & Southend electrification was commissioned in December 1958 and units of this stock (later Class 302) began running on the Colchester-Clacton-Walton section in March 1959. This section was also used for an advanced analysis of system performance in normal traffic conditions using the electronic digital recording techniques available at the time. Its purpose was to measure the external effects of the traction system, such as those on the low-current signalling circuits, on the Post Office

Below: Class AL2 (now 82) came from the Metropolitan-Vickers side of the AEI organisation and employed high-tension tap-changing instead of the low-tension scheme of the AL1s from AEI (Rugby). No 82.006 heads the Sundays 10.00 Glasgow-Liverpool at Glasgow Central on 23 June 1974, to take the train as far as Carstairs. */J. H. Cooper-Smith*

Below right: The prototype high-tension tap-changer for the AL2 locomotives. Note the chain and sprocket drive of the two sliders and the row of tappings traversed by the left hand slider./*GEC Traction Ltd*

telecommunications network, on broadcasting of all kinds and on the public electricity supply system. It was the first time it had been possible to study an electric traction system in this way.

By this time the eventual dominance of the semiconductor rectifier was becoming apparent but in the initial orders 274 of the 361 emu equipments were fitted with mercury-arc devices, as were 60 of the 100 locomotives for the LMR. For the most part these were single-anode rectifiers although two locomotive classes (later known as Classes 81 and 82) were equipped initially with three six-anode tanks of a proven industrial design modified to prevent splashing of the mercury pool. If one anode failed in a multi-anode rectifier, however, the whole tank had to be replaced, which was a laborious task unsuited to railway operating conditions where quick replacement of a faulty unit is obviously essential. Single-anode rectifiers could be changed individually in case of failure.

In either type of rectifier the current flows in the form of a stream of electrons emitted from an incandescent spot on the surface of a mercury pool. In a multi-anode rectifier the flow switches from anode

to anode as each becomes positive with respect to the cathode (the mercury pool) in turn, following the alternations of the supply voltage. The problem in the single-anode rectifier is that when its anode goes negative with respect to the cathode, the flow of electrons (ie the mercury-arc) is suppressed unless there is some means of maintaining it during the negative half cycle. Alternatively the arc must be restruck. A way round the difficulty was found in the 'excitron' rectifier by deflecting the arc to an auxiliary anode during the negative half-cycles. In the 'ignitron' the arc was extinguished and then restruck at the beginning of the positive half-cycle. Both systems had their advocates, and much was heard of them in the early days. Rectifiers can 'backfire' (ie conduct in the reverse direction) but this was less likely to happen in the ignitron because of the extinction of the arc. The ignitron therefore had the advantage of smaller size because anode and cathode could be brought closer together, with the added gain that the shorter arc resulted in a lower voltage drop across the rectifier. But precautions against backfires had still to be taken and so baffles were placed in the path of the arc, which prevented the volts drop from being as low as it might be. Nonetheless, the ignitron was often preferred despite its more complicated excitation arrangements.

The 'Com-Pak' rectifiers originally fitted in the Class 84 locomotives were an attempt to match the small size and low volts drop of an ignitron in an excitron but they had problems of their own and the advance of semiconductor technology made further development unnecessary.

The year 1960 was eventful. As a prelude the first of the ac locomotives being built for the LMR electrification was handed over to the LMR on 27 November 1959. The Manchester-Crewe section of the scheme was opened on 12 September 1960 and during the year locomotives of all five prototype classes emerged from their builders' works. Local services were worked by four-car emus with germanium rectifiers. All locomotives and motorcoaches were equipped for running on 25kV or 6.25kV but extensive civil engineering to provide clearances for the higher voltage made it possible to work at 25kV throughout the 31 miles of the Manchester-Crewe line. These works have been described in detail in O. S. Nock's *Britain's New Railway* (Ian Allan Ltd, 1966).

The locomotives were built to meet a common performance specification but individual contractors were free to follow their own ideas in the electrical design subject to the use of circuit-breakers, pantographs, earthing switches and voltage-sensing equipment specified by BR. Control was by tap-changing of two basic types. Classes 81, 83 and 85 had main transformers with separate primary and secondary windings, with low tension tap-changers operating on the secondaries. In Classes 82 and 84 the main transformer was an auto-transformer, ie a single tapped winding. Although physically one unit, the auto-transformer acts as if it had two windings, the primary consisting of the total number of turns and the secondary consisting of the number of turns between the selected tapping and the earthed end of the winding. In this case the tap-changer operates at high tension, with the advantage of handling lower currents. In the two-winding transformers the primaries were in four sections which were in series on 25kV and connected as two parallel pairs on 6.25kV. The auto-transformers had a 6.25kV input tapping about a quarter of the way from the earthed end of the winding. It was claimed by advocates of the two-winding transformer that the auto-transformer involved losses which were not incurred in their system. Soon, however the requirement of running at 6.25kV no longer existed on routes operated by locomotives and the auto-transformer system has been standardised in later locomotive construction.

All locomotives had similar driving controls, enabling the tap-changer to be notched up or back, step by step, or to run continuously in either direction until arrested by moving the controller to a 'hold' position. After maximum voltage (notch 38) the traction motors went into weak-field. Years later the same form of controller was used in the thyristor locomotive, No 87.101, although here movement of the handle varied the firing angle of the thyristors instead of operating an electro-mechanical tap-changer.

In the days of the APT it is hard to recapture the glamour of a maximum speed of 100mile/h but it was

this capability of the ac locomotives which made most impression on the general public. In brief the specification called for 90mile/h with a 475 ton train and up to 55mile/h with 950 tons, and a maximum weight of 80 tons. This was the era of the Bo-Bo high-speed locomotive, which was the wheel arrangement chosen. Later some of the strongest supporters on the Continent of the Bo-Bo rectifier locomotive as meeting all speed and adhesion requirements revised their opinion and returned to the Co-Co. Ratings of the designs for BR ranged from 2,950 to 3,300hp.

The styling of the locomotives by the various builders was uniform. It was remarked somewhat apologetically of the design in 1960 that 'there is a limit to what can be achieved by way of attractive appearance in what is in effect a rectangular box' but the effect achieved was functional and satisfactory, and has been little criticised. There was some controversy over the insistence on fully springborne motors with flexible drives, particularly as the latter were of Continental origin in the absence of proven British types. It had become almost a dogma in the electric traction industry that the springborne motor was a device adopted by ac railways on the Continent because their series motors would not commutate satisfactorily if axle-hung. Inevitably the question of whether the expense of flexible drives was justified was raised by an industry spokesman at the British Railways Electrification Conference in London in 1960 and he was told that the decision had been taken under considerable pressure from the civil engineers in the absence of definite information on the characteristics of the two methods of suspension. Tests to establish the effects on the track of each were proceeding. Flexible drives were, in fact, dispensed with in the next series of 100 locomotives (Class 86) which in due course demonstrated in the most practical manner that with 100mile/h speeds and intensive service conditions the axle-hung motor can cause deterioration of the permanent way.

The emus on Manchester-Crewe represented the first large-scale use of semiconductor traction rectifiers in the world. Each rectifier comprised 480 germanium diodes mounted on 10 pull-out trays and was carried in a case on the motorcoach underframe. Germanium is more sensitive to heat than its suc-

cessor, silicon, and so a motor-driven fan supplied cooling air at a rate of approximately 3,500cu ft/min. The same air flow cooled the smoothing chokes, the reactor used in the tap-changing operation, and the transformer oil cooler. On the opposite side of the underframe were mounted the transformer and the low-tension tap-changer. These were four-car units consisting of an open second battery driving trailer, second class motorcoach with luggage compartment, trailer composite, and driving trailer. The battery, battery charger and main compressor were carried under the battery driving trailer, the compressor being driven by a dc motor with its own germanium rectifier. The four axle-hung traction motors in the motorcoach were rated at 190hp (continuous) in full field and 207hp in weak field, at 975V. During acceleration the motor voltage was raised in 17 steps under relay control but the master controller only had the usual four emu positions. However, the progression could be held on any step, all of which could be used continuously.

The arrangements described were generally similar in all the emu stock of this generation whether with semiconductor or mercury-arc rectifiers. In ac traction equipments a supply for auxiliary services can be taken from an extra winding on the transformer, but single-phase ac is not suitable for all purposes; dc is required for battery charging and for the compressor drive, with its need for a high starting torque. Single-phase motors can be used for fans and pumps, usually capacitor-start-and-run machines, (ie similar to the domestic refrigerator motor but with the capacitor continuously in circuit instead of being cut out by a centrifugal switch). In the Class 83 locomotives, however, a rotary machine (an Arno converter) converted single-phase ac to three-phase for driving the oil and water cooling fans (the ignitron rectifiers were water-cooled), water pump, oil pump and traction motor blowers, all of which were driven by squirrel cage induction motors. This arrangement has not been perpetuated in later locomotive designs.

Not unnaturally there was some headshaking among engineers brought up in the dc tradition at the profusion of auxiliary machines and services in ac stock. I remember one of them reminiscing nostalgically on some public occasion about the simplicity of the Manchester-Sheffield dc motive power for which he had been responsible, and lowering his voice in case his *lèse-majesté* should be overheard. Something of the 'my country right or wrong' spirit was abroad in official railway circles in those days.

The main line from Manchester to Crewe is via Stockport. Between Manchester Piccadilly and Stockport a secondary line branches to the west of the main line and runs via Styal to Wilmslow, where the main

Top left: Class AL3 (83) came from English Electric. No 83.007 passes Oxenholme with the up 'Postal' on 11 June 1974./*Brian Morrison*

Left: No 82.003 on a long train of Palvans begins the long rise to the flyover which crosses the up and down main lines (foreground) about 1½ miles south of Rugby. /*Philip D. Hawkins*

line is rejoined. The Styal loop was used for the development and testing of the many new techniques involved in electrifying at 50Hz and also for training drivers in readiness for the opening of the first stage. Training had to begin before the first of the new ac locomotives were delivered in quantity and so the Metropolitan-Vickers gas turbine locomotive No 18100, which had formerly operated on the Western Region, was equipped with a pantograph, mercury-arc rectifiers and driving controls similar to those of the new designs in production. The rectifiers were glass

bulbs, a type still being used in substations at that time but hardly suitable for a mobile installation. However, they served their purpose for the short period required and No 18100 shared with four emus borrowed from the Eastern Region in the training of 206 instructors and drivers and 88 guards.

Power for the Manchester-Crewe electrification was taken from the CEGB at Heaton Norris and Crewe. With only two feeder stations some 27 miles apart for 31 miles of main route the scheme demonstrated one of the advantages of high-voltage ac over dc

Left: A train of tank wagons is hurried through Stafford by 83.002 on 30 July 1973./*M. Hall*

Above: GEC had its first major order for main line electric locomotives in the 10 units of Class AL4. No 84.006 is in the charge of an up parcels train passing Tamworth on 20 January 1975./*Philip D. Hawkins*

electrification, and this was reinforced by the fact that the railway had to provide less than seven miles of cable to link its overhead system with the Grid. A feature of which little had been said until then, however, was the need to provide 'booster' transformers every two miles at the lineside to avoid interference with Post Office telephone circuits. If the return traction current returned to the feeder points through the earth in the usual way there was the risk of induction in cables near the line. The boosters were 1:1 ratio transformers with their primaries in series with the contact wire and their secondaries connected across insulated joints in the rails. The voltage injected into the rails at these points 'boosted' the flow of current back to the feeder station and encouraged it to keep to the rails rather than stray through the earth.

Being still in the nature of a pilot scheme, Manchester-Crewe was used for testing three types of overhead construction – simple catenary, simple 'stitched' catenary, and compound. In the stitched version of simple catenary there is a short section of auxiliary catenary – the 'stitch' – at the supporting points and the droppers which carry the contact wire

are attached to the stitch instead of to the main catenary. At that time simple catenary was not considered suitable for speeds above 60mile/h but the stitched version was not used after Manchester-Crewe. Later sections of the LMR electrification between Euston and the North-West used compound catenary for high-speed stretches. Current collection at speed was continuously studied by the BR Research Department at Derby and by the time of the electrification extension from Weaver Junction to Glasgow it was possible to return to simple unstitched catenary throughout.

The boosters with rail return were not continued, either. In later work the transformers channelled the current into an insulated return conductor carried on the supports of the overhead system.

With Manchester-Crewe, rail travel at 100mile/h became an everyday experience. On a demonstration run before the start of public services a five-coach train headed by Class 83 No 3025 accelerated from a slowing for bridge reconstruction near Holmes Chapel to run some five miles at a minimum of 97mile/h and reached 102.3mile/h, still accelerating, between Goostrey and Chelford. *Change at Crewe* was the appropriate title of the commemorative book published by the London Midland Region. A glossary of terms was provided, among them 'Electric Locomotive' which was defined as: 'A hauling unit (for hauling coaching or freight stock) on which the electric motors for the movement of the train, the switchgear associated therewith and other apparatus are mounted; and having a cab containing apparatus for driving'.

With these words romance might seem to have flown out of the window but the new motive power continued to fascinate, and the traveller who had once watched steam billowing over the Cheshire plain could now gaze mesmerised at the ever-changing patterns traced, erased and recreated at lightning speed by the catenary system from which the 'hauling unit' at the head of the train drew its unflagging energy.

Much overshadowed by completion of the Manchester-Crewe scheme, the final steps on converting the 1,500V dc lines out of Liverpool Street to ac were taken between 4 and 6 November 1960. Preparatory work had been begun 18 months earlier. Here the two-voltage system was used for the first time. Liverpool Street-Shenfield-Southend was energised at 6.25kV, and the main line from Shenfield to Chelmsford at 25kV. Between Liverpool Street and Southend the existing copper section was retained and little alteration was necessary to the portal structures but there was a vast task in replacing insulators for the higher voltage. On the main line beyond Shenfield cantilever supports were used as on other ac sections but were erected within the existing portals and again all insulators had to be changed. The whole job was carried out with minimum interruption to the dense suburban and main line traffic. Specially uprated ac switchgear was installed to carry the heavy dc currents before the changeover was made. Supplies from the Grid were taken from the same points as before but 6.25kV transformers and ac circuit breakers were installed. Booster transformers and return conductors were provided throughout except between Bow Junction and Stratford.

By the time of the changeover the original three-car Liverpool Street-Shenfield sets (Class 306) had been converted for ac operation. The dc control equipment in the motorcoach was retained and a transformer/rectifier equipment installed under the centre trailer.

These sets were supplemented by four-car units built for the LT&S electrification from Fenchurch Street until a similar conversion of the Liverpool Street-Southend units (Class 307) had been carried out.

The dc/ac conversion out of Liverpool Street underlined another special requirement of 50Hz electrification. When electrified at 1,500V dc the lines had been equipped with 50Hz ac track circuits and impedance bonds. In order to separate the return traction and the signalling currents when 50Hz was used for traction it was necessary to change the track circuit frequency. In this instance $83\frac{1}{3}$Hz was chosen, generated by rotary converters. Frequency discriminating devices were incorporated at the relay end of the circuits and the local coils were energised by a second phase of the supply which was independent of that feeding the tracks. A relay would only close its contacts if both local and control coils were energised by current of the same frequency. If 50Hz traction current penetrated to the control coil in spite of the selective circuitry it could not make the vane rotate. These special measures had not been necessary on the Colchester-Clacton-Walton pilot scheme because there only one rail was needed for the traction return currrent and single-rail dc track circuits were employed.

In 1978 BR ordered 61 sets of thyristor control traction equipments for the new four-car units to replace the Class 306 sets dating from the first days of the Liverpool Street-Shenfield electrification. The new units are classified 315 and are similar to the Class 314 thyristor units for Glasgow but with an additional trailer (see Chapter 11).

Below: The AL5s were the first of the prototype locomotive classes to be equipped with semiconductor rectifiers. All were built by BR at Doncaster and equipped by AEI, Rugby. No 85.010, approaching Bescot Yard alongside the motorway on 21 August 1975 in this picture was one of the 30 originally fitted with germanium diodes.
/Philip D. Hawkins

7
Third-Rail Extensions

When the Modernisation Plan was published in 1955 the eastern limits of the Southern Region's electrification in Kent were Gillingham, Maidstone and Sevenoaks. The Plan gave high priority to extending electrification to the Kent Coast, and by the end of the year the Region had completed its own plans for carrying out the work in two phases, the first covering electrification from Gillingham to Ramsgate, including the Sheerness branch, and from Faversham to Dover; and the second dealing with the remainder of the project, including the main line from Sevenoaks to Dover via Tonbridge and Ashford.

At this period the Southern was engaged on its Change of Frequency scheme in the London area (Chapter 1). Certain technical features of this work set a pattern which was to be followed in both phases of the Kent Coast scheme and right through to completion of the Bournemouth electrification in 1967. The ones with which this chapter is concerned are: provision for increasing the condutor rail voltage from 660 to 750V; remote supervisory control apparatus; and the use of oil-filled cables for the 33kV supply to the traction substations. Although the Change of Frequency scheme area is equipped to operate at 750V the Kent Coast electrification was the first to operate at the higher voltage, followed by the Bournemouth line. It is intended that eventually all of the Region will be capable of operating at 750V.

Substations involved in the Change of Frequency scheme were controlled from control rooms at Raynes Park, Selhurst and Lewisham. The apparatus installed used telephone type relays, switches and uniselectors, one result of which was that the size of the mimic diagrams was much reduced compared with the equipment for the electrifications of the 1930s. The discrepancy switches (Chapter 11) could be mounted at 1in centres where several had to be grouped at positions on the diagram representing the feeds to multi-track sections. Whereas the diagrams in earlier control rooms had extended right round the walls, the new ones were on floor mounted panels 29ft 5in long and 7ft 7in high, presenting the whole area in the

same plane so that observation from the controllers' desk was easier, and the controllers worked in natural lighting by day, with scientifically planned fluorescent lighting at night – a contrast with the control room at Three Bridges for the Brighton electrification of which the official *History of the Southern Railway* said 'all daylight is excluded, and the artificial lighting of the interior is concealed, in order to avoid interference with the coloured lights on the switchboard'.

The new installations also economised in cabling by the number of items that could be controlled and monitored over one four-wire circuit (two wires for controls and two for indications) and they improved the speed of response. Similar apparatus was provided at Canterbury and Paddock Wood for the two phases of the Kent Coast electrification and at Eastleigh for the electrification to Bournemouth. More recently electronic systems have been used in additions to the existing installations and no doubt any completely new work of this kind would be electronic in the interests of continuity of supply of spares from an industry moving increasingly in that direction.

Oil-filled cable, as used in the Change of Frequency scheme, and subsequently in new work, undergoes the heating and cooling associated with the fluctuating railway load without its insulation deteriorating. The conductors of high-voltage cables of the previously used 'solid' type are insulated with paper tapes impregnated with oil-resin type compounds and the expansion due to heating when carrying current causes the lead sheaths to expand, and because of the non-elastic nature of the lead this is not compensated by restoring forces during cooling. In time this process leads to the formation of low-pressure pockets or 'voids' in which discharges may occur under stress, causing gradual deterioration of the dielectric.

In the oil-filled cable, low-viscosity oil is maintained under pressure within the cable sheath thus preventing the troublesome voids from forming. Full impregnation of the dielectric is achieved by the pre-pressured oil tanks which have become a familiar lineside feature on the Southern Region along the routes of the cable, being installed at intervals of approximately $\frac{1}{2}$ to one mile depending on the size of cable and profile of the route. These tanks contain gas-filled cells which contract or expand as oil flows out of or into the cable and thus pressure within the cable is maintained.

The earlier design of cables had copper conductors and reinforced lead sheaths and the oil was distributed from the oil tanks along the length of the cable by means of helical steel ducts, whereas cables installed on the Bournemouth electrification scheme and on replacements thereafter have aluminium conductors and corrugated aluminium sheaths, and the oil flows through the interstitial space between the insulated cores.

Whereas solid type cables are limited to an operating temperature of 65°C, because of the more efficient type of insulation it is permissible to operate oil-filled cables up to 85°C, with a consequent reduction in size of cable for a given load. The oil pressure is monitored by switches which transmit an alarm to the control room if it falls. A reserve supply can be connected to a pressure tank so that the section of cable affected can be kept in service without interruption of traffic until a convenient time for it to be isolated and examined for a possible leak. In normal conditions the life of an aluminium-sheathed cable today can be regarded as virtually unlimited. If a cable has to be cut and relocated because of track alignment, however, the oil-filled type involves more work. A solid cable with a dielectric not subject to voids would be ideal, and materials research has enabled such cables to be produced but they do not yet meet all the conditions of a main line railway installation.

The two phases of the Kent Coast electrification required 63 new substations, of which 32 were equipped with pumpless steel tank mercury-arc rectifiers and 31 with glass bulbs. In the Southern's third-rail electrification the tracks are fed in parallel from the

substation busbars, and track paralleling huts are situated mid-way between substations. At these points there is a gap in the conductor rails bridged electrically by a busbar in the hut, to which the conductor rails are connected through high-speed circuit-breakers. This arrangement gives three major advantages. Firstly, parallel feeding gives a reduction in electrical losses in the conductor rail, thereby enabling more power to be available for the trains; secondly, fault current levels are increased, allowing circuit-breakers to be set higher and so able to deal with heavier loads; and thirdly a shorter length of section is isolated in the event of a fault on the track.

The same basic design of truck-mounted air-break feeder circuit-breaker has been used throughout the Southern Region's postwar electrifications. The breakers are set to trip at currents between 5,000 and 10,000A and break the circuit in typically 14 or 15 milliseconds. As train service frequencies and electrical loads increased it became difficult with the original system of protection to discriminate between overloads due to traffic conditions and track faults. The Region therefore collaborated with the industry in developing a special relay – the Track Impedance Relay – to overcome the difficulty. This device, which is located at mid-section, measures, as its name implies, the volts/current ratio at that point. If this drops below a predetermined value, indicating that there is a fault on the track, the relay contacts close, completing trip circuits to the circuit-breakers feeding the section. With this arrangement higher circuit-breaker settings can be used, reducing the number of trips caused by transitory traffic conditions.

The Kent Coast electrification saw the first semiconductor substation on the Southern Region, brought into use at Hollingbourne on the Maidstone-Ashford line in 1962. By the time of the Bournemouth electrification all the substations were of this type. It is a measure of the progress in semiconductors that a standard 2,500kW rectifier equipment in the early 1960s used 360 silicon diodes, compared with 24 by 1978. Over that period diode voltage ratings increased from 600V to 2,000V and current ratings from 40A to 150A, with consequent reductions in the numbers which had to be connected in series and in parallel for a given load.

With steam under sentence, the Kent Coast scheme had to make provision from the first for alternative power to work locomotive-hauled trains. The choice for electric traction of boat trains such as the 'Night Ferry', summer reliefs to the Kent Coast resorts, inter-Regional services and certain freight duties was a locomotive with an updated version of Raworth's booster control system. This was the period of the high-speed Bo-Bo on the Continent, where the Swiss had given a lead in the BLS 4,000hp class and the Swiss Federal Re4/4s. In some mechanical features the new 2,500hp Bo-Bo for the Southern drew on Swiss experience. The Bulleid bogie of the earlier booster locomotives was dropped, replaced by an SLM bogie made under licence at Doncaster, where the locomotives were built, and fitted with SLM flexible drives. Both features were adopted because the new class was designed for a maximum service speed of 90mile/h. These were the first British electric locomotives to go into service with fully springborne motors, preceding the LMR 81 class by a few months.

Secondary suspension was in the form of a conventional bolster with centre pivot, the ends of the bolster bearing on laminated inverted springs outside the bogie frames. Rubber stops limited lateral movement of the bolster to $1\frac{1}{2}$in, and it was located longitudinally by horizontal traction links connecting it with the bogie frame.

There was only one booster set, and the four traction motors were connected in two parallel pairs. Motor rating (1hr) was 638hp at 675V. Auxiliary supplies came from a generator overhung on the booster instead of from a separate mg set, but traction motor cooling air was ducted from a single motor-driven blower instead of from blowers mounted on the booster shafts. Combined with the general advance in materials and practice since the 1940s, these equipment changes resulted in a 2,500hp locomotive weighing 77 tons against the weight of around 100 tons of the 1,470hp Co-Cos.

Another development seen for the first time on BR in these locomotives (later Class 71) was the form of driver's controller with 'run up' and 'run back' positions as well as provision for notching up manually step by step through the 33 running notches. There was a control positon on the offside of the cab for use in shunting, but without the run-up facility. The locomotive was equipped with a pantograph for use in sidings with overhead wiring and carried two collector shoes on each side of each bogie for third-rail collection.

Six series resistance steps were used in starting the booster set, switched by a camshaft which ran back to

Top left: No 71.002 arrives at Victoria with the 'Night Ferry' on 27 July 1974./*M. Hall*

Left: The Class 71 locomotives were fitted with pantographs for use in yards where overhead wiring had been installed. No 71.011, with pantograph raised, pulls away from Hither Green Down Yards on 2 February 1976 with a freight for Chatham which had arrived from the Eastern Region behind a Class 33 diesel electric. /*Brian Morrison*

restore resistance before a re-start when the supply was interrupted at gaps.

In 1956 BR had introduced six new main line emus and these formed the nucleus of the 4BEP and 4-CEP series, (later 410/1/2 and 411/1/2) for Kent Coast services. The basic formation was four cars, the end vehicles being motorcoaches with two 250hp traction motors each. In this stock the Southern moved away from individual contactor control to an air oil camshaft which has been the basis of all its equipments since that time. These were also the first of the Southern Region's main line trains with roller suspension bearings for the axle-hung traction motors. In this arrangement the suspension unit is a tubular casing, or 'cannon box' containing the bearings in which the driving axle revolves. An earth lead from the motor is connected to two brushes in brush-holders at the centre of the cannon box, the brushes being spring-loaded to bear on a copper track formed on the axles. The return path to the rails and earth is therefore through the axle itself and the wheels instead of via the roller bearings as would be the case if the motor frame were simply earthed direct to the bogie frame. Insulated liners in the motor suspension bearings insulate the motor frame electrically from the cannon box. This

arrangement was first used in Southern Region suburban stock in the 5300 series of 4-EPB units. Some of the same series also had the air-oil camshaft of the Kent Coast stock.

The principle of the air/oil motor driving the camshaft is shown in Fig 7. When magnet valves 1 and 2 are closed there is no pressure in oil reservoirs 3, 4, 5. Equalising valves 6, 7 are open, allowing oil levels in the three chambers to equalise. To rotate the camshaft clockwise valve 1 is opened and air from the compressed air system 8 enters right hand reservoir 5 so that oil is forced up to movement control valve 9 (right hand). Both movement control valves are operated simultaneously by movement control magnet valve 11 and in the present situation oil is forced by air pressure through 9 and causes vane 12 to move clockwise turing camshaft 13. At the same time oil will be forced out of the chamber through the other movement

Below left: A Hither Green-Dover freight rolls into the daylight from Elmstead Woods Tunnel on 16 May 1974. */Brian Morrison*

Fig 7 (*below*) Principle of the air/oil vane motor drive of a camshaft controller.

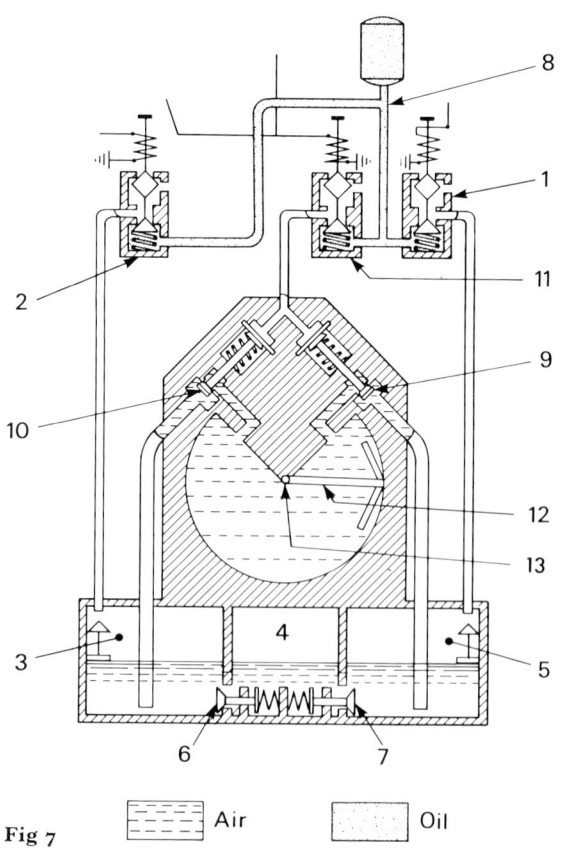

Fig 7

Air — Oil

control valve, 10, returning to reservoir 3. When the camshaft reaches the selected positon valve 11 is de-energised so that the movement control valves close and the camshaft is locked until the valves are again energised. For further clockwise rotation magnet valve 1 would remain energised, or for anti-clockwise movement 1 would be de-energised and 2 energised, allowing air to enter the left hand chamber.

The camshaft makes a partial rotation clockwise for series notching and then reverses for the parallel notches. Full parallel is also the 'off' position when an isolating contactor interlocked with the line switches is open. For weak-field the camshaft continues past 'off' and momentarily restores two sections of starting resistance before the weak-field running position is reached. Nine degrees before the shaft reaches full parallel a contact closes which alters the setting of the accelerating relay so that the steps into weak-field are taken at a lower notching current.

The sequence of events described above begins when the dropping of the accelerating relay makes a circuit to energise the movement control valve. As soon as the camshaft starts to rotate the relay is lifted by a control cam, which simultaneously closes a parallel pair of contacts through which the valve is held energised until the camshaft reaches its next position and the cam follower drops. The accelerating relay is now held up by the motor current and the camshaft remains locked until the current falls again to the notching value, when the sequence repeats. Series/parallel transitions are not controlled by the camshaft but by a separate air-operated switch group.

Protection of the motors in the Kent Coast stock was improved by a high-speed relay to detect reverse current flow. This can occur if there is a track fault near the train and the motors start to regenerate into it. The reverse current quickly wipes out the flux from the field windings, leaving the motors vulnerable to flashover if the fault suddenly clears and normal line volts are restored. The new relay acted in 5 milliseconds, compared with the 15 milliseconds of a normal overload relay, opening the line switches and inserting the full starting resistance.

The Kent Coast four-coach units provided 56 second class seats in the saloon type motorcoaches and 64 in a second class compartment trailer. The other trailer was either a compartment composite with 24 second class and 24 first class seats, or a buffet car. In this vehicle the buffet was adjacent to an open section with four seats and a table for passengers taking refreshments standing up. A side corridor communicated with a 17-seat saloon at the other end of the car beyond the kitchen. Early units had bogies with leaf spring primary suspension but improved on previous bogie designs by having hydraulic dampers for the bolster

Above: Coming from Liverpool Central via the Merseyrail Link line, a train of Class 502 units passes Hall Road en route for Southport on 8 June 1977./*D. A. Ule.*

and a torsion tube arrangement which resisted a tendency for the bolster to 'rock' about its longitudinal axis. Later units with Commonwealth bogies were the first on the Southern to have coil spring primary suspension.

Boat trains other then the 'Night Ferry' with its Wagons-Lits sleeping cars were generally formed of emu stock. At Dover and Folkestone it was necessary to detach a luggage-carrying vehicle from the trains and work it over non-electrified lines at the quayside. This requirement was met by the design of a motor luggage van able to travel to the port in multiple with emu stock and to operate independently on arrival under its own battery power. The 10 motor luggage vans (Class 419) built for the Kent Coast electrification were in fact the first dual-powered vehicles on the Southern Region, preceding the first electro-diesels. Power and brake equipment was the same as in the emu stock but they carried a 230amp/h battery to supply power away from the live-rail, and an mg set with a 200V output for keeping the battery charged during running on electrified lines. The motor of the set also drove a 70V generator for control and lighting supplies as in the emus. A compressor and exhauster ran on the 200V charging supply or could be operated from the traction battery. The vans could therefore

Top: Class 503 units carrying the Merseyrail insignia approach Birkenhead Park on a working from West Kirby to Liverpool./*Brian Morrison*

Above: New stock for the SR Kent Coast electrification included motor luggage vans for use on boat trains, with auxiliary battery power for working on non-electrified quayside lines. Class 419 mlv No 68005 heads an up boat train near Polhill on 30 May 1973./*J. H. Cooper-Smith*

Top right: Classes 410 (4-BEP) and 411 (4-CEP) were introduced for fast services on both routes to the Kent Coast. A Class 411/410/411 combination leaves Victoria for the Thanet resorts on 11 February 1978./*Brian Morrison*

haul vacuum fitted stock on or off the live-rail and could be used as light locomotives for handling a trailing load up to about 100 tons. They were of the same length, 64ft 6in, as the emu coaches and had a driving cab at each end, also a small guard's compartment. The rest of the interior was luggage space, divided into two sections of unequal size by an interior partition. Floors were strengthened so that pallet trucks could enter and manoeuvre inside.

The driver selected battery power by pressing a pushbutton. When he did so the shoes were raised pneumatically above conductor rail height and an indicator in the cab was illuminated. Battery condition was indicated by a state of charge meter. The automatic raising of the shoes on selecting battery power avoided the risk of their being damaged when returning to the live-rail from non-electrified sidings without ramps to guide shoes on to it. They were lowered on to the rail when the driver returned from battery to normal power.

The Kent Coast emus were the last Southern four-coach main-line sets with two-motor equipments in end motorcoaches. Since the Brighton replacement stock of 1964 (Class 421/1) the formation with one exception has been a four-motor motorcoach as an intermediate vehicle in the set, the end coaches being driving trailers. Although not associated with an extension of the third-rail system, the Brighton stock is considered in this chapter because in this respect it set a pattern to be repeated in much of the stock for the Bournemouth electrification. The exception referred to above was the Class 430 unit for Bournemouth trains with two four-motor motorcoaches of higher power.

In the 1964 Brighton stock (no longer confined to that division) the two 250hp motors in each motor-

coach bogie were permanently in parallel, the train starting with the two pairs in series. Notching was by a camshaft driven by an air/oil motor similar to that described above, but to relieve the contacts of having to carry the full current of four motors continuously it was backed up by an air-operated cam switch group which took the load on the running notches. Another switch group similar to that in the Kent Coast stock effected the series/parallel transitions. There were two rates of acceleration through the series notches. If the driver put his controller straight into weak-field the rate was 0.75mile/h/sec. If he set the handle at series or parallel the lower rate of 0.5mile/h/sec was selected.

Normally the mg set on each motorcoach supplied the auxiliary loads of its own unit only, parallel operation of sets being prevented by blocking diodes. The inter-unit control connections and the diode polarities were so arranged, however, that if one set failed the set in the adjacent unit automatically supplied its load. This stock also introduced a new type of shoegear. Instead of being suspended by links from beams between the axleboxes, the shoes were carried at the ends of arms resiliently supported from a point near the centre line of the bogie frame at their inner ends and at right angles to the longitudinal axis of the bogie. This arrangement is illustrated in Chapter 10.

All these emus work on sections of the Southern Region away from their original homes. In 1976 Class 411/3 (4-CEP) unit No 7153 was fitted with Commonwealth bogies and refurbished internally with fluorescent lighting and durable, damage-resistant surfaces replacing the original varnished wood and paintwork. All seating was in saloons except for a small compartment (unclassed) next to the van. The vestibule connections were modified to improve appearance and reduce costs. Other units have been dealt with similarly.

The Southern Railway's third-rail had reached Portsmouth in 1937, with much improvement in the holiday service to the Isle of Wight. In the Island itself, however, passengers continued to travel in steam trains of endearing aspect but not remarkable for speed or comfort. They did not survive the harsh realities of the postwar railway scene and it once seemed that the Isle of Wight would at length be without a railway service of any kind. A happy solution was found, however, by electrifying the line from Ryde Pier Head to Shanklin ($8\frac{1}{2}$ miles) and working it with reconditioned trains from the Central, Piccadilly and Northern City Lines of London Transport. These were three-car (Class 486) and four-car (Class 485) units, all having one motorcoach powered by two 240hp motors. The line was fed at 630V from sub-stations at Ryde St John's, Rowborough (near Brading) and Sandown. The principal electrical modification needed to the trains was removal of the negative shoe for the centre rail return on the London Transport system and reconnection of the motors for earth return through the running rails. Originally there had been line breakers on the positive and negative sides of the motors but these were now both reconnected on the positive side and reset with a 100A differential in tripping current. The separate switch for field weakening which had been London Transport practice was retained. On LT weak-field was not normally used in tunnel sections and the switch took the form of a 'flag' indicator something like the taxi driver's 'For Hire' flag as a precaution against the fact that weak-field had been selected being overlooked. On the Island, of course, there was no such restriction and the weak-field balancing speed of 46mile/h with a loaded train was useful in clearing the single-track section between Smallbrook Junction and Brading

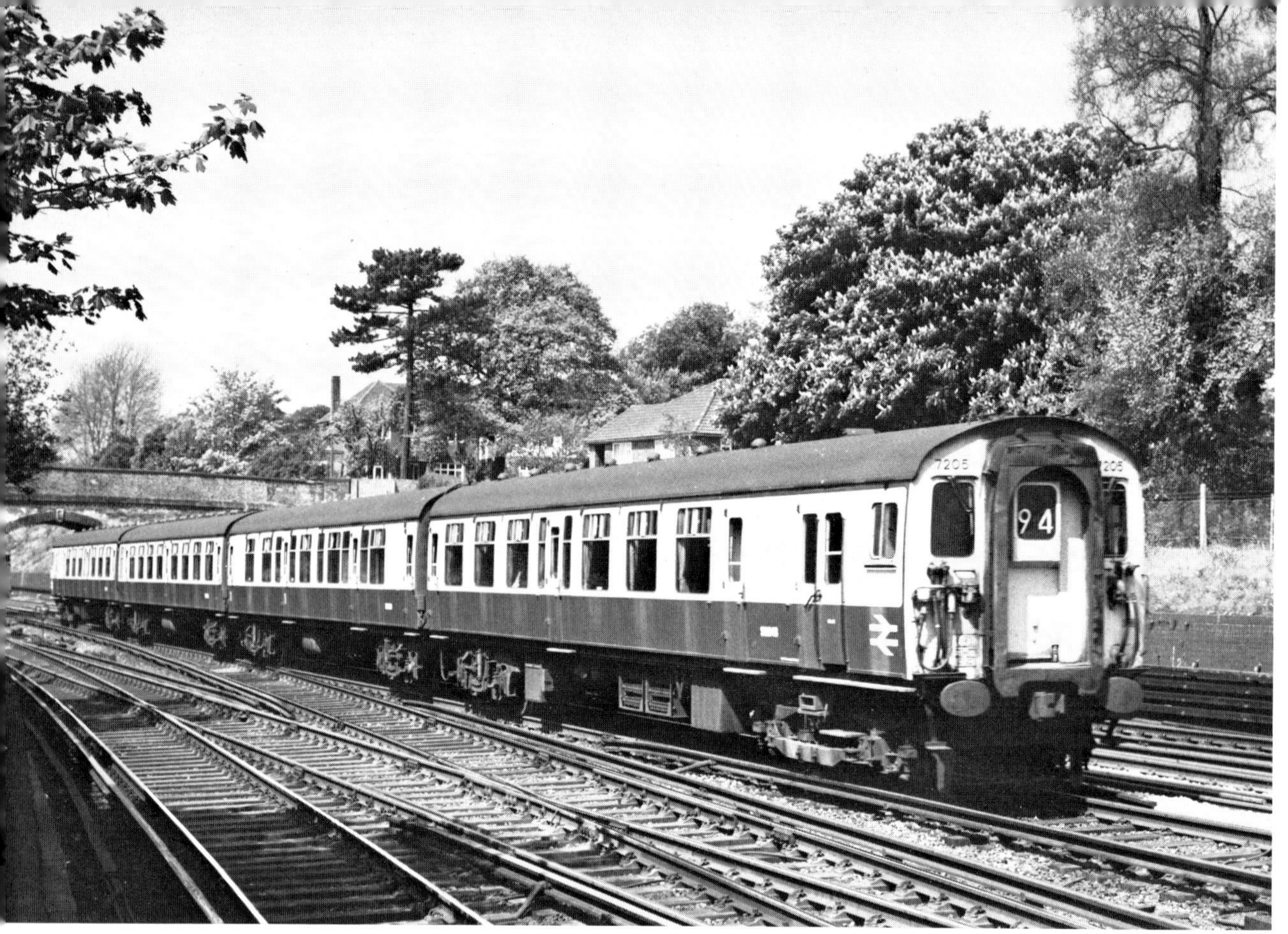
7205
94

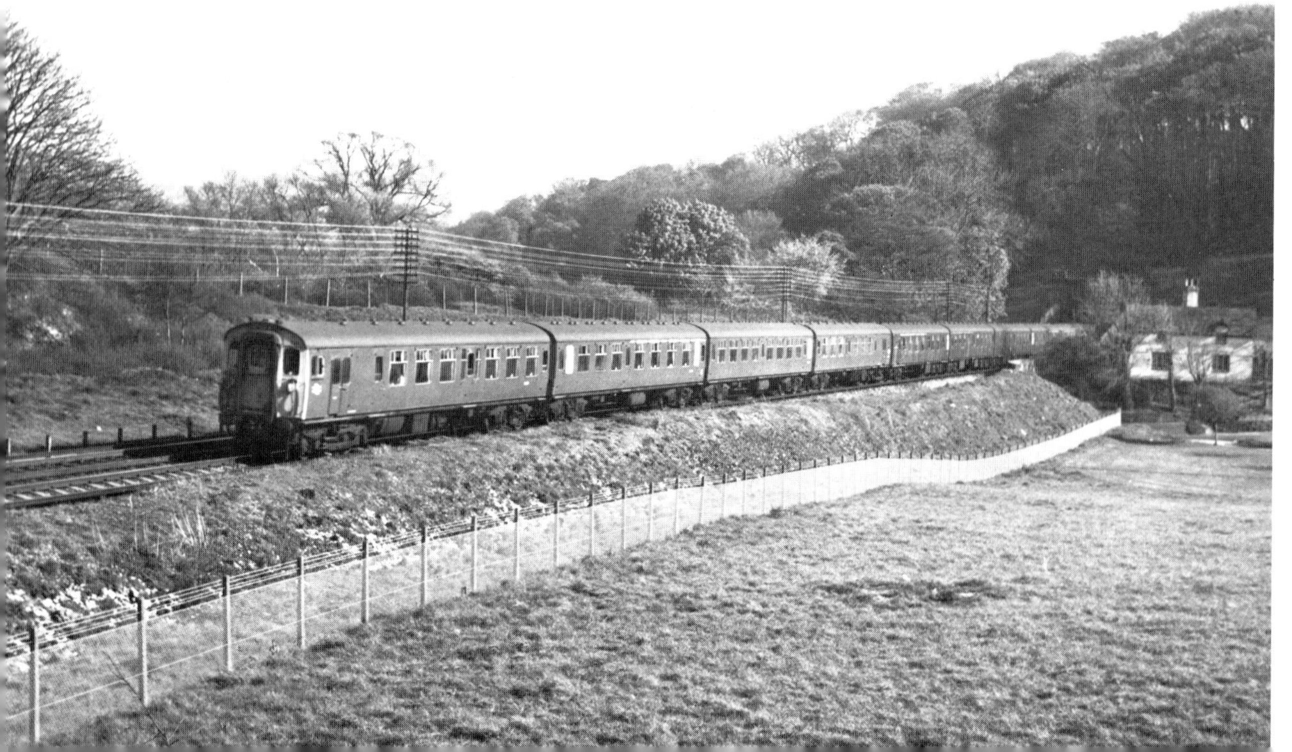

Above left: Class 411/2 unit No 7205 forms the 10.55 Victoria to Margate via Maidstone East, Ashford, and Canterbury West on 16 May 1974./*Brian Morrison*

Left: Class 411 units operate outside their native territory. No 7211 heads a Littlehampton to Victoria train at Patcham on 26 April 1968/*J. Scrace*

Above: A Class 411 leads a Victoria to Brighton semi-fast at Balcombe on 31 May 1968./*J. Scrace*

when working the short-interval summer holiday service. Accelerating rate remained 1.6mile/h/sec. Internally one section of seating was removed in the motorcoaches and two in the trailers to make room for three-tier luggage racks. The trains were painted 'Rail Blue' with yellow ends, the yellow extending round the side walls for a short distance.

The first Chairman of the British Transport Commission saw opportunities for extending and linking up what he called 'bits and pieces' of electrification around Liverpool and Manchester. A step in this direction, unforseen when he made the comment, was the conversion of the Manchester South Junction &

Altrincham line to 25kV in 1971 and the integration of its services with the Manchester-Crewe section of the LMR main-line. Action with some other lines which Lord Hurcomb clearly had in mind was taken later, the first results being the commisioning of the Loop and Link lines in Liverpool in 1977.

The Wirral lines of the LMS had been electrified in 1938 and the train service extended through the tunnel of the former Mersey Railway into Liverpool Central. The loop of today is a deep-level single-track tunnel forming virtually a 'turning circle' for trains from the Wirral arriving at James Street station after passing under the Mersey. Instead of proceeding direct to Central, they now take the loop line via Moorfields, Lime Street and Central, returning to James Street ready to continue their journey back to the Wirral.

The new alignment of the loop left part of the Mersey Railway tunnel between James Street and Central free and it has been absorbed into the route of the second new underground line in Liverpool – the Link. Liverpool Exchange station was closed in 1977 and the Southport/Ormskirk-Liverpool electric service which had terminated there now enters the new link tunnel just north of the site of the former terminus. First station on the link is Moorfields, where

Above: A Portsmouth Harbour-Victoria train passes Amberley on the Mid-Sussex line on 12 June 1968. Buffet accommodation is provided in the leading Class 410 unit. /*J. Scrace*

there is escalator interchange with the loop platforms on a lower level, and the line continues under the city to another interchange station with the loop at Central. Beyond Central the link joins the former Cheshire Lines Committee tracks from the old High Level station, which were electrified to Garston as part of the new works. On the other side of Liverpool the branch from the Liverpool-Ormskirk line at Walton Junction was electrified as far as Kirkby and a through electric service between Kirkby and Garston via Liverpool was instituted. At the time of writing, an extension of electrification from Kirkby to Wigan was in prospect. It was also likely that the third-rail would be extended from Garston to Hough Green on the borders of the Merseyside Passenger Transport Executive's area, with longer term extensions in view for serving Warrington, Widnes and St Helens. Local train services in the PTE area are operated by British Rail for the Executive under the name 'Merseyrail'.

The loop and the link services provide direct interchange between two busy suburban systems which were previously separated, involving surface travel across the city centre to go from one to the other. Many who live in the area can travel by rail throughout between home and work, and the numbers who already do so without a change could be increased by the electrification extensions proposed. Travellers to

Liverpool from further afield have the convenience of access from Lime Street to all local rail services without having to take a bus or taxi, or walk through crowded streets.

Services on the loop and link lines were launched in 1977 with the existing Wirral and Southport line stock, delivered to the LMS in 1938 and 1939 respectively, with additional Wirral line units supplied to the London Midland Region in 1956 which were basically similar to their forerunners. Train formations on both lines were based on a three-car unit (motorcoach-trailer-driving trailer) but the Southport line fleet included additional motorcoaches and trailers, enabling five-car trains to be made up with a motorcoach at both ends.

As representative of their period, some details of the 1939 Liverpool-Southport stock are of interest. The four 235hp motors of the motorcoach were controlled as individual pairs, each pair having its own series/parallel electro-pneumatic contactor control equipment. Weight per horsepower was 19.6lb, which compared with 40lb per horsepower for the motors of the original stock of 1904. The motor fields were tapped at approximately 70% and 43% of the main field turns, the latter being the weak-field running step. In the late 1930s totally enclosed motors were still general in emu stock, and an English Electric advertisement of 1938 drew special attention to the fact that the new machines for the Southport line were 'of the self-ventilated type, the incoming air being drawn from the roof of the coaches through flexible ducts. This arrangement, while adding slightly to the weight, has proved its value in providing motors with clean air, free from snow, brake shoe dust and other foreign matter, thereby materially reducing motor maintenance'.

Although there are no through passenger services between the loop and link lines, which are on different levels, rolling stock can be exchanged over a connecting line from James Street to the point where the link enters the former Mersey Railway tunnel. All trains therefore had to be modified to conform with Department of Transport requirements for running in single-track tunnels. End doors were provided for detraining passengers in emergency, and power bus-lines between motorcoaches and driving trailers removed. Current is therefore collected only by the shoes on the motorcoaches and fed direct to the power equipment. Considerable resiting of conductor rail gaps took place in consequence.

New stock for the loop and link line services was already under construction when the lines were opened. These three-car units, Class 507, are generally similar to Class 313 (Chapter 12) but with dc equipment only. They have the same air secondary suspension and chevron rubber primary suspension, and rheostatic braking combined with air braking under Westcode control providing three normal rates of braking and one for emergency. Passenger accommodation is all second class, with 234 seats and provision for some 324 standing passengers, who have handrails within easy reach throughout the length of the cars. The rate of acceleration is 2.25mile/h/sec. Thirty Class 507 units were scheduled to go into service in the Spring of 1979 and to be followed by a programme of gradual replacement of Wirral line trains with 43 further units in the early 1980s.

New traction substations for the loop and link lines and extensions were provided at Central in Liverpool; Walton Junction and Fazakerley, serving the Kirkby extension; and Aigburth and Brunswick on the extension to Garston. They are fed at 11kV, with vacuum interruptors on the ac side and equipped with semiconductor rectifier units of 2,500kW rating. Two units are installed at Central and one at each of the other substations. The conversion of glass bulb rectifiers at the older substations to similar equipment was put in hand on the Wirral section and a longer-term programme was drawn up for corresponding work on the Southport/Ormskirk lines. At first the supply to the live rails remained at 650V as previously but with provision for raising it to 750V after replacement of all the old rolling stock.

Power supplies for the Merseyrail system are now under remote control from Hall Road. A computer based electronic scanning system has replaced the old relay type systems which separately controlled the Mersey-Wirral lines from Birkenhead North and the Liverpool, Southport and Ormskirk lines from Hall Road.

The new system has the capacity to control 68 substations, which is the total envisaged for complete electrification of the Merseyrail commuter network; at present 27 substations are controlled.

A mimic diagram shows the whole system from the electricity board supplies at 11kV to individual track feeders, including the state of all remotely-controlled switches.

There are three controllers' desks which include visual display units and keyboards through which the system is controlled. The mimic diagram is updated continuously by the computer and visually and audibly draws the controller's attention to any changes on the system. The controller can then, using his vdu, bring up a detailed coloured diagram of any part of the system by typing in the appropriate instructions. The vdu picture consists of 'animated' symbols of the equipment, and the computer will only accept the controller's instructions if the equipment is actually on display on the vdu on the desk from which the instruction is typed in. An associated DEC writer provides a print out record of all instructions and operations, largely dispensing with manual logging and having the advantage that if an incident has to be investigated subsequently the record shows the full sequence and timing of events. Two way communication with the computer informs the operator through the vdu if an incorrect instruction has been given, no action being taken until the mistake has been rectified. Another safeguard is an 'inhibit' facility which 'freezes' any selected item of equipment so that its state cannot be changed until the instruction is cancelled by the controller.

The computer program is stored on a magnetic disc, and a copy is held on magnetic tape cassettes. If the power network requires changing for any reason a modified program can be prepared on a standby computer and once tested can be transferred to the cassettes, which can then be used to up date the program in the 'duty' computer without taking the machine off line.

A TEC (Tunnel Emergency Communication) system in the tunnels enables a driver in case of need, to cut off current from the section of track in which his train is standing and call the Electrical Control Room, or to communicate with the signalbox at James Street. The driver's telephone handset has flexible leads attached which he can clip on to wires on the tunnel wall without leaving his cab when an emergency arises. A selector switch and pushbuttons for communication in these circumstances are fitted on a telephone unit in the cab. The selector switch also has positions for driver-to-guard communication (used in Classes 502 and 507) and for public address (used in Class 507). Driver to guard communication in Class 503 is by Loudaphone. Crews are provided with a tool which can be applied by hand to the tunnel wires to obtain an emergency isolation when it is not possible to use the normal TEC system procedure.

Although this book is concerned mainly with traction equipment, the extent of the non-traction loads which have to be catered for in an underground city railway equipped to contemporary standards of service and amenities must not be overlooked. Lighting, lifts and escalators are the ones most apparent to the traveller but they include destination indicators, closed circuit television for platform surveillance and many others. Main and emergency supplies are taken from independent sources at all stations, including Hamilton Square on the former Mersey Railway section as well as those on the loop and the link. At Moorfields the emergency source is a standby diesel-alternator set which takes over without a break in the supply if the mains fail. Where sources are at high voltage (11kV, 6kV or 25kV) the local supplies are taken through packaged transformer substations of 315kVA or 500kVA capacity, installed singly or in pairs as necessary. The 25kV supply is the emergency source at Lime Street, being taken from the main line traction supply. At this station the normal supply is taken from the substation for the main line terminus.

Below: Refurbishing of Class 411 units began in 1976. First to be dealt with was 7153, seen here at Gatwick Airport on a train to Victoria during trial running on the Central Division during March 1978./*C. Burnham*

8
Achievements and Setbacks

In the mood of confidence engendered by the success-ful launch of main line ac traction between Manchester and Crewe a few weeks previously, the system was inaugurated in Glasgow on 7 November 1960. This was a first instalment of 52 route-miles covering the line from Airdrie to Helensburgh and branches. It was a route through extraordinarily varied surroundings, with industrial areas, residential suburbs, the shores of Loch Lomond, the banks of the Clyde, and the $1\frac{1}{2}$ miles of almost unbroken tunnel below central Glasgow through Glasgow Queen Street Low Level station. It was also the first electric railway in Scotland, a fact noted with unwonted lyricism in the publicity brochure, *Glasgow Electric*, published to mark the occasion:

'Out of a cutting above the River Clyde and into the sunshine there flashes a train at speed. Its coaches are painted the bright blue of the kingfisher, gay against the softer greens and browns of the fields, and its windows, almost unbroken in length, flash cheerfully. An old man on a chair at a cottage door on the hillside looks down to see that the three coaches ripping along so fast and so purposefully do so as by dark magic; vaguely he misses the smoke and steam, the glowing fires and heaped coals of the engines of his young manhood. At least, he has lived long enough to see the electric train come to Scotland.'

These were the 'Blue Trains' of Glasgow, and with their rounded countours and wrap-round windows they brought a panache to the emu which it had previously lacked. The formation was a three-coach unit of centre-gangway stock consisting of driving trailer, motorcoach and battery driving trailer, providing 238 seats in all. Mechanical parts were built by the Pressed Steel Co Ltd at Linwood to BR requirements, with the Design Research Unit responsible for the external appearance and interior detail. The air-operated double sliding doors were recessed so that the maximum body width of 9ft 3in permitted by the British loading gauge could be utilised. This stock

later became Class 303 and was supplemented in 1967 by the Class 311 units of similar design but with traction motors of 222hp instead of the original 207hp. Class 311 had silicon rectifiers from the start whereas Class 303 originally had mercury-arcs. The silicon cells were oil-cooled by pumping the main transformer oil through the rectifier cubicles by means of the normal circulating pump. The cubicles contained a number of large-diameter tubes through which air flowed as a result of the normal movement of the train in sufficient volume to dissipate the heat losses of the transformer, smoothing choke and rectifiers without requiring motor-driven fan.

The electrical equipment for the original trains supplied by Associated Electrical Industries Ltd included four single-anode excitron rectifiers of a type which by 1960 had given over 130,000 miles of trouble-free running in one of the motorcoaches on the Lancaster-Morecambe-Heysham lines. In cold weather the rectifiers could be warmed up before load was applied by operating them with a resistance across their output designed to pass 100A at first notch voltage, this arrangement being brought into action by thermostats. Interlocks prevented the line contactors from closing to supply power to the motors until the warm-up was completed and the resistor switched out. The fan for cooling the rectifiers was mounted in the same underframe equipment case and the air was normally expelled through shutters at the rear but under cold weather and light load conditions the shutters were closed by an electro-pneumatic control brought into action by thermostats so that air re-circulated inside the case.

Tap-changing was on the secondary side of the transformer. In any tap-changing system there is a moment during transition when both taps concerned are connected and would short-circuit the section of winding between them without precautions being taken. In this case a resistor was connected momentarily across the tappings, and the same resistor was also used to provide additional steps of voltage control between those derived from the tappings. The tap-changer was a motor-driven camshaft, and it was so arranged that it could not come to rest with the resistor in circuit.

The four traction motors of the motorcoach were permanently connected in series-parallel, but the mid-point of each series pair was connected to a centre tapping on the transformer secondary so that effectively the machines were in parallel, operating at 975V with ratings of 190hp, 165A, in full field and 210hp, 180A, in weak-field. Maximum service speed was 75mile/h.

All motive power at this period was equipped for dual-voltage (25/6.25kV) operation and the equipment for automatic changeover between the two voltages was standardised for locomotives and emus. The procedure was similar at neutral sections between changes of phase. An aws receiver mounted on a bogie was actuated by aws type track magnets fitted on the sleeper ends outside the running rails approximately 100ft before the neutral section preceding a change of voltage or phase. Deflection of the receiver armature interrupted the closing and holding circuits of the main circuit breaker, which opened before the 'dead' section of overhead wire was reached. When the pantograph had passed the neutral section and was again in contact with energised wire, a measuring circuit detected the voltage present and if necessary operated the voltage changeover switch to make the appropriate connections at the input to the main transformer. In the locomotives with high-tension tap-changers this was done by selecting an input tapping, but in equipments with tapped secondaries the primaries were in four sections which were connected in series or parallel as necessary. After this change of connections had been made, or the sensing circuit detected no change in voltage (as in passing through a neutral section between two phases), the main circuit-breaker was reclosed. This automatic power control (apc) system had been tested on the Colchester-Clacton-Walton pilot scheme. It was first used operationally on the Glasgow lines during driver training.

Restricted clearances in the Glasgow area made several 6.25kV sections necessary. The longest was from Carntyne to Westerton ($8\frac{3}{4}$ miles); the Springburn, Bridgeton and Milngavie branches totalled some $6\frac{1}{4}$ miles; and the loop through Clydebank Central added approximately another 4 miles. For these sections power was supplied through sub-feeder stations at Finnieston and Westerton, which were linked with the Parkhead feeder station by a 25kV cable route laid in concrete troughing. The gas-filled cable in this installation was the first of its kind on British Railways. Gas is an alternative to oil as an internal cable insulator which expands and contracts with changing temperature without risk of the 'voids'

which form in solid insulation in similar conditions and lead eventually to breakdown. Charging cylinders for the nitrogen were installed at Parkhead, Finnieston and Westerton. Intermediate charging points were provided at certain cable joints along the route at intervals of 1,500–2,000yd. All these 6.25kV sections have now been converted to 25kV.

There were other main feeder stations at Dalreoch and Motherwell, the latter being sited to serve future electrification south of the Clyde. In order to provide a feed at the Airdrie end of the line, Motherwell was connected to a sub-feeder station at Coatbridge by a 25kV oil-filled cable. The location of the power control room at Cathcart was also chosen with a view to the coming extensions south of the city.

The national, local and technical press were taken on a tour of inspection of the line a day or two before public services began. The proceedings included a demonstration of automatic voltage changeover and the representative of *The Engineer* noted that:

'No action was required by the motorman, who on starting from Westerton under clear signals on the 6.25kV section advanced his controller at once to the full-speed position. On approaching the changeover point the process of opening the circuit-breaker, throwing the changeover switch, reclosing the circuit-breaker and notching up again to weak-field followed automatically but with imperceptible effect on the train.'

Electrification of the Eastern Region services from Liverpool Street through the north-east suburbs to Chingford, Enfield Town, Hertford and Bishops Stortford followed on the heels of the Scottish Region's opening in Glasgow, the inaugural day being 16 November, 1960. Initially the main line to Bishops Stortford along the Lea Valley was not electrified but Bishops Stortford trains followed the Enfield Town line to a junction south of Bush Hill Park station from which there was a connection some five miles in length to the main line immediately south of Cheshunt. This connecting line had not been used for regular passenger services since 1908. The old track and ballast were removed and the whole section relaid with standard flat bottom track. Originally the first station going north had been Churchbury and the line had been known as the Churchbury loop. After renovation and lengthening of platforms, as was carried at the other two stations on the loop. it was renamed Southbury. The junction with the Lea Valley line at Cheshunt was remodelled to allow higher speeds. On the main line a new station, Harlow Town, was built on the site of the former Burnt Mill station to serve Harlow New Town and was the first in the country to be built specifically for the needs of a New Town population. The former Harlow station become Harlow Mill.

The 42 route-miles of the new electrification included a considerable proportion at 6.25kV but as the low-voltage section was continuous from Liverpool Street to Cheshunt, including the Chingford and Enfield Town branches, there was only one voltage changeover point. On the other hand there were more neutral sections than usual because supplies were taken from five feeder stations. All had direct connection with CEGB or Area Board lines and were situated at Bethnal Green, Silver Street, Wood Street (Chingford branch), Rye House (Hertford East branch), and Bishops Stortford, but the last named was a standby as far as services south of Bishops Stortford were concerned, having been provided in anticipation of an early extension to Cambridge. The overhead system was mainly simple catenary although there were short sections with stitch wires for comparative purposes. In 1969 the main (Lea Valley) Cambridge line was electrified at 25kV between Clapton and Cheshunt. Conversion of the 6.25kV sections in North East London has been programmed for the early 1980s.

British Railways works at York built 52 three-car emus for the services to Chingford and Enfield Town, while Doncaster built 19 four-car units for those to Hertford East and Bishops Stortford. The formations followed the standard pattern of driving trailers as the end vehicles and an intermediate motorcoach. The three-car sets (Class 305/1) were centre-corridor throughout, and second class only. The four-car sets (Class 305/2) had an additional trailer with three side-corridor first class compartments separated from an open second section by toilets for each class. There were also two toilets in the second class open driving trailer. The motorcoach and the other driving trailer were second class compartment vehicles.

Traction equipment for all these emus was supplied by The General Electric Co Ltd, which equipped the motorcoaches with a smaller version of the Compak mercury-arc rectifier fitted in the Class 84 locomotives. They were liquid-cooled but with anode, cathode and tank in a single circuit instead of the anodes having a separate circuit as in the locomotive version.

All motorcoaches had 200hp traction motors and a maximum service speed of 75mile/h. The three-car unit, designed for inner suburban work with frequent stops, had an accelerating rate of 1.35mile/h/sec, but the four-car unit accelerated at 1.1mile/h/sec, which was adequate for its longer inter-station runs. Control was by tappings on the transformer secondary combined with intermediate resistance notches, 20 voltage steps being obtained with only nine tappings.

There were intermediate and final weak-field steps, only the latter being a running notch. In the final step the field was tapped, and a proportional reduction was made in the value of the permanent field shunt by connection to a tapping on the resistor. Control switching was shared by two air-operated camshafts which were interlocked so that they operated alternately under the control of a common escapement mechanism. This dual arrangement was adopted to provide maximum mechanical spacing between the elements in the successive steps. In notching back, current was broken by separate contactors, allowing the camshafts to return quickly to 'off'.

The launch of the new services in Glasgow and north-east London was followed with dramatic suddenness by an outbreak of technical troubles on an unprecedented scale. Glasgow suffered the most serious incident on 13 December 1960 when the guard and seven passengers were injured by an explosion in a train near Renton which blew off the cover to the transformer oil conservator in the guard's compartment. This was one of five occurrences affecting transformers in the 'Blue Trains' and on 18 December 1960 they were withdrawn from service. They did not carry passengers again for 11 months.

In the London area the new rolling stock was in trouble from the start and extensive replacement of services by dmus was necessary. The occurrences were serious enough in both parts of the country to be the subject of an inquiry carried out by Brig C. A. Langley, Chief Inspecting Officer of Railways, into an episode in which, as he put it, 'troubles even of a minor kind had repercussions on the service causing much inconvenience and delay to passengers with consequent adverse publicity.'

Considering the incidents in the Glasgow area, Brig Langley found that the explosion of 13 December was probably caused by oil in the conservator vaporising and being unable to escape although a larger vent had already been provided. It was probably ignited by a spark from a contactor in the low-tension cupboard in the guard's compartment. The general conclusion regarding the transformers in the Glasgow trains was that they were not always strong enough to withstand the frequent application of severe short-circuits to which they were subjected in service, and there was little doubt that the short-circuits resulted from backfires in the rectifiers. The backfires in turn arose from overheating or an unfavourable temperature differential between anode and cathode. Irregular operation of the automatic power control equipment also caused severe over-voltages and these would have contributed to the transformer failures had they occurred at the same time as the backfires. He noted that one cause of irregular apc operation had been vandalism in the shape of throwing lengths of wire on the overhead system – a diversion with which electrical control room staffs are still unhappily familiar. There had been trouble from the operation of overload relays during trial running of the Glasgow trains, probably as a result of rectifier backfires, but 'the true significance had not been appreciated at the time'.

Discussing the Eastern Region troubles, the report noted that as soon as public services began on 21 November 1960 they were disrupted by failures, the most serious being breakdown of traction motors and battery chargers. Rectifiers also gave some trouble, traced to restricted flow of coolant caused by electrolytic action on the ferrule of a hose. In summer a 'blanket' of hot air travelled along with the train, producing a temperature around the cooling fan inlet several times higher than atmospheric shade temperature. A more fundamental problem of the Compak rectifier was that every time the voltage was excessively reduced or lost in the excitation circuit the rectifiers had to be re-ignited. After more than four or five rapid make/break operations the rectifier excitation might lock out for an unspecified time. This could happen with loss of contact between pantograph and contact wire. If the circuit opened during temporary loss of excitation in some rectifiers, conditions likely to cause voltage surges could be created. In a general comment on this design, the report said: 'they are complicated pieces of equipment with duplicate circulating pumps and no fewer than five thermostats to control the temperature limits. They are mounted in a confined space under the floor of the motorcoach and at present they require excessive maintenance.' The words can be regarded as an elegy for a rectifier developed at great expense of research effort to combine the best features of the excitron and the ignitron in a form suitable for traction. By the time they were published the incentive to overcome their problems had gone with the arrival of the semiconductor diode.

The GEC traction motors proved vulnerable to the quick make/break 'chopping' action of the circuit-breaker as a train passed through neutral sections. There was a tendency in some quarters at the time to attribute the various troubles to the BR dual-voltage system, but it must be remembered that neutral sections occur where there is no change of voltage as well as at changeover points, and on the North East London electrification with its five different sources of supply these sections were relatively numerous within a short route-mileage although only one of them, at Cheshunt, was associated with a change of voltage.

In 1961 the Shenfield-Chelmsford section of the ER main line to East Anglia was electrified at 25kV, necessitating voltage changeover at Shenfield for trains running to and from the 6.25kV section between Shenfield and Liverpool Street. Six transformer failures occurred because of circuit-breakers remaining closed when passing through the 6.25/25kV section, leading to further modifications of the equipment. Conversion of the 6.25kV section to 25kV had reached Gidea Park by 1979 and was due for completion to Liverpool Street in 1981.

In the meantime electrification of the London, Tilbury & Southend line from Fenchurch Street to Southend and Shoeburyness had been in progress and it had been hoped to provide a full electric service in the autumn of 1961. This had to be deferred and a service of electric interspersed with steam trains operated instead because of insulation troubles which developed in the traction motors of the LTS stock. This was an unexpected as well as an unwelcome development for these trains had run without trouble on the Colchester-Clacton-Walton pilot scheme, in north-east London as replacements for the troubled GEC trains, and on the Liverpool Street-Shenfield-Southend Victoria service pending conversion of the dc stock. A programme of rewinding was put in hand and the full electric service between Fenchurch Street and Shoeburyness was introduced on 18 June 1962. Brig Langley's report emphasised that these troubles had no connection with the voltage surges and other phenomena associated with the dual-voltage system.

Without criticising the dual-voltage system as such, the report made it clear that it created conditions in which trouble could occur. It was noted that the Compak rectifier faults occurred mainly when running on 6.25kV. There had been irregular operation of the voltage changeover equipment, and cases of the transformer tap being switched to 6.25kV while running on 25kV, together with occasional faulty operation of the air-blast circuit-breakers. It was clearly desirable to reduce the number of voltage changeover points, and in 1962 new clearances were approved which made it possible to complete the electrification of the LMR main line from Manchester and Liverpool to London at a uniform voltage of 25kV.

It remains to add that Glasgow's 'Blue Trains' began running again on 2 October 1961. On 27 May 1962 the services south of the Clyde from Glasgow Central round the Cathcart Circle to Neilston, and to Motherwell via Kirkhill, Newton and Uddingston were electrified. The section from Newton to Motherwell is now part of the electrified West Coast main line. The event passed off 'without incident'. From that time until the LMR electrification was completed to Euston via the Trent Valley line in 1965 opening ceremonies were muted in comparison with their former exuberance.

Was the decision to use dual-voltage ac 'bold and courageous'? So mused *The Railway Gazette* editorially at the time of Brig Langley's report, using the brigadier's own words, much favoured at that period for describing any project of which the wisdom might be questioned. A correspondent in the paper's 22 June 1962 issue was forthright: 'You ask if the British Transport Commission was bold and courageous' he wrote. 'The answer is that it was not bold and courageous: it was just plain stupid and untutored'. Others had their doubts without putting them so bluntly, and they often centred round a phrase in the report which noted in respect of circuit-breakers 'chopping' on 6.25kV that the effect was four times greater on the secondary and tertiary windings than on the 25kV lines and surges up to six or seven times the normal peak were recorded. The first part of the statement was a matter of simple arithmetic and cannot have been overlooked, but it does seem as if the effects of the four-to-one difference in voltage on the particular circuits and components used had been under-estimated. Clearly the principle was sound and worked well for years where the two voltages had to be retained, but the early problems involved much expensive modification and even rejection of equipment, and their effect on the railway image was deplorable.

While the troubles on the North-East London trains were being sorted out, electrification of the Eastern Region main line beyond Shenfield was continuing at 25kV. It reached Chelmsford in 1961, and Colchester in 1962, linking up there with the hitherto isolated Colchester-Clacton-Walton section. In the summer service of 1962 some through trains of outer-suburban electric stock were run between Liverpool Street, Clacton and Walton. Delivery of the express emus built for the service (Classes 309/1/2/3) was delayed by the chief electrical contractor's preoccupation with suburban emu failures, and this new stock did not enter traffic until 7 January 1963. The equipment was by GEC, but the company's Compak rectifier had had its day and the power circuits were designed round silicon rectifiers with the cells supplied by Westinghouse as sub-contractor. The last of the equipments supplied by GEC for the North East London electrification had in fact included a silicon rectifier of this type.

Rolling stock for the new Clacton trains was built at York and comprised initially 15 four-car and eight two-car units. The four-car units followed the now established pattern of battery driving trailer, motorcoach, trailer and driving trailer, and in eight of them one vehicle was a griddle car. Motorcoaches were powered by four 282hp motors. Balancing speed of a four-car unit in weak-field on level track was 90mile/h, which was the highest permitted on the route, but the maximum service speed was 100mile/h. The new trains were considered at that time as forerunners of a fleet of express emus for other parts of the ac system but this was a concept not to be realised until the coming of the electric APT.

Inter-tap control with resistances was carried a step further in these units, 20 voltage steps being provided with only four transformer secondary tappings. During a tap-change a resistor was connected momentarily across the two tappings concerned to block circulating currents. It was then disconnected from the lower tapping and power was fed from the higher-voltage tapping to the rectifiers through the resistance. On this step, therefore, the voltage at the rectifiers was that of the higher tapping less the volts drop in the resistance. Next the resistance was short-circuited in three steps, the rectifiers finally being connected direct to the tapping, after which the sequence continued until the full transformer secondary voltage was applied. Three electro-pneumatic contactors were used for resistance notching, which simplified the design of the tap-changer itself and enabled all steps to be provided without reversal of camshaft movement. The traction motors were connected in series-parallel with an equalising connection between the mid-points of the two motor circuits to reduce the rise in voltage on the motor driving an axle which slipped. If slipping occurred it was detected by a relay and notching was arrested. The permanent resistive shunts across the motor fields to divert ripple current were tapped and were partly by-passed to provide the weak-field step.

The rectifier was a bridge circuit with eight parallel strings of six diodes in each arm. The diodes were mounted on cooling fins over which air was blown by a fan, but they themselves were in sealed chambers so that the air flow did not come in contact with them. Output was 1,250V nominal.

All vehicles were carried on Commonwealth bogies. In the Commonwealth design the axleboxes are carried by equalising beams, and the bogie frame is supported on the beams by coil springs. The bolster also rests on coil springs, with hydraulic damping of vertical movements and rubber stops to check excessive sideways movement. Tractive forces are transmitted by traction bars connecting the bolster with the bogie frame. The bars have rubber pad mountings which, together with their bending moments, allow for normal sideways movements.

Four-car units seated 36 first class and 176 second class passengers (reduced to 144 in the griddle car sets). First class seating was in compartments except for a saloon section, with tables in the driving trailer adjoining the griddle car. Second class seating was in saloons except for compartments in the motorcoaches. The stock was double-glazed and sound-insulated between body panels, under floors and in the ceilings. In the griddle cars the self-service counter was between a saloon section with two tables and movable armchairs at one end and a saloon seating 24 at the other. The pre-inflation 'traveller's fare' offered an 'Angus Steak in Hamburger' for 1s 9d (about 11p) or for 3s (15p) if served with a fried egg. The 'Tartan Plate' (Entrecote steak with egg and tomatoes) cost 6s 9d. Contemporary comment, beginning to interest itself with the appearance of electric trains, was not altogether happy with the front end design and thought that something more distinctive than the maroon livery then standard for main line stock might have been chosen, but these were the opinions of the intellectual elite. To many travellers they did look like main line trains, vastly different from the original Shenfield electrics and the Southend Victoria or LT&S stock which followed.

The performance was lively. Cecil J. Allen rode on the press trip and found the journey 'extraordinarily stimulating'. Of the return run from Clacton he wrote: 'so the lightning time was achieved of 17min 3sec over the 21.9 miles from Colchester to Chelmsford start-to-stop, and if that were not enough, what about 8min 41sec for the 9.6miles from Chelmsford to Shenfield start-to-stop, this time against the grade?' The stock was designed for an 85min Liverpool Street-Clacton service with four intermediate stops. This was still the schedule of the 18.00 from Liverpool Street in the summer service of 1978 but the early-riser in Clacton catching the 06.17 could be in London in 82min. Some trains by that time had a minute or two added to their times to allow for additional stops at stations between Chelmsford and Colchester where populations have grown since electric traction was inaugurated. It was acknowledged that the power was more than adequate for the service, but this was because of the design forming the basis for possible future emus working on more difficult routes. In 1974 four of the two-car units were increased to four-cars, forming Class 309/4. In their early days the trains carried rectangular destination boards above window level – a useful arrangement in view of the division of the Clacton and Walton portions at Thorpe-le-Soken.

During the troubled early 1960s work on the LMR electrification was rolling steadily forward. On 1 January 1960 electric working began between Crewe and Liverpool. It was extended to Stafford in January 1963, to Rugby in November 1964, and in September 1965 electric freight trains began working to Willesden. In November of the same year there were partial electric services at Euston, followed by full electrification at the terminus at the beginning of 1966, with accelerated services from 18 April, although at first by the Trent Valley line only, the routes to the north-west via Birmingham and via Stoke-on-Trent being electrified in 1966–67. The 25kV electrification from Glasgow to Gourock and Wemyss Bay belongs to the same period.

In their earliest days railways represented the spearhead of engineering achievement. As time went on their specialised characteristics and requirements tended to lead them into paths of their own, parallel rather than overlapping with the main highways of technical progress even in their early use of electrical apparatus in signalling and communications. Electrification brought them closer to the main streams of development, and this was seen particularly in the LMR scheme with its concentration of signalling and power control in a few centres, the remote supervisory systems being closely allied to current industrial practice. Similarly, in areas peculiar to the railway such as overhead current collection new materials and methods finding their way into industry were adapted to the railway environment. It was a period of general technical advance, stimulated by a stream of new electronic devices, and there were important changes in practice over the years that electrification between Euston and the north-west was in progress.

One of the technical developments with the most far-reaching effects on electric traction has been the improvement in insulating materials. For one thing it helped British Railways to demonstrate to the satisfaction of the Ministry of Transport that the overhead line clearances which had been worked to at first could safely be reduced. As early as 1960 the Chief Inspecting Officer had recommended that 6.25kV sections should be kept to a minimum. In many places, however, the use of the higher voltage would have involved very costly work in raising bridges, opening out tunnels, and so on unless smaller clearances could be accepted. By chance an accident enquiry at Colchester led to some special tests being made to show that flashover was unlikely to occur across a gap of more than 2in. When this was established it was followed up by a series of experiments extending over several months in all kinds of severe conditions. Some of them were witnessed by Brig Langley, including a demonstration in Crewe tunnel when even the full blast of a steam locomotive exhaust on the overhead system did not cause a flashover

Right: With their top speed of 90mile/h, the Eastern Region's Class 309 sets for the Liverpool Street-Clacton-Walton services were expected to herald a breed of high-speed emus, although the electric APT was then unheard of. Class 309/2 buffet car units Nos 612 and 613 form a down Clacton service on Brentwood Bank on 19 May 1977./*Brian Morrison*

across a 2in gap. Brig Langley recalled later that the trials 'proved beyond doubt that lower clearances could be accepted with safety'. New standards of 8in static and 6in passing clearance were approved by the Ministry of Transport in August 1962. They enabled the whole of the London Midland Region electrification to be carried out at 25kV. Much research on current collection at speed was carried out at this period but the promise of simple catenary throughout was not yet achieved. High-speed sections on the main line to Euston were equipped with compound catenary but an improved form of simple catenary with 'sagged' contact wire was installed on the 85mile/h section between Colwich and Stoke-on-Trent. During this period, too, the development of glass fibre insulating materials enabled many of the porcelain insulators used originally in the structures and in the overhead lines themselves to be replaced by smaller and lighter components. The most noticeable advance was an insulator of little larger cross-section than the contact wire which enabled neutral sections to be reduced from an original overall length of 714ft to only 15ft (see Chapter 11). The same device was used as a section insulator, replacing the original cumbersome arrangement of porcelain insulators and metal runners to provide a continuous conducting path for the pantograph. The new insulator was spliced into the overlapping contact wires. The glass fibre insulating core had ceramic beads threaded over it throughout its length to protect it from wear by pantographs.

Booster transformers with return conductors to prevent interference with Post Office circuits were installed between Liverpool and Crewe, and from Crewe southwards, but in parts of the London and Birmingham areas they were not required because of improved screening of the telecommunications circuits. Altogether some 90% of the route was given booster transformer protection. On the Manchester-Crewe section, where the return was through the rails, transformers were spaced about a mile apart but elsewhere, with return conductors, the spacing is about two miles. They are not an inevitable feature of 50Hz electrification and there have been cases of their being removed as no longer necessary.

The last of the prototype locomotive classes for the LMR electrification was Class 85, of which 20 were built at Doncaster and 20 at Crewe, all having electrical equipment supplied by Associated Electrical Industries (Rugby). Semiconductor rectifiers were considered to have proved themselves sufficiently in emus on the Lancaster-Morecambe-Heysham pilot scheme for them to be adopted in these locomotive installations, 30 of which had germanium diodes and 10 silicon. This type of rectifier saved space and weight compared with the Class 81 locomotives, which otherwise had similar electrical equipment, and so the opportunity was taken to install rheostatic braking. The braking resistors for all four motors were built into a unit with the blower for cooling them. During braking the motor fields were separately excited from the secondary winding of a transformer with its primary fed from the main transformer via the tap-changer so that excitation was controlled by the power handle after the driver had operated a power/brake changeover switch.

The germanium rectifiers were made up of diodes connected in strings of eight mounted in withdrawable trays. There were 20 trays with 64 diodes in each. The silicon rectifiers occupied 12 trays with 28 diodes in each connected in strings of seven. Both types were ventilated by fans. Since those days both the voltage and current ratings of semiconductor diodes have been progressively improved with corresponding reductions in the number required for a given duty. All germanium rectifiers have been replaced by silicon.

9
Enter Electronics

The first germanium traction rectifier in 1955 was greeted with some reserve in the railway press. Germanium was an unfamiliar material and its uses at the time were mainly in low-current applications. It was associated with the transistor, and today one reads with surprise contemporary references by persons who should have known better to 'transistor locomotives'.

The mercury-arc rectifier had exploited the 'free' electron, not confined to a conventional conductor but flowing from cathode to anode through a mercury-vapour atmosphere. The semiconductor rectifier of germanium or silicon organises the random movements of electrons within the material. For this process to be possible the slice of material must first be treated in such a way that one zone has an excess and the other a deficit of electrons. The critical factor in the operation of the device is the junction between the two zones.

When a suitably treated semiconductor slice is connected in circuit with an alternating voltage, the positive voltage half-cycle can be considered as marshalling the electrons into an orderly column which then advances irresistibly across the junction and round the circuit. In the negative half-cycle their cohesion is lost; a few straggle back across the junction, forming what is known as 'leakage current', but to all intents and purposes the current flow is blocked and the device has acted as a rectifier, allowing current to pass in one direction only.

The above is, of course, an over-simplification. The current flow in the 'forward' direction is not entirely unopposed. There is a small drop in voltage and consequent generation of heat. In the reverse direction a voltage exceeding the rated value will cause the leakage current suddenly to increase, and in these circumstances the heat produced can destroy the properties of the device. Semiconductor devices are also sensitive to ambient temperature, germanium much more so than silicon, which was why germanium had only a short life as a traction rectifying material.

In a transistor there are two zones with an excess and one with a deficit of electrons, or vice versa, and consequently two internal junctions. The transistor can act as an amplifier, an oscillator, or a high-speed switch, and in present-day control systems it is found in all these roles. It is, in fact, a necessary adjunct to the thyristor, or controlled semiconductor rectifier, which depends for its operation on the generation externally of pulses of accurate timing, length and shape.

A controlled rectifier delivers a variable dc output voltage from a fixed ac input voltage. Mercury-arc rectifiers will act in this way if fitted with a grid electrode and considerable use was made of the property in industrial installations, but only on a limited scale in traction. Grid control can also be used to operate a rectifier as an 'inverter', giving the effect of a reversed current flow, and this capability was used at certain 3,000V dc substations on the South African Railways to return power to the ac distribution system from locomotives using their regenerative braking. More might have been done with grid control of mercury-arcs had it not been for the rapid development of the thyristor as a controlled rectifier for high powers.

The thyristor is basically similar in formation to a transistor, but with an additional 'deficit' zone, and it has a third terminal connected to an extra electrode called the 'gate'. No current flows between the main electrodes during positive half-cycles of voltage until the device is 'triggered' by applying a pulse of current to the gate. Normal conduction follows until the applied positive voltage falls nearly to zero; during the negative half-cycle only a negligible leakage current passes as in a normal diode. The trigger pulse is repeated to initiate conduction during every positive half-cycle and the point on the incoming voltage wave at which it occurs determines the output voltage from the device. If firing is fully retarded, ie at 180 degrees, there is no output. As firing is advanced the output voltage rises, until at zero degrees, ie at the beginning of the half-cycle, the full input voltage appears at the output and the device behaves like an ordinary diode.

Positive and negative as used here are relative terms. In a practical rectifier the devices are connected in groups so arranged that each half-cycle of the supply appears as positive to one or more groups and is therefore provided with a conducting path. The flow of direct current into the circuit is continuous. This is known as full-wave rectification. A full-wave diode rectifier is shown schematically in Fig 8. The arrangement is called a 'bridge' circuit and in practice each arm of the bridge would be formed by a number of devices in series-parallel.

The thyristor offered the traction engineer the possibility of attaining his long-sought goal of stepless voltage control, but even before the device was fully proven for high-power applications some interesting steps in that direction had been taken. In 1960 the motorcoach of Eastern Region Class 302 unit No 312 – the last of its series – was equipped with silicon rectifiers and other technical improvements, one of them being a regulating transformer with a continuously variable ratio. The main tapped transformer was retained, but as each tap was connected, the regulating transformer came into action to raise the voltage applied to the rectifiers smoothly to that of the next tap. This continuous control was obtained by means of rollers travelling along a bared conducting path on the regulating transformer winding. The rollers were driven by a pilot motor at a speed controlled automatically to maintain a constant accelerating current in the traction motors. According to the conditions in which the unit was accelerating the time for a full traverse of the rollers varied from about $2\frac{1}{2}$sec on level track to a maximum of about $7\frac{1}{2}$sec on the steepest up grade. At the/end of each traverse the next tap on the main transformer was selected in the normal way, but as the motors were already receiving the voltage corresponding to that tap there was no sudden rise in current.

The regulating transformer system, developed by The English Electric Co Ltd in conjunction with Brentford Transformers Ltd, was overtaken by the rapid advance of thyristor control to produce a similar effect but in the meantime there had been another experiment with notchless control applied to a locomotive. An AL3 (Class 83) locomotive, No 3100, was fitted with silicon rectifiers instead of the ignitrons of the rest of its class and with a system for the smooth build-up of voltage from tap to tap corresponding to that of the regulating transformer but this time achieved without moving parts or pilot motor. The control elements were four transductors connected between the main transformer and the rectifiers, each consisting of a power winding carrying the traction current and a control winding carrying a dc supply at a variable low voltage. The current in the control winding varied the impedance of the power winding and hence the voltage applied to the rectifier: it was variable in

small steps by resistances switched by a separate camshaft controller under the control of the driver's normal power handle. In a later stage of the experiment in 1963 the switched resistors were replaced by magnetic amplifiers arranged in a closed loop system to control traction motor current at any value selected by the driver up to any pre-set speed. The whole system was planned around the eventual use of thyristors (then known as silicon controlled rectifiers) and the transductors were not regarded as more than a temporary expedient pending the availability of semiconductor devices of suitable capacity.

By the mid-1960s the power thyristor had arrived. Experiments with two different forms of thyristor control were carried out in British Railways emu motorcoaches but the one which became the basis of future development was phase angle control on the principle described earlier in this chapter. Again the motorcoach of unit 312 was involved, the regulating transformer system being removed and thyristors substituted for it, the main silicon diode rectifier remaining unchanged. The main transformer, however, now had only one tapping, at the centre point of the secondary winding. In operation, the thyristors were first connected to the centre tap and fully retarded. Firing was then advanced at a rate which maintained the correct accelerating current until they were fully conducting and behaving like diodes, the motors receiving the full voltage of the centre tap. At this stage contactors operated to bring the main diode rectifier into action and reconnect the thyristors to the full-voltage tapping on the transformer. At the same time their firing angle was quickly fully retarded. To continue acceleration the angle was again advanced to raise the motor voltage to the full operating value. Top speed was attained by field-weakening in the usual way.

This installation was notable as an early application of industrial 'logic' modules for controlling current during acceleration by adjusting the thyristor firing angle, initiating the tap-change, and finally weakening the motor fields. The modules were assemblies of electronic components on printed circuit boards, each with a particular function. Basically they comprised 'gates' which produced a control signal at their output terminals when a particular set of conditions was present at their input, supplemented by amplifiers of various kinds. The mode of operation was what is known as a 'closed loop' or sometimes a 'servo'. A reference signal representing the required accelerating current was fed into the system from the driver's controller, and a signal proportional to the actual motor current was continuously compared with it. When the motor current tended to fall with increasing speed, for example, the system produced an output which advanced the firing of the thyristors to close the gap between the reference and actual current signals. Further elements detected when the thyristors were fully advanced and initiated the tap-change. On the 'second time round,' with the thyristors again fully advanced and current falling with the motors at full voltage, a second comparison circuit consisting of an amplifier with two inputs came into action. One input was a 'reference' representing the current at which field weakening was to take place, the other was a signal representing motor current as before. As long as the signal from the motors exceeded the reference the amplifier gave no output, but as soon as the two coincided it switched to full output and operated the weak-field contactors. All the functions of electro-mechanical relays in a conventional control system were thus performed by static components.

The tap-change limited the range of control which the thyristors had to provide. To cover the full operating voltage range of the motors would have resulted in a poor power factor and excessive harmonic interference with the supply. Subsequent practice has eliminated the tap-change but still restricts the range of control of individual thyristors, by splitting the full voltage range into two or more stages. The principle is illustrated in Fig 9 which shows the basic circuit for the control of one of the four traction motors in the BR thyristor locomotive No 87.101 of Class 87/1. It comprises two 'mixed' bridges (ie a combination of diodes and thyristors), A and B, each fed by a separate secondary winding on the main transformer and connected in series. When both bridges are fully conducting, therefore, the voltage applied to motor M is the sum of the voltages across the two secondaries, and is the normal operating voltage of the machine. It will be noted that the field winding is not in series with the armature as in the usual traction motor but is connected to a separate source of excitation, itself controlled by thyristors. Separate excitation is not an essential feature of thyristor control but it enables maximum advantage to be derived from it in respect of operating characteristics.

At starting, only the thyristors in bridge A are triggered. An essential difference between a diode and a thyristor is that the diode *always* conducts in one direction, but the thyristor conducts *only* when 'turned on' by a trigger pulse to its gate. In the starting condition, therefore, thyristors T_3 and T_4 can be regarded simply as open switches. Operation begins with thyristors T_1 and T_2 fully retarded. As they are advanced, the rectified voltage of bridge A increases and current flows through motor M via diodes D_3 and D_4 in bridge B. As these devices are not rectifying at this stage, being presented only with a dc voltage in their 'forward' or conducting direction, they are said to be 'freewheeling'.

When T_1 and T_2 are fully advanced the motor is running at half voltage. Thyristors T_3 and T_4 in bridge B are now triggered, fully retarded at first but with gradual advance. Bridge B is now rectifying the input from its secondary, and its voltage is added to bridge A, where T_1 and T_2 are fully conducting and acting as ordinary diodes. When the advance of T_3 and T_4 is completed, motor M receives its full operating voltage.

During acceleration the armature current is measured and the field current controlled to maintain a constant tractive effort, so that the tractive effort/speed curve of the locomotive is similar to that of one with ordinary series motors. After full operating voltage is attained, field excitation is reduced by retarding the thyristors in the field control circuits so that the motors run with weakened fields and reach maximum balancing speed.

Fig 8 (*below*) Full-wave rectification with a bridge rectifier.
Fig 9 (*below right*) Simplified power circuit for thyristor control of a single traction motor.

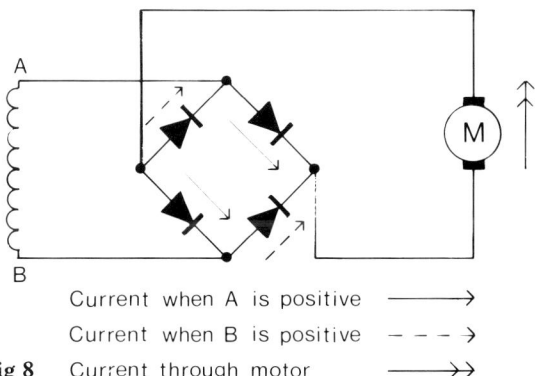

Current when A is positive   ⟶
Current when B is positive   - - - ⟶
Fig 8   Current through motor   ⟶⟶

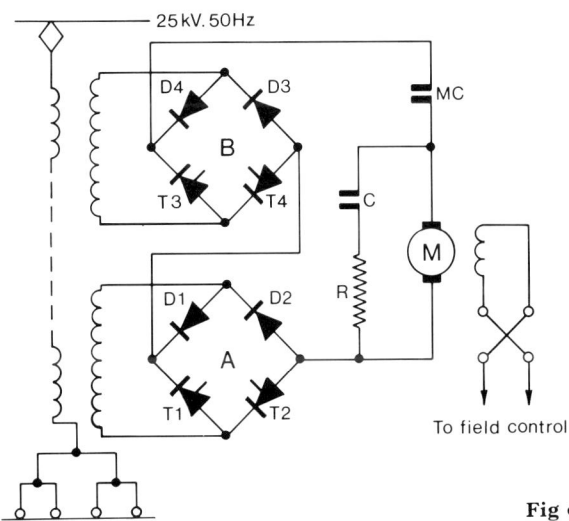

Fig 9

With separate field excitation a locomotive or motor-coach is inherently less liable to slipping if an axle loses adhesion. With a series motor the effect of slipping is cumulative, since increased armature speed reduces current in both armature and field, and the weakened field allows the speed of the slipping axle to rise further. Separate excitation holds the field strength constant or can actually increase it. These possibilities combine with stepless build-up of voltage and absence of sharp increases of current during acceleration to give thyristor motive power the ability to make use of the maximum tractive effort of which it is capable in all conditions of load and rail adhesion. The electronic circuits which control the thyristors are compatible with various types of 'closed loop' systems which allow the driver to preset tractive effort and maximum speed and then concentrate on observing signals and the road ahead while the equipment observes his instructions with an accuracy and consistency much better than can be expected with manual control.

A resistor R can be connected across the motor armature for rheostatic braking by closing the braking contactor C. The motor is isolated from the supply by opening motor contactor MC, and operates as a separately excited generator with its excitation controlled by the field circuit thyristors, giving stepless control of braking effort.

Not only has the thyristor made it possible to dispense with the tap-changing transformer in ac traction but it can provide stepless control without resistances on dc systems. When a dc supply is connected to a load such as a traction motor the full voltage is not developed across the supply instantaneously. A very quick acting switch would allow the supply to be disconnected while the voltage in the circuit was still at a low value, although rising. By repeating this very rapid on/off switching process the motor could be operated at any voltage up to the full value of the supply by varying the time for which the switch was closed. We are talking here in terms of the switch being closed for about one-hundredth of a second, and the change from the open to the closed condition occurring in millionths of a second. No mechanical switch could operate at these speeds, but the same effect can be produced with a thyristor. Here then is a method of controlling the voltage applied to a traction motor without resistances and the loss of energy as heat which they entail. To begin with, the 'on' periods of the switch are very short and minimum voltage reaches the motor. As they are increased the voltage rises, and when finally they become continuous the voltage at the motor equals that of the supply.

Switching the thyristor to its conducting state, when it is the equivalent of a closed switch, presents no

problem, being effected by a pulse at the gate electrode as already seen, but when the supply is dc there is a problem in switching off. Once a thyristor has been triggered into the conducting state it continues conducting until the applied voltage ceases or is reversed. With ac the voltage passes through zero at the end of every half wave but in a dc system the voltage is constant. A second thyristor, known as the 'quenching' thyristor, has to be used for the turn-off process. The rapid on/off switching 'chops' the supply into short pulses and so the circuit is called a 'chopper'.

A basic chopper circuit is shown in Fig 10. Thyristor T2 is the quenching thyristor and its function is to charge the commutating capacitor C. T2 is triggered to start the process. There is a rush of current into C, which stops when the capacitor is fully charged with its left-hand plate at supply voltage. Because no more current can flow into the capacitor, T2 switches off. T1 is now triggered so that current can flow through the motor. With T1 conducting there is a circuit round which C can discharge via L, D1 and T1. A reverse swing of current, such as would normally occur in a circuit with inductance and capacity, is blocked by D1. The charge on C1 is now reversed, the right hand plate being at supply voltage.

To turn T1 off, T2 is triggered and raises the left hand plate of C to supply voltage, which causes the

Fig 10 (*below*) Basic chopper circuit for controlling traction motor voltage without the use of resistances.

Right: The last of the AL3 locomotives, No 3100, was fitted with transductors for smooth control of voltage between taps and other refinements foreshadowing later electronic systems. It was reclassified AL3/1 and is illustrated on a test train near Stafford./*GEC Traction Ltd*

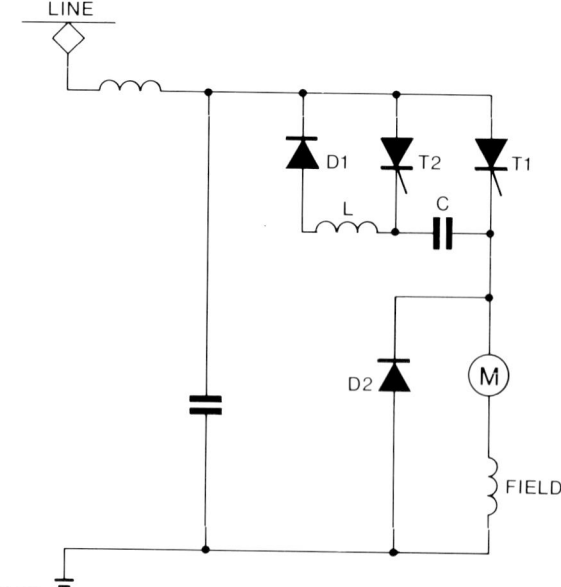

Fig 10.

right-hand plate to rise to twice supply voltage. With the condenser once more fully charged, no more current can flow through T2, which switches off, and since the potential across T1 has been reversed, this thyristor switches off as well. Both thyristors are now ready for the next cycle. For full-voltage operation of the motor T1 conducts continuously and T2 is not triggered. Diode D2 is called the 'flywheel' diode. In accordance with the Newtonian law, every action produces an equal and opposite reaction. Therefore, when the current through the motor is cut off, the energy stored in its windings tends to keep a current

flowing. D2 provides a path around which it can circulate, helping to smooth the pulsations of current through the motor by filling the gaps between them. For full-voltage operation of the motor T1 conducts continuously and T2 is not triggered. In practice the circuit is modified so that the high voltage – twice the supply value – used to turn off T1 does not appear in the load circuit.

Chopper control is of particular interest to rapid transit dc railways where stations are close together and starting resistances are in frequent use. Maximum savings are achieved when regenerative braking is

provided, the chopper controlling the motor field excitation in this phase of operation to regulate the braking effort. The rapid action of thyristor switching enables both regenerative and rheostsatic braking to be used as appropriate. The system continuously senses the ability of the supply to accept regenerated power and adjusts the ratio of regenerative to rheostatic braking accordingly within 0.005sec.

The switching action of thyristors produces harmonics which can cause adverse effects both in the main supply system and other apparatus connected to it, and in nearby signalling and telecommunications circuits. Adoption of thyristor systems in Britain has therefore been cautious and the subject of extended trials. On British Rail the motorcoach experiments of 1966 were not followed up until the appearance of the thyristor-controlled Class 87/1 locomotive No 87.101 in 1975 although in the meantime orders had been placed with ASEA in Sweden for the power equipments of the electric version of the Advanced Passenger Train in which the control is by thyristors. By the time the first APT power cars began trial running in 1977 considerable experience of harmonic effects and how to neutralise them had been gained. Chopper control raises interference problems similar to those of phase-angle control.

In order to assess the effect of chopper control in a busy suburban railway environment, in 1978 BR ordered a 750V dc chopper equipment from GEC Traction Ltd for installation in a Southern Region 4-SUB emu of Class 405/2. The next generation of SR commuter stock, however, has resistance control similar to the dc side of the Class 313 equipments. These four-car units are Class 508 and generally similar to the Merseyrail 507s.

Outside the power circuits of locomotives and motorcoaches the scope for electronics in control systems is vast, ranging from the simple substitution of devices using transistors and thyristors for electro-mechanical relays, to closed loop control schemes requiring minimum intervention by the driver. A major step in this direction was taken in the Southern Region Class 74 electro-diesel locomotives of 1967 (converted from Class 71 electrics), which were needed for certain traffic requirements of the Bournemouth electrification. Problems were encountered partly because electronic components of proven reliability for traction service were not available at that period, and also because the locomotives had to go into service before final development was completed. Early availability was poor and the class incurred some odium among

Left: Thyristor locomotive No. 87.101 (Classified 87/1) heads a test train during experiments to establish the effects of thyristor control on signalling and telecommunication circuits./*BR*

ill-informed observers, many of whom were still lamenting their lost Bulleid Pacifics on the Bournemouth line. But if there is no experiment there can be no progress and some useful lessons were learned for the future. Specialist electronic manufacturers whose products had stood up to many thousands of hours of service in aircraft were often incredulous when they discovered how difficult it was to mount printed circuit boards securely in their racks in the vibrating interior of a locomotive.

In parallel with the development of the phase-controlled thyristor and the thyristor chopper for traction has gone that of the inverter for converting dc into ac. This device first became familiar in rolling stock for providing ac for fluorescent lighting from a battery supply. High power versions today will produce ac power for traction, and three-phase power at that, bringing another old aspiration of the traction engineer

closer to his grasp – the use of three-phase traction motors with similar characteristics to the conventional series machine and the same flexibility of speed control. This subject is dealt with in a later chapter, but it is mentioned here to show how the advent of electronics has broken down the barriers that were once expressed in phrases like 'the battle of the systems' and 'ac and dc countries'. The engineer who can manipulate electric power as he wishes need no longer be a partisan of any particular form.

Below: One of the PEP units was converted to thyristor control and ac operation as a prototype for new stock on the Glasgow suburban services. The converted set, renumbered 920.001, passes Dalreoch during trials in 1976. */F. McKechnie*

10
New Generations-Third Rail

The Southern Region's electrification to Southampton and Bournemouth in 1967 was certainly a third-rail extension and as such could have been considered in Chapter 7, but it also began a new phase in the Region's operating practice. In the 1930s the Southern Railway was already considering the need for motive power to work over non-electrified lines bordering its electrified network and had proposed auxiliary battery power for its first booster locomotives. The study was taken up again after the war, by which time it was considered that the booster set might be driven by an 800hp diesel engine through a magnetic coupling when operating away from the live rail, and that the diesel might provide additional power when necessary on electrified track. These ideas would have involved complicated circuitry and were dropped, the principal requirements for diesel working being scaled down to movements in non-electrified sidings, dockside areas and during track possessions.

Discussion next turned to various ratios of diesel to electric power. At one stage a 1,200hp electric equipment with a 200hp diesel auxiliary was proposed, combined in a centre-cab layout. This was later changed to 1,500hp electric and 500hp diesel ratings in an end cab design with unoccupied space in the body used for luggage, but the Operating Department did not need this facility. A final change of plan took place in 1956 when the Southern dual-power locomotive as known today took shape on the drawing board and for the first time acquired the name 'electro-diesel', echoing in more elegant form the name 'boosel' which had been bestowed unofficially on the proposed diesel-assisted booster locomotive. Authority to build six prototype electro-diesels of 1,600hp electric rating and 600hp diesel was given in 1959. These were the locomotives later classified Class 73/0.

A second long-standing Southern objective was compatibility of control between different types of motive power. An initial step was taken in 1951 when a 27-wire train control cable was adopted in place of the 8-wire or 12-wire cables used previously, and wires were allotted for switching functions necessary for

achieving a highly flexible new operating policy expressed as: 'application of the multiple-unit principle to any formation of modern electric stock with electric or diesel-electric locomotives as might be required by the traffic pattern.' This overall compatibility was seen in practice in the Bournemouth electrification.

The two classes of electro-diesels, 73/0 and 73/1, are basically Bo-Bo electric locomotives with resistance and series/parallel control. This classic method was chosen because it was thought desirable to use equipment already developed, and no suitable booster set was available. In any case, the 'gapping' problem was not serious because the diesel engine could extricate the locomotive if it stalled, and large openings in the bodysides and roof had a tunnel effect which created sufficient airflow over the edge-wound strip resistors for all notches to be considered as continuously rated in normal circumstances.

The generator in the diesel set was basically the machine used in the Hastings demus but with its continuous rating raised from 600A to 900A. The 600hp 4SRKT diesel engine was as used in the SR Hampshire diesels but with improved silencing and electric fan drive. In choosing a well-tried design, the Region accepted an engine of about twice the power required for shunting duties but probably this is not now regretted for the electro-diesels sometimes travel considerable distances on diesel power.

The locomotives have separate, and interlocked, electric and diesel power handles. On electric power the driver can notch up step by step or let the equipment run up under accelerating relay control. Class 73/1 also has a 'shunt' position corresponding to the standard emu controller. The four weak-field notches can be used in series or parallel in both classes, but the procedure for using series weak-field is simpler in the 73/1 class. In both designs notching is by motor-driven camshafts.

An interesting comment on driving the electro-diesels was made in a letter received by the present writer commenting on an article on 'notching up' in *Railway World*. A Southern Region driver wrote:

'To mention the Southern electro-diesels . . . the resistances are all shorted out at a mere 15mile/h when the controller is put to series run-up. Put it to parallel run-up and they are shorted out all over again by 30mile/h. In the case of the few freak trains like those carrying long welded rail, booked at 25mile/h, you just put the reverser handle to series forward and the controller to weak-field run-up and you get a suitable speed between 15mile/h and 30mile/h without using resistances at all'.

An unusual feature of the diesel control scheme in both classes is that series/parallel switching takes place, transition occurring automatically when generator excitation reaches maximum with the motors in series and minimum field. At this point the resistance camshaft comes into action, switching resistance into the motor circuit to avoid a current peak. Operation of the diesel power handle automatically retracts the shoegear within the loading gauge.

Traction motors are not interchangeable between the two electro-diesel classes, but the Class 73/1 motors are fully interchangeable with those of the 4-REP

emus and the roller suspension bearing assemblies have the standard emu arrangement of central brushes for traction current return. Bogie frames are identical with REP and VEP stock although the design of the coil springs is altered to allow for the difference in loading. Class 73/0 locomotives have a gear ratio of 63:17 and a maximum operating speed of 80mile/h. The ratio was changed to 63:19 in Class 73/1 for a top speed in normal running of 90mile/h. The motors of this class have sustained an overspeed test at 3,300rev/min. Class 73/1 was also equipped so that the diesel engine start sequence was fully automatic after pressing an 'auxiliary power on' button in the cab of an emu running in multiple with it.

Below: Replacement of express stock on the Central Division began with the Class 421 (4-CIG) units in 1964, quickly followed by the Class 420s (4-BIGs). The 16.00 Victoria-Brighton non-stop emerges from Quarry Tunnel on 2 July 1970 with Class 420/1 No 7039 in the lead. /*J. H. Cooper-Smith*

Below right: Class 421 unit No 7318 heads the 13.40 Victoria to Brighton semi-fast past Balcombe Tunnel Junction on 18 June 1978./*J. Scrace*

By the time the Bournemouth electrification was undertaken the semiconductor rectifier was established for traction substation use and this influenced the decision to continue with the third-rail at 750V beyond its existing limit on the main line at Sturt Lane Junction. Among other possibilities, thought had been given to a protected third rail at 1,500V, but although this would have halved the number of substations the reduction in cost would have been insufficient to offset the cost of additional rolling stock to compensate for loss of interavailability, while the shoegear for a protected system would not have been compatible with a 750V top contact rail. But the forward volts drop through a silicon rectifier is only about 5V, compared with 24V in a mercury-arc device, and here a saving in the number of substations could be achieved. The extension of the third rail from Brookwood to Bournemouth and over the Lymington branch from Brockenhurst required 19 new substations and 20 track paralleling huts. There were 13 between Basingstoke and Bournemouth, where 16 mercury-arc installations would have been necessary.

Four of the most heavily loaded substations on the main line section already electrified had their mercury-arc rectifiers – glass bulbs or pumped steel tanks with water cooling – replaced with silicon. The first five substations on the newly electrified four-track section from Brookwood to Basingstoke were equipped with 2,000kW silicon units at a spacing of approximately 3½ miles. Beyond Basingstoke the spacing was increased, the maximum being 4.7 miles. On this section most of the substations had two 1,000kW units but at Eastleigh and Bournemouth two 1,500kW units were installed to cater for the extra load of sidings and depots.

Power for the extension was obtained at Basingstoke, Southampton and Bournemouth and distributed to the substations by a ring main of 0.15sq in oil-filled 33kV cable with aluminium conductors and sheath. At each substation the supply to the rectifiers was taken through an oil switch. When this was closed, and a 750V dc output establish, contactors closed automatically to connect the rectifiers to the busbars. Relays were arranged to trip the track circuit-breakers and the oil switch if in fault conditions current was detected as flowing back from the live rails into the

Above: The 13.17 Littlehampton-Victoria calls at Hove on 28 April 1971, Class 420/1 No 7038 leading./*J. Scrace*

Right: Unit No 7341, one of the 1970 batch of 421s (421/2), leaves St Denys with a Bournemouth-Waterloo stopping service on 22 June 1970./*John H. Bird*

substation. The breakers also tripped if there was a substantial fall in track voltage, such as could be caused by a track fault. These precautions were, of course, additional to the normal protection by tripping on overload current.

The major operating development of the electrification arose from the method adopted for giving a through service by London trains to stations between Bournemouth and Weymouth. Haulage by electric locomotives to Bournemouth and by diesel-electrics over the non-electrified section beyond was not practicable because of limited platform lengths at Waterloo. Twelve-coach trains plus locomotives could not be accommodated and light locomotive movements at the terminus would have been an embarrassment at peak periods. It was therefore decided to form Bournemouth-Weymouth trains of a four-coach powered unit at the London end, propelling one or two four-coach trailer sets. The procedure is now well known. Trailer sets have a driving compartment with standard emu equipment at each end. The down train is driven from the leading trailer unit cab. At Bournemouth a Class 33 diesel-electric backs on to the front of the train and hauls one or both trailer sets on to Weymouth.

For the return journey the diesel-electric locomotive does not run round its train at Weymouth but propels it, controlled from the leading driving trailer cab by a standard four-position emu controller supplemented only by an extra push button for starting the diesel engine. Electrical signals corresponding to the four controller positions are transmitted over wires in the 27-wire control cable to the locomotive at the rear, where they are translated into different values of air pressure which act on the engine governor in the same

way as when the locomotive is being driven from its own cab.

Before these methods of working could be introduced the Region had to demonstrate that propulsion of long trains at high speed was safe. Many test runs were made with a 12-coach train of emu stock propelled by an electro-diesel locomotive, and detailed records of the forces on train and track were taken. Speeds up to 100mile/h were attained on the trial stretch between Tonbridge and Ashford. The Ministry of Transport was satisfied, and push-pull working on a scale and at speeds not hitherto seen in this country became in due course a daily event.

The Bournemouth-Weymouth push-pull operation was only one of the facilities made available by the Southern's development of the multiple-unit system. The whole range of possibilities was summed up at the time in the following words:

'The way is now clear for any combination of interconnection and reversibility of rolling stock and locomotives on the Southern Region which may best suit operating needs – the electro-diesel locomotives are interchangeable with the high-power motorcoaches; the diesel-electric locomotives can supply heat, light and compressed air power to them and can be remotely controlled from them. Furthermore there is a push-

button on the driving desk in the new multiple-unit trains which initiates the engine starting cycle of any diesel locomotive marshalled in the train and can bring in also the auxiliary battery power of one of the Kent Coast luggage vans.'

The high-power motorcoaches mentioned above are the power cars of the 4-REP (Class 430) units for the Bournemouth-Weymouth service. York built an initial batch of 22 of these vehicles, which form the first and last coaches of a 4-REP unit. There are four 365hp traction motors in each motorcoach. A Class 73/1 electro-diesel can replace one motorcoach and the unit can still operate to its normal timings with eight trailer coaches. The two intermediate vehicles in a 4-REP are a buffet car and a brake first, the motorcoaches being second class saloons.

Buffet cars, brake firsts and the vehicles of the first 28 four-car trailer sets (4-TC – Class 491) were converted from former locomotive-hauled coaches. The 4-TCs consist of second class saloon driving trailers, a brake second and a first class vehicle. Three 3-TC sets formed of second class saloons were also built originally but later converted to 4-TCs. A TC driving trailer can replace one motorcoach of a 4-REP.

For semi-fast services 20 four-car units of new stock were built, the motorcoaches and trailers coming from Derby and the driving trailers from York. These were classified 4-VEP (Class 423) and have since been built in large numbers. The 4-VEP formation of driving trailer, motorcoach, trailer and driving trailer is the same as the 4-CIG and the electrical equipment and shoegear arrangement are also similar. The shoes are on the driving trailers and interconnected with the motorcoach by buslines.

While writing this book I was able by courtesy of the Southern Region to ride to Bournemouth in the cab of the 10.30 from Waterloo. At the rear of the train when I joined it was 4-REP No 3001, the driver being in the leading 4-TC unit. The control layout in the 4-TC cab is simple and practical. The master controller handle is on the right of the desk. It is biassed upwards by a spring and a slight downward pressure must be maintained while running. If the handle is released and allowed to lift, the air brake pipe will be vented applying the brake, and, via an air-controlled electrical governor, the power to the traction motors will be cut off as in most 'dead man' devices. The handle moves horizontally through positions numbered 1 to 4 to select shunt, series, parallel and weak-field characteristics. Notch 1 is used only for shunting movements in depots etc.

The stock has automatic wheelslip correction which in case of slipping opens the line breakers, runs the resistance camshaft to the 'all resistance in' positon, and re-applies power. Under conditions of low wheel to rail adhesion the driver can hand notch the power cars, overriding the normal continuous automatic acceleration, but the inspector who rode with me assured me that in his experience the train 'would look after itself' under the control of the wheelslip correction system. If slow running is necessary for permanent way work, fog, or other restrictive conditions, speed is controlled by alternating between notches 2, 3 or 4 and 'off' rather than by using the shunt notch for 'crawling'. To return from a higher to a lower notch the power handle has to be moved back to 'off' and then advanced to the required position, direct 'runback' being confined to the automatic wheelslip correction process.

The reverser handle is on the left of the power handle and is interlocked with it so that the power handle cannot be moved until 'forward' or 'reverse' has been selected, while the setting of the reverser cannot be changed unless the power handle is 'off'.

The driver's instruments are a 'duplex' gauge showing main reservoir and air train pipe pressure, brake cylinder pressure gauge and a speedometer. A group of indicators on the right of the desk show if an electrical supply is available for the electro-pneumatic brake, the occurrence of an earth fault in the control system, and the presence of line volts at the shoegear, in our case on the 4-REP at the other end of the train. Should a control earth fault occur the unit may continue running but must be taken out of service at the earliest opportunity.

The indicator and reset pushbutton of the standard BR aws (automatic warning system) are to the driver's left. When the audible warning of a restrictive signal aspect is received (red, yellow or double yellow) the driver acknowledges it by pressing the reset button, which changes the indicator disc from all-black to alternate black and yellow segments as a reminder to the driver that he has acknowledged the warning and is taking appropriate action, ie shutting off power. Failure to acknowledge would lead to an automatic brake application after a delay period. Black and yellow is displayed until the train passes over the next track magnet.

Our train formation was a 4-REP propelling two 4-TCs. Each unit has its own lt power source – a motor-generator set and a battery. In the 4-REP it is carried under the first class brake vehicle. Should the mg set fail on the REP or any of the TCs an alternative

Top left: The traditional 'Brighton' route from Victoria to Portsmouth via Sutton and Dorking was used only by a few peak hour trains from the new timetable of May 1978, most of the service being re-routed via Three Bridges to serve Gatwick Airport and Crawley. On 27 January 1978, in the last days of Bognor-Portsmouth via Dorking, every hour off-peak, Class 421/1 unit No 7314 heads a 12-car formation out of Mickleham Tunnel bound for the Mid-Sussex line./*John A. M. Vaughan*

Above left: Class 421/2 unit No 7379 arrives at Wokingham with the 13.02 Reading-Waterloo service on 19 March 1977. /*L. Bertram*

Above: Until 1971 ex-Southern Railway 4-COR units continued to work Waterloo-Portsmouth expresses. On 13 September 1964 unit No 3106 leads the 12.50 Waterloo-Portsmouth Harbour on to the Portsmouth line at Woking. /*Brian Stephenson*

control supply is available from sound unit(s) in multiple via a network of blocking diodes. If a 4-REP motor-coach has to be moved by itself, the control supply is tapped off a potentiometer across the 750V traction supply. There is no shoegear on the 4-TCs, which may run diesel-hauled over non-electrified lines, and their mg sets are connected to a 750V heating supply which is taken from the 4-REP and fed to every vehicle in the train by train heating jumpers between coaches.

The buffet/restaurant car in the 4-REP has its own mg set to provide 200V for the catering equipment. Provision is made for the set to run automatically at intervals under the control of the refrigerator thermostat when the unit is berthed with perishables in store.

Train lighting is taken off the 70V lt supply in each unit, In the event of loss of line volts to the mg set, the

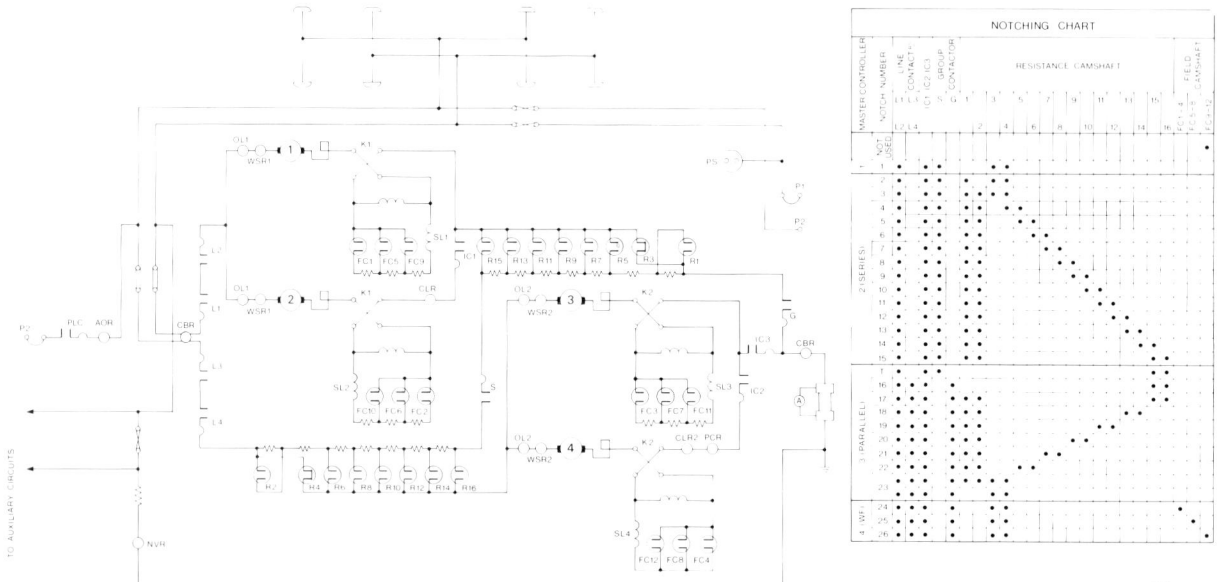

Fig 11

emergency lights remain on, fed from the unit battery until the voltage falls to 50.5V at which value they are cut off, leaving only safety lights (eg red blinds in rear route indicators) supplied.

Each motorcoach in the 4-REP is powered by four 365hp motors. The two machines in each bogie are connected in permanent parallel. Series/parallel control is similar to that described in Chapter 2 for a two-motor equipment, the pairs being in series at starting and then switched into parallel. Separate camshafts control the resistance and weak-field steps but they are operated by the same type of air/oil actuator as in the Kent Coast stock (Chapter 7). A full 4-REP power circuit is shown in Fig 11 together with a notching chart from which the operation of the contactors on each step can be followed. Contactors belonging to cam-operated groups are circled. Because of the high-power of this equipment, individual electro-pneumatic contactors (G and S) are used for transition. There are three stages of field-weakening by means of divert resistances but only the third stage is used as a running notch.

Four types of relay protection are provided:

1　No-volt relay (NVR) to disconnect the motors and re-insert all starting resistance on loss of line volts.
2　Current-balance relay (CBR) having one coil at the 'entry' and the other at the 'exit' end of the circuit. Normally both coils should carry the same current, but if a fault in the circuit allows current to pass to earth at some intermediate point, the current in the two coils will be different and the relay will operate to open the line breakers.

Fig 11 (*above*) Complete power circuit and notching chart for a Southern Region 4-REP (Class 430). The black spots in the chart show the contactors closed in each step of the control sequence.

Fig 12 (*below right*) Shoe arm, height-limiting beam and shoe of a 4-REP motorcoach:
1 Attachment to bogie frame,
2 Cable connections,
3 Shoe arm,
4 Shoe,
5 Height-limiting beam,
6 Axlebox bracket supporting height-limiting beam.

3　Wheelslip relays (WSR) also employ current comparison as the basis of operation. When an axle slips, its motor accelerates and takes less current due to the increasing back emf. The relay detects the imbalance of motors on either bogie and acts to cut off power as described earlier.
4　Polarised current relay (PCR) is provided to detect reverse current flow and disconnect the motors from the line. For example, a short-circuit on the track could cause the motors to regenerate into the fault, resulting possibly in a flashover.

A faulty motor can be isolated by preventing the line breakers to its bogie from closing, ie failure of one motor on a coach will result in half-power running if isolation on that coach is selected.

Shoegear on the 4-REPs is similar to the design introduced in the 4-CIG stock as briefly referred to in Chapter 7. Each shoe is carried by a cantilever arm suspended from resilient rubber pivots on the bogie frame and supported at the outer end on an elastic stop carried on a height-limiting beam attached at each end to the inner side of an axle-box (Fig 12). Minimum height of the shoe is maintained by the height adjustment bracket, which is adjusted when wheel diameters change. Unlike the straight arm employed on the 4-CIGs, the 4-REP arm is angled to pass between the primary springs and the swing links. Shoes are of cast iron, weighing approximately 50lb each, and the weight supplements the pre-tension in the rubber pivots in providing pressure on the live rail. Some modifications were made to the original design to allow for speeds up to 90mile/h, at which it was found that shoes could come adrift too easily. The cable terminal on the arm is now connected to the shoe by a copper ribbon that will tear off in emergency.

Two power lines running through the unit interconnect the shoes on both motorcoaches. The method of interconnection is such that the last shoe to leave the live rail at a gap never breaks the load of more than four motors. Fig 13 shows the arrangement, which should be studied in conjuction with the following tabulation of how the motors are fed in series and in parallel both normally and at a gap.

Series

1 Normal. All shoes on conductor rail.
Coach (1): S1 feeds all (1) motors, and there is also a feed to them from S2 shoes on (2).

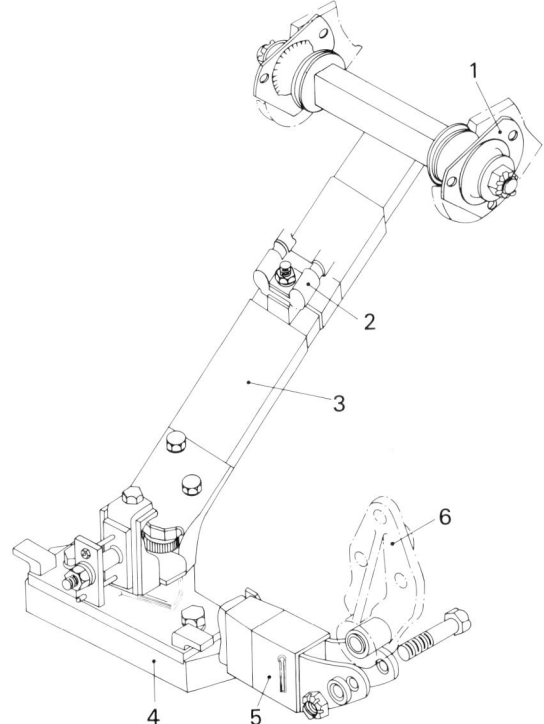

Fig 12

Coach (2): S1 shoes on (2) feed all motors on this coach, and they are also fed by S2 shoes on coach (1).
2 Last shoe on conductor rail
2.1 Direction A
S2 shoe on (2) is last to leave, breaking current to all four motors of coach (1). NB. Current to coach (2) motors was broken when S1 on that coach left the rail.
2.2 Direction B
S2 on (1) is last to leave, breaking current to all 4 motors on (2), S1 on (1) having broken current to (1) motors.

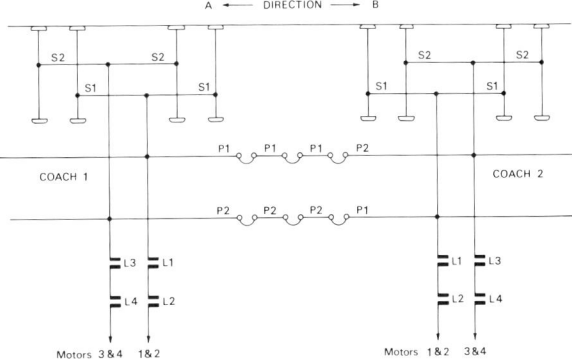

Fig 13 *(above)* Interconnection of shoes between the two motorcoaches of a 4-REP unit.

Parallel

1 Normal, all shoes on conductor rail. All motors on each coach fed through L1, L2.
Coach (1): S1 feeds (1)'s Nos 1 and 2 and (2)'s Nos 3 and 4 motors; S2 feeds (1)'s Nos 3 and 4 and (2)'s 1 and 2 motors.
Coach (2): S1 feeds (2)'s Nos 1 and 2 and (1)'s 3 and 4 motors; S2 feeds (2)'s Nos 3 and 4 and (1)'s 1 and 2 motors.
2 Last shoe on conductor rail
2.1 Direction A
S2 shoe on (2) breaks (2)'s Nos 3 and 4 and (1)'s Nos 1 and 2 motors; (S1 on (2) broke (2)'s 1 and 2 and (1)'s 3 and 4).
2.2 Direction B
S2 on (1) breaks (1)'s Nos 3 and 4 and (2)'s 1 and 2 motors; S1 on (1) broke (1)'s 1 and 2 and (2)'s 3 and 4 motors.

The foregoing may seem a digression, but watching the manipulation of the controller in a multiple-unit train gives no idea of the interesting things going on all the time further down the formation, the variety and intricacy of which should earn the emu more respectful attention than it usually gains as it flashes past.

We return to the cab of the 10.30, where the Louda-phone was just announcing when I arrived that the fitters who had been working in the 4-REP at the rear since the train arrived from Bournemouth had cleared a fault. But our departure had been slightly delayed and it was 10.34 when the guard's bell signal sounded in the cab to give us the 'right away'.

Movement of the power handle to Notch 2 got us moving out of the station and on towards Vauxhall at steadily rising speed, the driver soon advancing to Notch 3 so that the motors could switch into parallel and continue to accelerate. There is a 40mile/h restriction round the sharp curve through Vauxhall station and power was cut off to observe it. At the time of my journey speed was limited to 60mile/h as far as New Malden, $9\frac{3}{4}$ miles from Waterloo, and on restoring power after Vauxhall the driver did not go beyond Notch 3, coming back momentarily to Notch 2 to keep within the limit.

By Nine Elms the controller had been set in Notch 4 for the first time, allowing the equipment to go into weak-field, which occurs at about 40mile/h. Speed had reached 60 before power was cut off to coast through Clapham Junction at 40. The line rises from Clapham towards Wimbledon, but acceleration after the slack was rapid and we coasted again past Earlsfield and

through Wimbledon station at 60mile/h. With the station behind us the controller went back to Notch 3 for the level running ahead, then into Notch 4 after passing New Malden and leaving the restricted area.

Speed had risen to 86 at Esher and we touched our first 90 on the level at Byfleet. On the rising gradients which follow, the needle dropped back slightly and power was cut off through Woking. Then the lever was back to Notch 4 and we raced for the summit beyond Pirbright Junction. With no sound to be heard from the motors, which are away at the back of the train, it was easy to misjudge the speed and one missed the sense of urgency in the changing pitch of the hum as the machines accelerate. Only the trilling of the aws bell at every colour-light signal was added to the ordinary train noises heard by the passengers in the coaches behind us. But the speedometer needle was creeping upwards and in the dip past Pirbright was back at 90. Speed remained around this level as far as Hook, although by that station we had begun coasting in readiness for a 40mile/h speed restriction at Newham. Once clear of the pw work a return to Notch 4 brought speed back to 80 before we coasted again to pass Basingstoke at 65.

Taking power again in Notch 3 we were up to 80 by Worting Junction, now taken unchecked by Bourne-

mouth trains thanks to track improvements. At Roundwood, the summit point of the line, we were doing 90 and shut off power, holding that speed through Micheldever and Winchester with only a brief restoration of power in Notch 3. At Shawford we were coasting again, still at 90, and had just gone up to Notch 4 when our first adverse signal was sighted – a double yellow. As we approached the aspect changed to green even before we had reached the aws magnet, but we were now approaching Eastleigh where, irrespective of signal aspects, an aws magnet sounds the cab siren as a reminder of the 60mile/h speed restriction ahead. Eastleigh station was passed in exactly the 62min allowed from Waterloo.

Recovering from the slack, Notch 4 brought speed up to 68 on the rising gradients after the station, but then power was cut to observe a temporary 20mile/h speed restriction and a return to Notch 4 did not raise speed to much above 50mile/h before we had to slow drastically to negotiate the very acute curve at Northam where the 'new line' to Dorchester left the original London & Southampton Railway main line to its terminus near the docks. The course of the old line could be seen ahead until the view was sharply cut off by a bank as the train swung sharp right into a cutting and tunnel. It was an appropriate introduction

Left: After the 4-CORs, Classes 420 and 421 formed Waterloo-Portsmouth trains. One of these formations is seen on the former LSWR 'Portsmouth Direct' line south of Buriton Tunnel on 8 October 1972./*Philip Hollingbery*

Above: The 4-PEP high-density suburban units which began running in the Southern Region in 1971 were precursors of several classes to follow both for third-rail and overhead systems (including the 313s which run on both). Prototype unit No 4001 is illustrated here./*BR*

to 'Castleman's Corkscrew', the Southampton-Weymouth line promoted by the Wimborne Solicitor, Charles Castleman, which wound westwards in a large loop, by-passing the future resort of Bournemouth. Here was visual railway history, and it was easy to imagine the driver of a Beattie 2-4-0 in 1847, when the line was opened to Dorchester, having much the same impression as my own of passing from one railway to another as his engine ground round the sharp bend at Northam Junction after the long straight stretches and sweeping curves of the main line so far.

We now ran slowly through the suburbs of Southampton to pull up in its rebuilt station at 11.44, in 100min from Waterloo as scheduled. Perhaps if it had not been for the temporary speed restrictions a minute

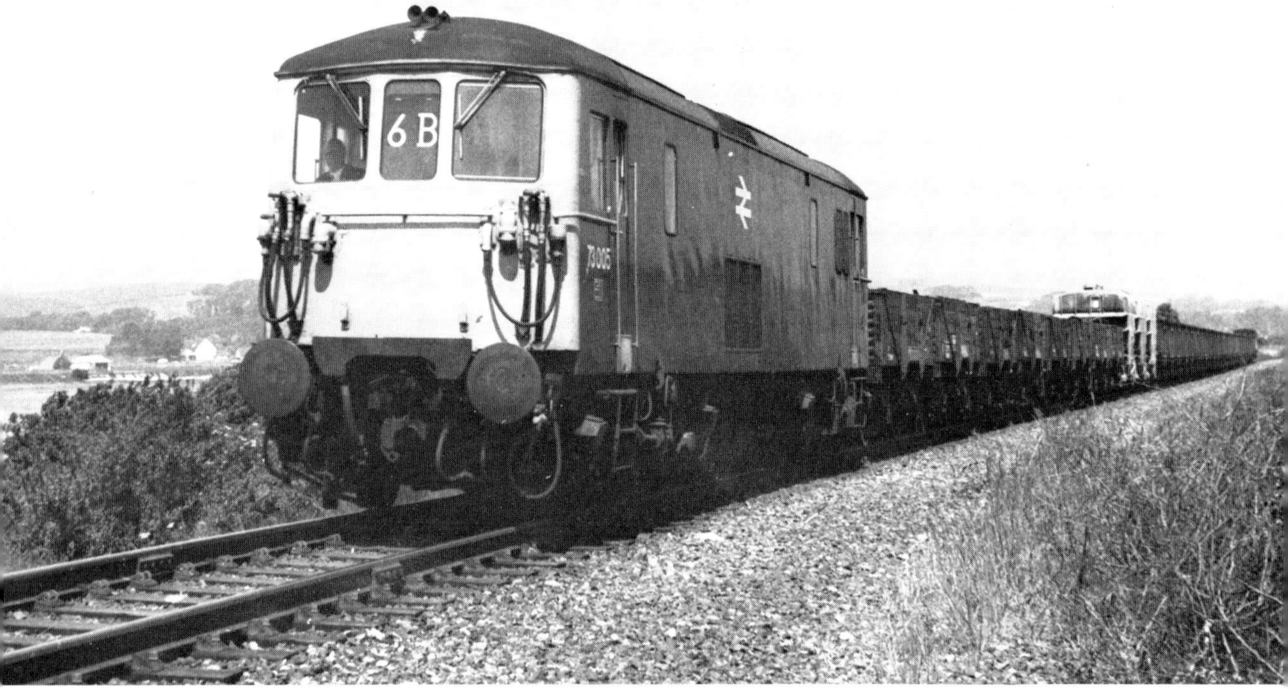
6B

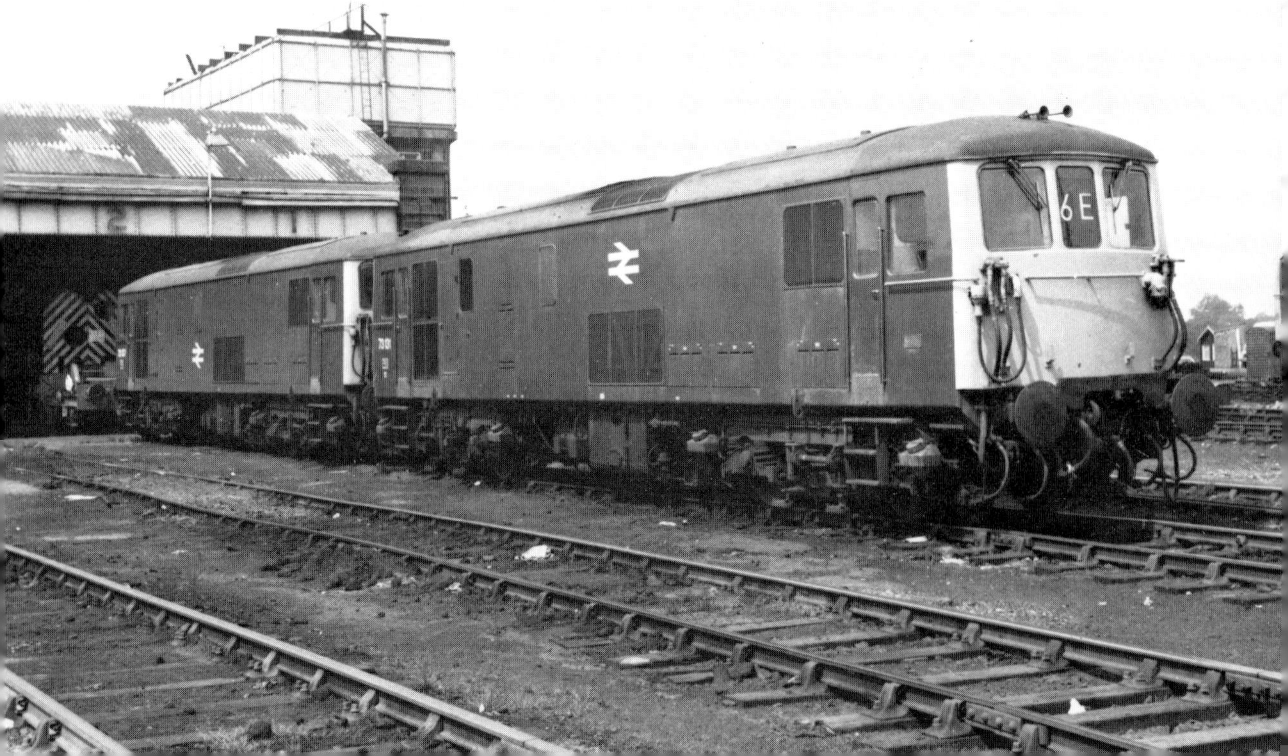
6E

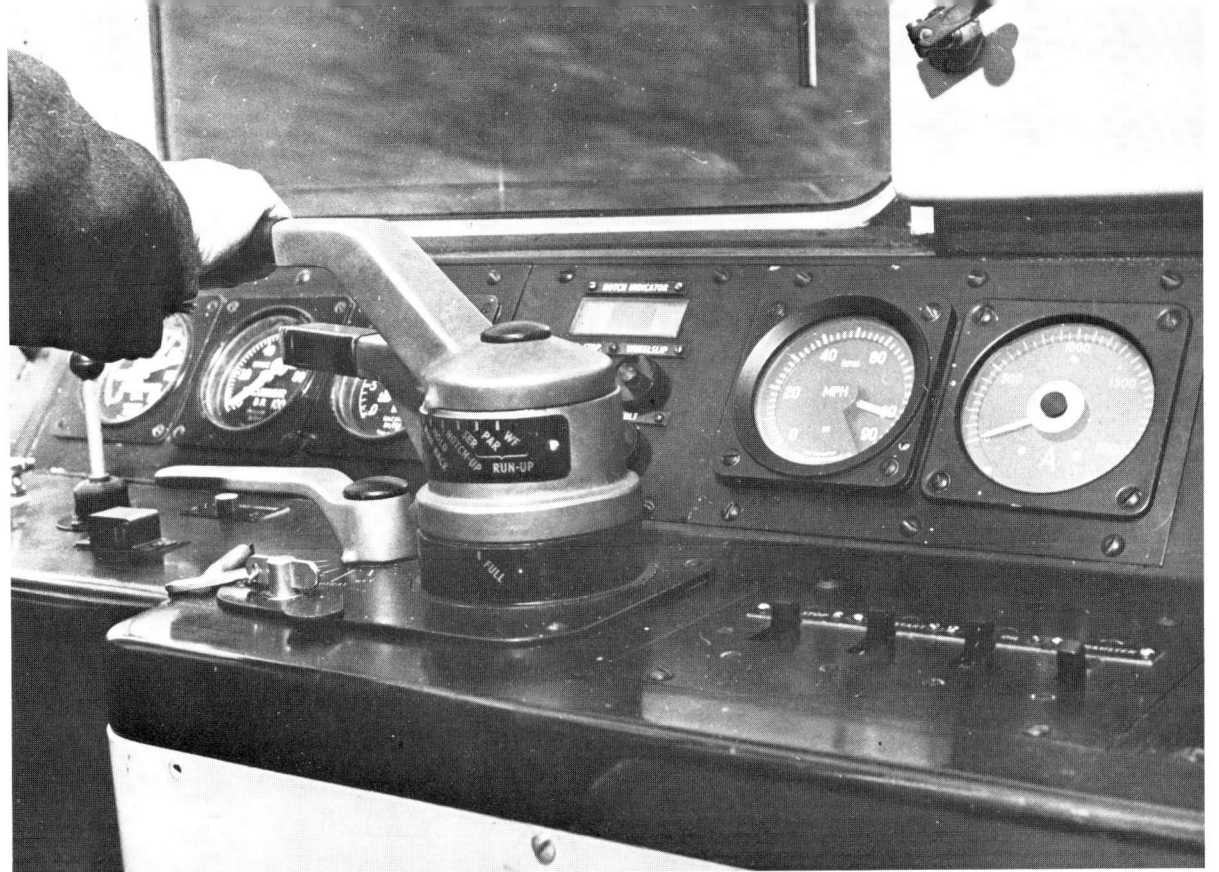

Top left: A train of empty coal wagons and three loaded cement wagons runs beside the River Adur en route from Beeding sidings to Brighton, headed by Class 73 electro-diesel No 73.005./*R. E. Ruffell*

Left: The second series of electro-diesels, Class 73/1, appeared shortly before completion of the Southern Region electrification to Bournemouth. Nos 73.131 and 73.137 are at Hither Green mpd on 22 June 1977./*J. Scrace*

Above: Controls of a Class 73 locomotive. The driver's hand is on the electric controller. The handle immediately below controls the 600hp diesel engine./*BR*

or so of the time lost before departure might have been regained, but it would not have been easy. At 11.47 we were off again, going straight into Notch 3, but coming back to Notch 2 for the speed restriction at Redbridge. Clear of this check, the controller was set in Notch 4 to accelerate, but power was soon cut to observe the 65mile/h restriction on this section. At the 90mile/h sign after Lyndhurst Road station the controller went back to Notch 4 and we topped the rise at Beaulieu Road at 80, accelerating to 84 before coasting to observe a 75mile/h restriction. Returning to Notch 4, speed had risen to 86 when a double yellow was sighted. Coasting at 80, the brakes brought

our speed down to 60 for another restriction approaching Brockenhurst, where a single yellow at the home signal warned us that the starter was 'on' and brought us to a stand in the platform. Signal Engineer's staff on the station told us we should have to pass the next two signals at danger, the track circuits being out of action. The message was given to the guard over the Loudaphone and we pulled away in Notch 2, soon going up to Notch 3 to pass the Brockenhurst advanced starter at about 40. After further acceleration in Notch 4, a spell of coasting was required to observe a 75mile/h limit; then back to Notch 4 and 84 at New Milton, rising to 90 after the station. A brief drop to 80 was followed by another 90, held until power was cut approaching Christchurch to pass the station at 60mile/h. A 90mile/h sign was an invitation to return to Notch 4, although with little likelihood of reaching the line speed on the short run remaining to Bournemouth. We did, in fact, get up to 65 near Pokesdown before cutting power to coast to a standstill in Bournemouth station at 12.16. The run from Southampton had taken 29min, only 1min over the allowance despite the unscheduled stop at Brockenhurst and the necessarily cautious restart past the two signals at danger.

Since the opening of the Bournemouth electrification the boat train traffic to Southampton has been

Right: No. 73107 heads a Royal Special from Waterloo to Southampton Docks in Clapham Cutting on 4 August 1977. */J. Scrace*

Below: Class 74 electro-diesel No 74.001, first of the 10 converted from Class 71 electrics, heads a Southampton-Clapham van train at Eastleigh on 29 December 1975. */F. R. Kerr*

Above far right: The standard design of substation for the Bournemouth electrification. This 3,000kW installation at Bournemouth comprises two 1,500kW naturally air-cooled rectifiers and switchgear. A reservoir for the oil-filled feeder cable is seen in front of the transformer to the right of the substation building./*GEC Rectifiers Ltd*

Below far right: Class 430 4-REP unit No 3012 heads two 4TC sets forming a train to Waterloo at Bournemouth on 15 November 1976. In the bay platform is Class 423 4-VEP No 7716 on a stopping service./*Brian Morrison*

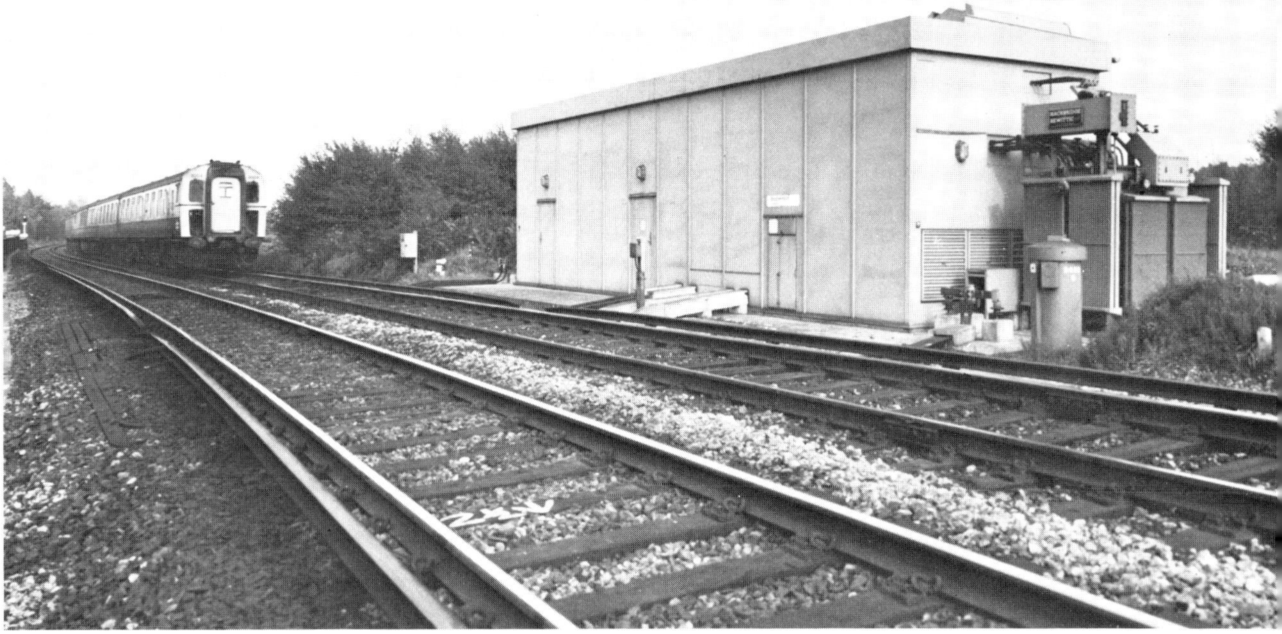

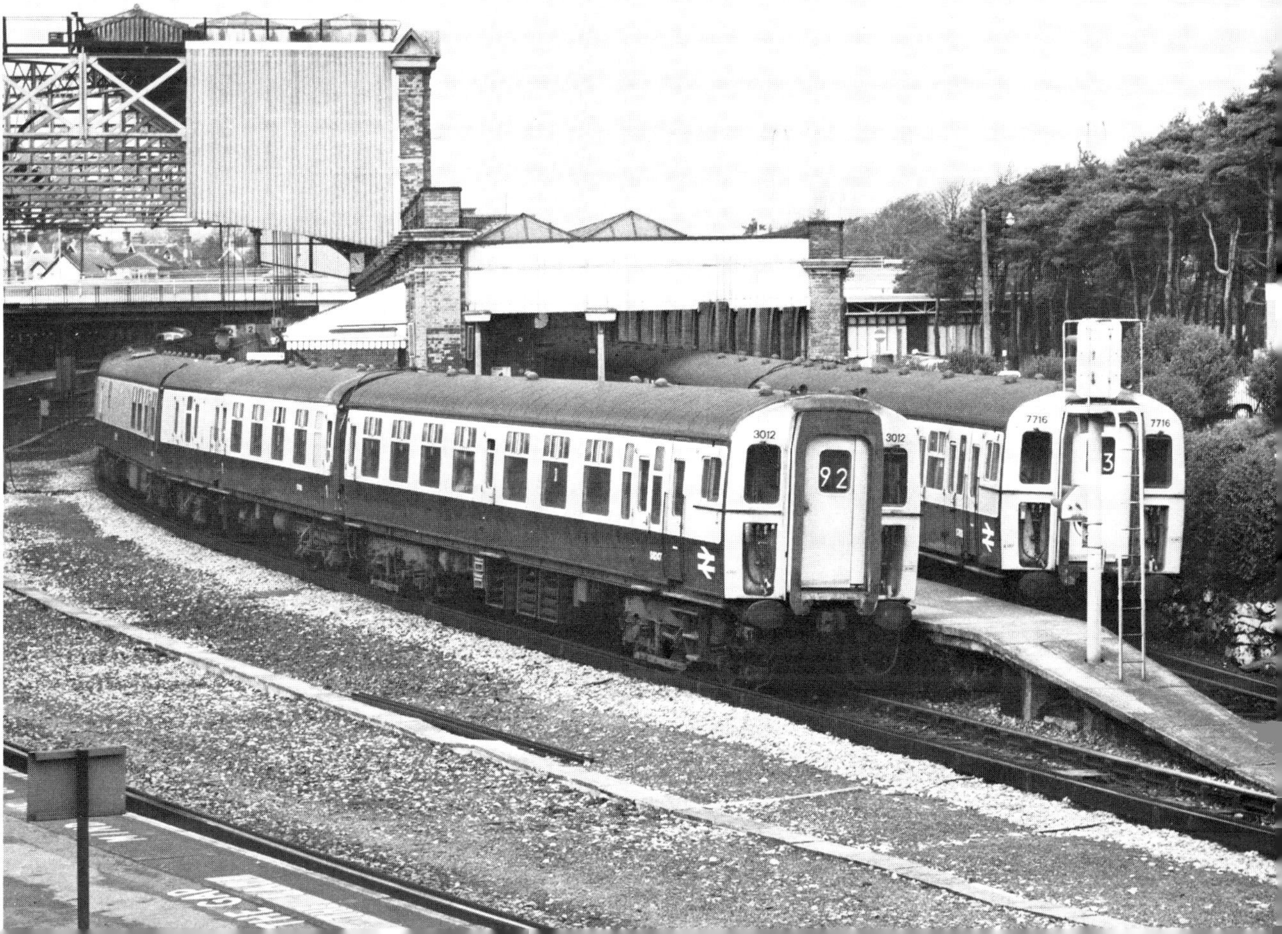
3012
92
7716
3

much reduced, mainly serving seasonal cruises instead of regular liner sailings. When the scheme was planned provision was made for working locomotive-hauled boat trains at speeds comparable with the emu services by converting ten Class 71 electric locomotives to electro-diesels, since this would give them mobility on dockside lines and auxiliary power for carriage heating. The conversions, Class 74, retained the 2,500hp booster installation for live-rail working and added a 650hp diesel set. The idea of driving the booster with the diesel engine had by this time been dropped and the engine was coupled to its own electric generator which provided an input to the booster when on non-electrified track. Room was made for the diesel set inside the locomotive by removing the traction motor blower of the Class 71 and incorporating blowers with the booster in place of the original flywheels, experience having shown that the inertia of the armatures was sufficient by itself to maintain an output through conductor rail gaps. Booster excitation was controlled by thyristors instead of resistances.

Although a locomotive in the normal sense, Class 74 was viewed simply as a 'tractive unit' in the austere Southern Region philosophy of the day, being capable of working in multiple with emu stock, electric, diesel-electric and other electro-diesel locomotives, controlled from a remote cab if necessary. The problems encountered with this early application of solid state and closed loop technology have been mentioned in Chapter 9. With changing traffic patterns on the Bournemouth line it was found that locomotive-haulage requirements could be met with Classes 33 and 73/1 and the last of the 74s was withdrawn in 1978. The Southern Region's Chief Mechanical & Electrical Engineer, W. J. A. Sykes, once said that the lesson he learned from the Class 74s was 'never convert anything'. Their misfortune was being ahead of their time, and perhaps not being fully understood

by the operators. A Class 74 used to work an up morning business train starting from Poole, which meant using its diesel engine from Poole to Branksome on mostly adverse gradients often as steep as 1 in 60. Speed with the diesel averaged around 20mile/h, but the train was given the same timing as if it had a 1,550hp Class 33. Inevitable late arrivals at Branksome did not endear it to the commuters.

For suburban stock the Southern remained faithful to the formula of two motorcoaches per four-car unit, each with two 250hp motors and control by individual electro-pneumatic contactors, using the type of equipment supplied for the 4-EPBs in 1951. An mg set was carried under each motorcoach and collector shoes one on each side, were fitted to the motor bogies only except in two-car units, were the driving trailer was similarly equipped on one bogie. Camshaft control came in with the Kent Coast stock as mentioned earlier, but the six units built as prototypes for the 4-BEP/CEP series, Nos 7001/2 and 7101-7104, still had individual contactor control. Camshafts were fitted to the last ten SAP units and some late EPBs but the first major change did not come until the high-density prototype stock (PEP) of 1971 which had a 100hp motor driving every axle of the four-car unit and rheostatic braking. In 1978 orders were placed for the traction equipment of 58 new four-car suburban units to be known as Class 508. They are generally similar to the Merseyrail 507s and share with them a common ancestor in the GN Suburban 313s as far as general arrangement and the dc traction equipment are concerned. In this convoluted genealogy the expert will discern hereditary influences stemming from the 4-PEPs.

Below: The 14.40 Bournemouth-Waterloo slow, formed of Class 423 unit No 7829, approaches Brockenhurst on 30 March 1978./*D. Kimber*

11
New Generations-Overhead

The second half of the 1960s was a watershed period, with the LMR scheme between Euston and the North West in full operation and work on the extension from Weaver Junction to Glasgow in its early stages. This had been authorised after a period of hesitation in which it was feared that the experience and man-power amassed during the earlier project might be allowed to disperse and go to waste.

When electrification reached Euston, new rolling stock was required for outer suburban services running fast or with only one or two stops between London and Watford. Intermediate stations on the tracks originally electrified by the LNWR in 1917/22 at 630V dc continued to be served by London Transport trains and the LMR Class 501 three-car units which had replaced the stately 'Oerlikon' sets in 1957. Fifty new outer suburban sets originally classified AM10 (now Class 310) were built at Derby. These four-car units were equipped with disc brakes, becoming the first large scale application of discs on BR. Electrically they were important for the simplification resulting from cooling the rectifiers and transformer by the natural airflow under the coach. The diodes were mounted inside a finned aluminium casing, from which they were insulated by beryllia washers. As well as being an insulator, this material is a good conductor of heat, which could therefore pass from the diodes to the fins, which were cooled by the motion of the train. The transformer was in a tank with external tubes through which the oil was pumped. Tank, tubing and oil pump formed a single unit mounted under the coach and naturally cooled. This arrangement dispensed with the oil radiator and fan used in earlier ac emus, reducing both maintenance and noise level.

A simple form of tap-changing was adopted. The secondary of the transformer had equal tapped and untapped sections, each delivering half the motor voltage when all turns were in circuit. Progression to half-voltage was made on the tapped section alone by means of individual contactors. At the half way point the load was transferred to the untapped section of the winding and all the tap-changing contactors were opened. For further progression the tapping contactors were operated again with both halves of the winding in series until full volts were applied to the rectifier.

Successors to the original five prototype classes of ac locomotives began entering traffic in 1965. These were Class AL6 (now Class 86), in which S. B. Warder, the BRB's Chief Electrical Engineer, made certain changes based on experience with the earlier types. The most controversial was the return to axle-hung motors. In a list of British contributions to ac traction practice, Warder once boldly included: 'Nose-suspended axle-hung motors for locomotives, technically proved that special designs incorporating full suspension are an unnecessary expense.' Events proved his confidence to be premature. He also designed the transformer and traction motors to give the required high-speed performance without field-weakening, thereby simplifying the control system. This arrangement, too, proved to bring certain penalties and was not repeated. The equipment was further simplified by omission of switching for dual-voltage operation, the locomotives being designed after it had been found possible to use 25kV throughout the LMR electrification.

Semiconductor rectifiers for locomotives had come in with Class 85, which were divided between germanium and silicon. The 100 locomotives of Class 86 all had silicon rectifiers and the number of cells was dramatically reduced. Rheostatic braking was fitted as in Class 85 but in the new locomotives was controlled by the air brake lever through an air-operated regulator. The previous arrangement had been to control the rheostatic brake with the electric power handle after operating a power/brake changeover switch. This linking of the air and the rheostatic brake is now normal practice in BR equipments with rheostatic systems.

Class 86 also introduced the principle of splitting the electrical power equipment into individual 'power packs' for each traction motor. The power pack comprises the silicon rectifier, smoothing choke and blower for the motor concerned. Associated control gear is mounted in a frame adjacent to the pack. The same air stream, drawn in through louvres in the body side, cools the rectifier, choke and motor. Each power pack is fed from its own secondary winding on the traction transformer and the whole unit can be isolated in the event of a fault, leaving the other power packs unaffected.

The new class soon became popular for its reliability, although footplate crew criticised it for a hard ride. The effect on the track was more serious, and with electrification to Glasgow close at hand steps were taken to improve matters, it being accepted by then that the damage was attributable to working heavy traffic at speeds in the 100mile/h range with locomotives having a high unsprung mass and stiff secondary suspension. It is true that 100mile/h speeds were being run by 'Deltic' diesel-electric locomotives on the East Coast main line, but these were of Co-Co wheel arrangement and the axle load was $17\frac{1}{2}$ tons compared with $20\frac{1}{2}$ tons in the Bo-Bo electrics.

As originally built Class 86 had a bolsterless bogie, the body being supported directly on the bogie by a coned rubber type of pivot which could twist to allow rotation and bend to allow transverse movements of the bogie relative to the body. A similar arrangement had been used in Class 81. It was impracticable to install a conventional swing bolster in the same bogie frame, apart from which the move away from bolster, swing links and spring plank was in line with contemporary thinking. A system known as 'flexicoil' had been developed on the Continent (where, indeed, the

coned rubber pivot had originated) in which coil springs of special design formed the sole body support and at the same time controlled lateral and rotational movements, assisted by dampers. Tractive forces were transmitted through the bogie pivot which was clamped between rubber buffers allowing it to 'float' with the movements of the suspension while continuing to transmit tractive effort.

A flexicoil system was tested in a Class 86 locomotive and gave encouraging results. Meanwhile a new bogie was being designed for additional locomotives needed for the Anglo-Scottish services, with flexicoil suspension to improve the ride and a flexible coupling between frame-mounted motors and the driving pinion to reduce the unsprung load. Three Class 86 locomotives were fitted with the new bogie and classified 86/1. Out of the remaining locomotives of this class it was decided to fit 58 with flexicoil suspension and, while retaining axle-hung motors, to relieve the un-

Below: A Class 501 unit bound for Watford climbs Camden Bank out of Euston on the 630V dc tracks on 6 May 1973. /*Brian Morrison*

Right: At Richmond, 501s on the North London line service meet London Transport's District Line trains. The two are seen side by side as a 501 from Broad Street brakes to a standstill on 8 November 1975./*Roland Hummerston*

Below right: A new generation began with Class AL6 in 1964. First of the series was No 3101, here shown in its original form. The class now has three subdivisions./*BR*

sprung weight by fitting resilient wheels with rubber between the tyre and wheel centre. These became Class 86/2 and have since with their Class 87 partners shared the task of providing the backbone of high-speed services on the LMR electrification. Unmodified Class 86 locomotives were reclassified 86/0 and confined as far as possible to duties not requiring continuous 100mile/h running, but this series is also to be fitted with resilient wheels.

High-tension tap-changing was chosen for Class 85 and repeated in Class 87. The input from the overhead line was taken via the pantograph and a roof-mounted circuit-breaker to a tapped auto-transformer, from which a variable voltage was selected by the tap-chan-

ger and fed to the primary of a fixed-ratio traction transformer. This had four secondaries, each supplying one of the rectifier/motor power packs mentioned previously, but there were now only 16 diodes per rectifier instead of 96 as in Class 86. As long ago as 1966 a speaker at a technical conference predicted that 'the tap-changer is the next conventional item doomed to disappear'. It was partly wishful thinking, for a tap-changer has to carry out mechanically a sequence of precisely timed switching operations and those first fitted in Class 86 locomotives gave some trouble at first. Later the whole series was modified, and further minor changes were made in those fitted in Class 87 locomotives to improve reliability.

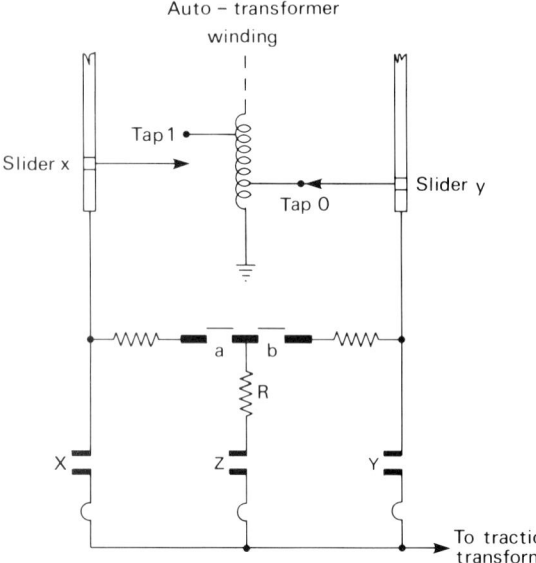

Above: One of the basic 86s (Class 86/0), No 86.039 arrives at Euston on 27 June 1975 with the 08.10 ex-Manchester. /*John E. Oxley*

Right: The riding qualities and effect on the track of the 86s and their axle-hung traction motors called for investigation, leading to experiments with 'flexicoil' suspension. The coil springs of this type of secondary suspension are seen here on a bogie of one of the modified locomotives./*BR*

Fig 14 On-load tap-changing.

The switching in a tap-changer is arranged so that in going from tap to tap the circuit to the rectifiers is never broken. At one stage two taps have to be connected to the circuit at the same time, and at this moment a resistance must be introduced so that the section of transformer winding between the taps is not short-circuited. In changing from tap to tap the tap-changer makes 9 moves. There are 38 taps on the Class 87 unit, or 342 moves from starting to full voltage, and these are made in 25sec if the tap-changer is run up by its electric motor drive unchecked, as for example when restoring power after coasting through a neutral section.

Auto – transformer winding

Slider x

Tap 1

Tap 0

Slider y

X

a b

R

Z

Y

To traction transformer

Fig 14

The moves are made by sliders acting in conjunction with a changeover switch. Fig 14 shows the sequence of operations for one tap-change. Consider slider y on tap o and contactor Y closed. All other switches are open so that the circuit to the load (ie the traction transformer primary) is via y and Y. At this stage slider x is between taps o and 1 but is isolated electrically because contactor X is open. The sequence of events in changing the connection of the traction transformer from tap o to tap 1 is then as follows:

1 Slider x moves to tap 1.
2 Changeover contacts a close.
3 Diverter contactor Z closes. Taps o and 1 are now connected together through resistance R, which prevents short-circuit current from flowing between them.
4 Diverter contactor Y opens, transferring the load to slider x. R is still in circuit so that the voltage applied to the load is now that of tap 1 less the drop in R.
5 X diverter contactor closes, short-circuiting R; load voltage is now tap voltage and the tap change is completed.

In the remaining moves Z opens first, then changeover contacts a, and slider y moves to a position between taps o and 2 in readiness for the next change. This time, however, contacts b of the changeover switch close to connect R to slider y.

While having much in common mechanically with Class 86, the traction motors of Class 87 had a one-hour rating of 950kW (1,274hp), making the class the first 5,000hp electric locomotives on BR. The machines had to be accommodated in the same space as in a Class 86 bogie, which could have caused electrical problems at the higher output. They are therefore fitted with an additional winding, known as a 'compensating' winding, lying in slots in the main pole faces to ensure good commutation in weak-field. The armature shaft is hollow and is toothed internally at one end to form a gear type coupling with the drive shaft, which passes through the centre of the armature shaft with a clearance of between $1\frac{1}{2}$ and 2in. The other end of the drive shaft is coupled by a universal joint to the pinion shaft in the gearbox. Since the gearbox is axle-hung, the pinion and gearwheel are at fixed centres, but the universal joint and gear coupling accommodate movements of the frame-mounted motor relative to the pinion shaft. This is a compact and light arrangement compared with the types used in the prototype locomotives of Classes 81 to 85. Class 87 was equipped for multiple-unit control of a second locomotive; a similar arrangement has been extended to Class 86.

As in all the LMR electric locomotives the driver of a Class 87 can either notch step by step by hand or allow the tap-changer to run up with its motor drive, checking it by returning the power handle to 'hold' if current rises too fast. When I rode in the cab of a Class 87 from Crewe to Carlisle at the head of the

12.05 Birmingham-Glasgow-Edinburgh, an 11-coach train of 360 tons, the driver hand-notched away from every stopping place. The intervals between taking each notch varied and were judged to keep the motor ammeter pointers in the green sectors of their scales. Some notches were taken in quick succession; on others the dwell was longer. The process of going through the 38 steps took three or four minutes and by the time the notch indicator was showing 100% (full voltage) speed was usually nearing 100mile/h. When the pointer climbs above 100% the locomotive is in weak-field.

The driver must release and depress the pedal of the vigilance device every 60sec or an emergency brake application will begin after a delay of 5–7sec. Alternatively a switch on the driving desk may be operated if more convenient. Either action resets the equipment for a further 60sec at the end of which time an audible warning is given. Acknowledging an aws warning also resets the vigilance device.

Restarting from Wigan, speed had reached 100mile/h at Coppull Hall Box after 4½ miles of climbing with a steepest stretch of 1 in 104 to Boar's Head and a final 1 in 119 to the summit. The pattern was repeated after Preston, the speedometer reading 100mile/h some 4min after the start notwithstanding the initial climb out of the station. We were now entering a stretch where the driver has to remember 26 changes of line speed on the way to Carlisle. Approaching Lancaster the home signal was at red, but cleared as we approached, showing that the driver had correctly controlled his speed through the timed track circuit, which must be occupied for at least 23sec or a train will be brought to a standstill before being allowed to proceed over the turnout into the platform.

The line falls from Lancaster to Carnforth and we reached the 100mile/h only 3min from the start with the notch indicator still only at 80%. The driver continued notching to full volts and the locomotive went into weak-field while climbing the 1 in 134 to the summit at milepost 9½. A speed restriction of 90mile/h at Hincaster Junction, where the line is rising at 1 in 173, was observed without using the brakes by running the tap-changer back to reduce power.

From Oxenholme it is uphill all the way to Grayrigg but the seven miles only took 6min although a crop of speed restrictions kept speed below 100mile/h and power was cut briefly to coast through a neutral section. If we had failed to do so, the circuit-breaker would have opened automatically but would have had to break the full load current. Furthermore, by notching back ahead of the neutral section the tap-changer is ready to run up as soon as line volts come on again. The brief 'wink' of the line volts indicator lamp in the cab shows how short the interruption of supply is at the latest type of neutral section.

After Tebay we were on the final stage of the climb to Shap, watching the slow creep of the coloured scales under the pointers of the ammeters. Would they swing round until the pointers were at least in the yellow sector? Even this modest touch of drama was denied us; they got no further than the top of the green and five minutes after passing Tebay we were passing the summit at 90mile/h. Sometimes drivers have to reduce power to observe this limit. Now it was downhill all the way to Carlisle, with one more stop at Penrith.

Some impressions remain unaccountably clear. At every station the restart was heralded by the sound of

Right: No 86.202 waits in the loop at the north end of Beattock station during test running on 3 May 1973. This is one of the three locomotives equipped with Class 87 bogies having both flexicoil suspension and traction motors with flexible drives. They now form Class 86/1./*Derek Cross*

Top right: In Class 86/2 flexicoil suspension and resilient wheels have overcome the earlier problems of the class. No 86.240 awaits departure from Euston with the 10.55 to Manchester on 27 June 1975./*John E. Oxley*

Far right: The transformer and tap-changer of a Class 86 locomotive. The tank at the top is the oil conservator and together with the 'lead-in' insulator to its right is above roof level when the unit is installed./*GEC Traction Ltd*

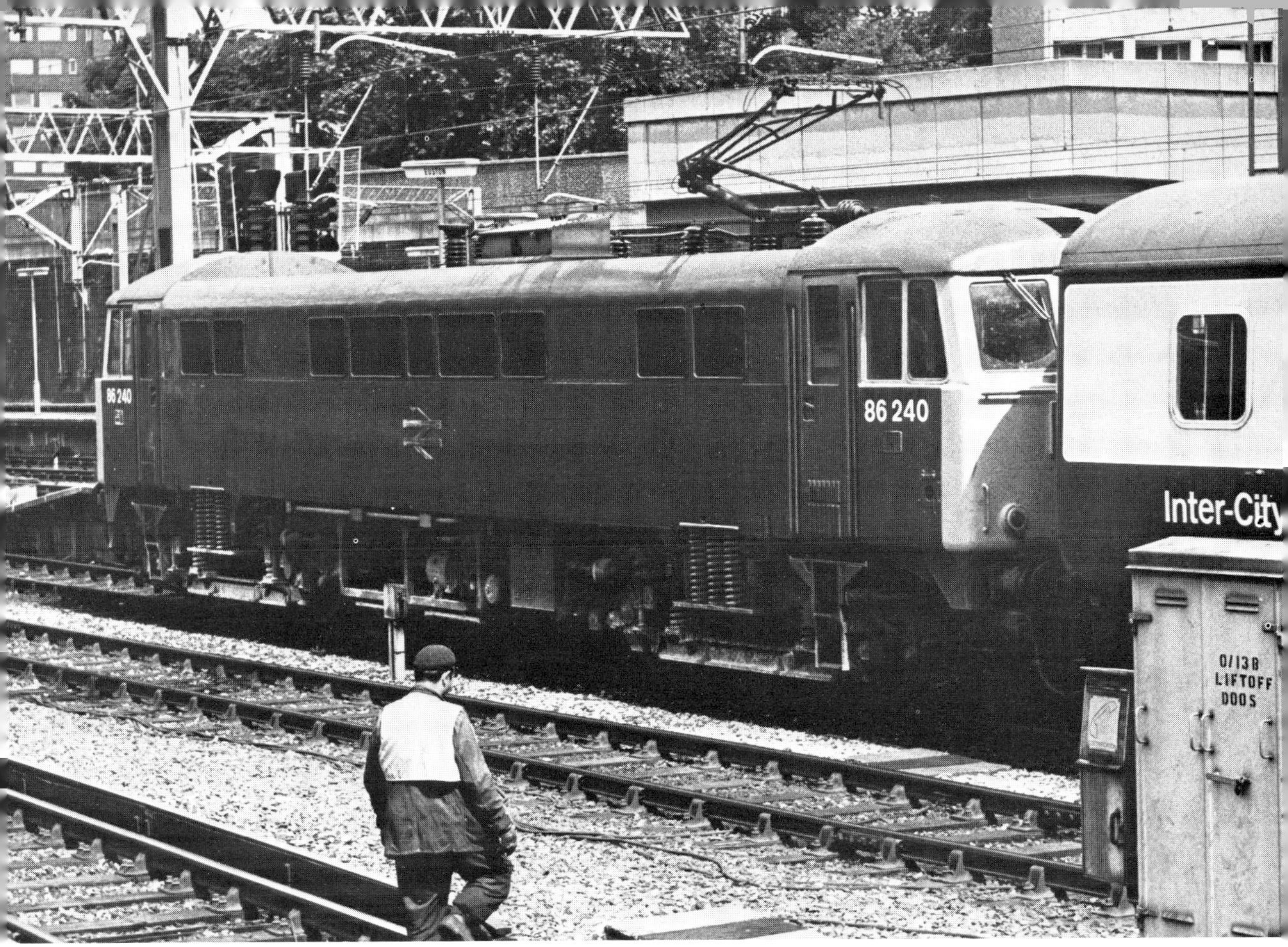
86 240
86 240
Inter-City

Test Car 4

AEI
ENGLISH ELECTRIC

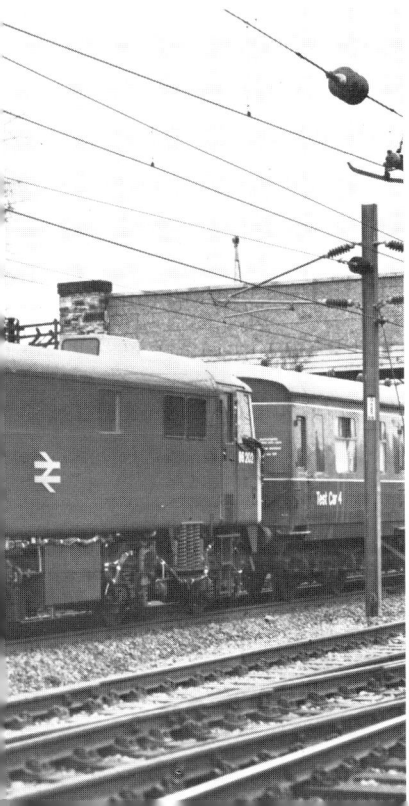

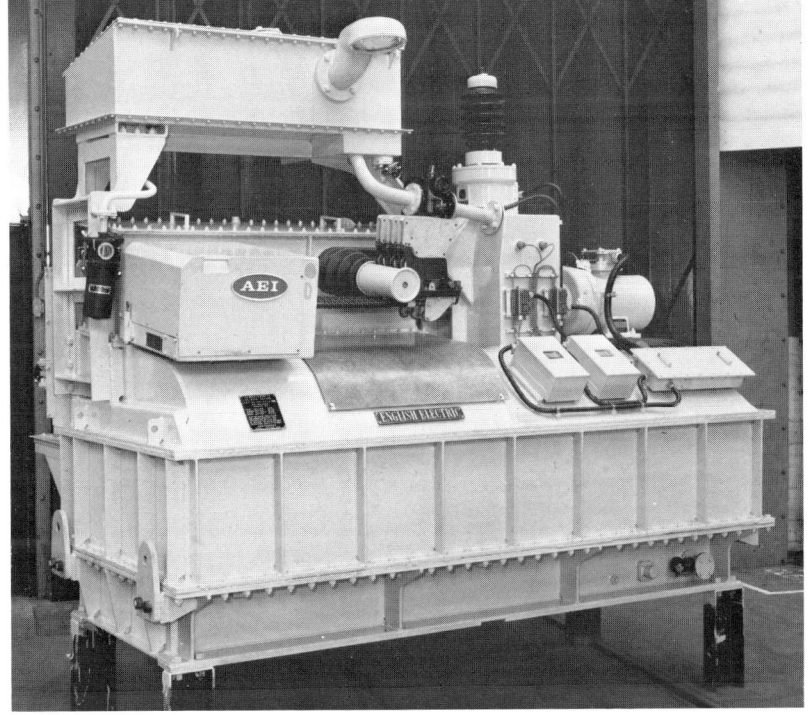

the traction motor blowers starting up. They close down when the reverser is returned to 'off' when the train has come to rest and are switched on when it is returned to 'forward'. The familiar sound of an mg set is absent, for in an ac locomotive auxiliary supplies are taken through a transformer and converted to dc by a static rectifier when necessary. The only rotary machines in a Class 87 are the blowers, the compressor and the fans which cool the resistors during rheostatic braking. A sudden short rattle and jerk while travelling at speed provoked the laconic comment 'stones' from the driver, all too familiar with the practice of throwing objects on to the track. At the time I made my trip there was a bottleneck in servicing the dampers of the flexicoil suspension and at times I felt as if I was riding on the top of a large jelly, the base of which was being rhythmically prodded. The effect on the legibility of my notes was not good and I sympathise with the journalist quoted by Francis Williams in *Our Iron Roads* who tried to write shorthand during a trip on the footplate of the Dover night mail but achieved little more than a curiosity for 'any ardent student of Pitmanian lore'.

Most of all I remember the sense of isolation from the outside world when we could do no more than speculate about the reason for the urgent waving of a very large yellow flag at the trackside to warn of a diversion on to the slow line to by-pass some unknown hazard – perhaps the discovery of a cracked rail.

The years during which the LMR electrification was in progress were a time of development in remote control and supervisory systems throughout industry, based increasingly on solid state electronics. On the railways the new methods were applied at first to signalling, and an electronic remote control system was installed at signalboxes on the Manchester-Crewe electrification in 1960.

Remote control of power supplies to the overhead system has much in common with signalling. Control room staff must be able to operate numerous items of equipment dispersed over a long distance, and be provided with a continuous indication of their state. The control room diagrams are similar to modern signalling control panels, although they only show the main overhead line circuits and their connections with the Grid system instead of being a detailed track diagram. In the first stages of the LMR electrification the power control systems were based on Post Office type relays and uniselectors and various forms of selective coding were used so that large numbers of items connected to a common circuit could be addressed individually from the control room and any item could signal a change of state to Control when it occurred. Electronic systems provide the same facility but with a much improved speed of response. They are normally based on some form of 'scanning', in

which the control station addresses outstations in a continuously repeated cycle and receives from each item in turn an indication of its state.

When the West Coast main line electrification was extended from Weaver Junction to Glasgow the power installations on this section were controlled over new electric systems from the existing control rooms at Crewe and Cathcart. Previously Cathcart had covered only the area of the Glasgow suburban electrification north and south of the Clyde. Northward from Acton Grange, Crewe controls the feeder stations at Parkside (Warrington), Catterall (near Garstang), and Natlands (near Kendal). The busbars at these points are fed with 25kV ac from transformers in nearby CEGB substations and are connected through circuit-breakers to the overhead catenary system from which the trains collect power. Average distance between feeder stations is about 30 miles (48km). At intervals of about 7 miles (11km) between feeder stations the catenaries are connected through circuit-breakers to busbars in track-sectioning cabins at the lineside. If a fault occurs on the overhead system or in a train equipment, the supply to the point affected must be cut off. The feeder stations and track-sectioning cabins together provide switchgear for this purpose at relatively short intervals so that the length of line de-energised when the first protective action is taken is minimised. The West Coast main line track-section-

ing cabins controlled from Crewe are at Acton Grange, Euxton, Preston, Bay Horse, Hest Bank, Burton & Holme, Grayrigg, and Tebay (this last jointly with Cathcart).

Most feeder stations have two inputs from the CEGB Grid, which are connected to separate sections of the station busbar. Both busbar connections can be connected together, however, by closing a circuit-breaker called a 'bus coupler' if one input fails or is out of service. In this way a supply to the contact wire can be maintained.

The catenary system is not continuous between feeder stations and track-sectioning cabins but is erected in lengths of up to 6,000ft (1.8km). These are known as 'tension lengths', being tensioned by weights

Below left: After trials on certain Class 86s, the crossed arm pantograph was adopted for all Class 87 locomotives. No 87.001 was the first of the series. With the 86/2s, the 5,000hp Class 87 provided motive power for the principal West Coast main line express duties. Note the jumpers for multiple-unit working and the central headlamp./*BR*

Below: Driving position of a Class 87 locomotive. The power handle is on the extreme right. The two large dials on the instrument panel show brake pipe pressure and speed. To their right are the scales of the motor ammeters (one for each bogie) and the notch indicators, the second notch indicator showing the setting of the tap-changer in the rear locomotive when two are working in multiple./*BR*

at each end and anchored in the centre at an 'anchor span'. The lengths overlap at their ends so that a pantograph is continuously in contact with energised contact wire, and they may be connected electrically through a switch, usually manually operated, called an 'isolator'. Tension lengths singly or in multiples can be isolated completely from the supply by opening the isolators, although this must only be done on instructions from the control room after power has been cut off. This is a further method of minimising disturbance to traffic after an incident of some kind. Overlapping catenary sections as described are called 'insulated and switching overlaps'. In some circumstances, as at crossovers and other trackwork, sections of contact wire which meet must be separated electrically from each other, which is done by insertion of a short 'section insulator' in the system.

The 25kV ac system of traction is single-phase, but it operates from a three-phase Grid system. In order to balance the load on the Grid the traction supply is distributed between the phases where connections to the Grid are made at feeder stations. Sections of catenary connected to different phases must be insulated from each other, and so 'neutral sections' are inserted in the overhead system at feeder stations and at track-sectioning cabins mid-way between them.

The neutral section is 15ft (4.6m) long and comprises two sets of insulators in series with an earthed section of catenary between them, approximately 6ft (1.8m) long. The latter arrangement is a backup precaution to ensure that in the event of an arc being drawn by the pantograph across one or other of the insulators, this would trip the circuit-breakers protecting the system and there would be no paralleling of the two separated phases of the supply. Normally this situation is avoided by means of track magnets on either side of the neutral section which through the automatic power control (apc) system on the locomotives and emu stock cause their circuit-breakers to trip and reclose before and after passing under the neutral section. Additionally, as seen already, drivers are instructed to notch down their power controllers. A novel feature of the insulators, which are cut into the contact wire, is that they are of almost the same cross-section, and their make-up comprising ceramic collars interspersed with ptfe washers threaded on to a glass fibre rod, enables the pantograph to pass over the system without a physical break.

When locomotives are working in pairs on heavy freight the two pantographs will be on separated sections of the contact wire at the same time but each draws its supply independently. In Class 87 locomotives, which are fitted for multiple control, the power circuits are not interconnected, the jumper cables between them being for control purposes only.

The control room diagram at Crewe shows the whole of the area covered, extending southwards to the boundary near Rugeley of the area controlled from Rugby, and showing both routes to Manchester together with three outstations on the 1,200V dc Manchester-Bury line which are controlled by the same electronic system as the West Coast main line from Acton Grange northwards. The board is normally 'dark', the purpose of its indicator lamps being to inform staff of changes in the situation needing their

attention. Operation is on the principle of the 'discrepancy switch'. That is to say, at every point on the diagram where a piece of switchgear is represented, there is a small rotary switch operated by a bar that can be gripped between finger and thumb. When the associated circuit-breaker is closed, the bar is in a position which bridges a break in the circuit as represented on the diagram. It therefore represents electrical continuity, or 'circuit-breaker closed'. If the circuit-breaker trips, however, the indication of the switch is no longer correct and a light in the switch unit flashes to show that a discrepancy exists. A buzzer warning is given at the same time. The operator then moves the switch to the 'circuit-breaker open' setting and the flashing stops.

To close the breaker the switch is moved back to its 'closed' setting and flashing resumes, showing that the system has selected the breaker in readiness for reclosure. The operator then turns a separate 'close' button in a group of buttons on the diagram associated with the feeder station or trackside cabin (TSC) where

Left: The magnet frame of a Class 87 traction motor, showing the pole faces of a main pole and an interpole, and the turns of the compensating winding which lies in the pole faces./*GEC Traction Ltd*

Below left: A Class 87 traction motor with the drive shaft partly withdrawn. The teeth of the gear type coupling at the end of the drive shaft mesh with corresponding teeth on the inside of the hollow armature shaft, allowing some relative axial movement./*GEC Traction Ltd*

Below: Another view of a Class 87 motor showing the resilient rubber coupling on the end of the drive shaft to connect it with the pinion shaft in the separate gearbox./*BR*

the trip has occurred. If the fault has cleared, the breaker closes and extinction of the flashing light shows that the operation is completed. By a similar procedure any circuit breaker can be opened from the control. When operating switchgear connected to the electronic system at Crewe, selection and operation are virtually simultaneous with the movement of the panel controls. Outstations south of Crewe are still on the older relay system and there is a perceptible delay of a second or two between calling for an operation and seeing its completion signalled.

Control and indication signals on the electronic system are sent in the form of pulses of two different frequencies, representing the '0' bit and the '1' bit of a digital code. Every outstation has an 8-bit address and the control station calls each in turn in a continuous sequence. If no change has occurred in the condition of its switchgear since it was last addressed, an outstation simply responds with its own address code. If a change has taken place, however, it answers with a 56-bit message showing the present situation in full. The message is decoded by the control room apparatus and the appropriate discrepancy lights flash as necessary.

To ensure that no change is missed during a scan, when each scan is completed it is followed by an update scan addressed to two outstations at a time (eg 1 and 2, 3 and 4, and so on) until all have had a second chance to respond. The complete cycle of events therefore consists of 8 alarm scans alternating with 8 update scans each covering two outstations at a time, the whole process taking only 6sec. When it is necessary to operate a circuit-breaker from the control room the operator can break into the normal scanning procedure at any moment by turning one of the discrepancy keys to select a particular item of equipment. He will do so when sections of the overhead equipment have to be isolated for maintenance or safety reasons, or to maintain power supplies if there is a failure at a feeder station.

Certain discrepancy switches on the panel are covered with caps as a reminder that they must not be operated without consultation with the power supply authority, as in the case of bus-couplers at feeder stations, or with an adjacent control room. Cathcart must be consulted, for example, if Crewe needs to take power from Penrith by closing the bus-coupler in the TSC at Tebay. If the supply voltage at feeder stations differs materially from normal, under-voltage or over-voltage lamps are illuminated on the panel. There are similar indications at various 'signalling supply plinths' where power is taken normally from the local Area Board at 415V, but can be derived through standby transformers from the 25kV traction supply, or additionally at certain locations from a standby diesel set. The control room has direct telephone communication with the CEGB. Reports of undervoltage sometimes come from drivers who note some loss of performance and a tendency for their locomotives to draw heavier currents. Problems of this kind can be ironed out in consulation with the CEGB which has its own switching centres and facilities for adjusting voltage levels if necessary.

The visitor to Crewe, noting that the diagram extends to Tebay on the approach to the 1 in 75 climb to Shap summit, expects illogically to sense something of the excitement which that name has stirred in generations of railway enthusiasts. But the locomotives of today sail up the bank with their ammeters barely registering in the yellow sector and certainly not creeping towards the red. The most likely causes of circuit-breakers tripping are not overloads caused by power demand but transient faults caused by vandalism, birds and icing conditions, and they were put in that order by the Chief Con-

troller at Crewe when I visited the control room. Vandalism includes such lethal practices as throwing or dropping lengths of wire over the catenary, probably with fatal consequences for the vandal if he has not let go of the wire before contact is made. Combating such practices by talks and film shows in schools continues to be a major task for the public relations staff of the railway. The behaviour of birds is more reasonable although equally lethal to themselves. In bad weather they sometimes shelter under bridges, perching on the contact wire. When the wire

Right: This view of a Class 87 bogie before installation of the motors shows the 'floating' pivot seating through which the tractive forces are transmitted, and the lateral dampers. The pivot 'floats' to allow for movements of the body on the flexicoil springs./*BR*

Below: A close-up view of the primary and secondary suspension coil springs of a Class 87 bogie. Note the dampers above the axle boxes on each side of the flexicoil spring group./*BR*

Far right: No 87.001 rolls a down express over Shap Summit on 24 July 1976./*C. R. Davis*

begins to vibrate on the approach of a train they are disturbed and spread their wings to fly away. But the clearance under a bridge is small, and particularly with the larger birds their wings may touch the brickwork, forming a short-circuit to earth. Ice and icicles similarly can form paths of good conductivity if atmospheric pollution is present, by-passing insulators. The resultant short-circuits have been known to cause as many as 150 trips during an eight-hour shift in the control room. This sort of situation was more common in the early days of electrification when steam

and diesel locomotives were still in use under the wires.

The staff in the control room consists of a chief controller and two assistants. Much of their work is routine, such as arranging isolations of sections of catenary so that maintenance can be carried out, or testing the operation of switchgear after the rectification of faults. When a 'burglar alarm' sounds, it does not necessarily mean that there has been a break-in but simply that staff have entered a feeder station or TSC to inspect or attend to the equipment. If a trip does occur the prescribed procedure is to allow up to two minutes for making enquiries and if no serious incident is reported to attempt to reclose the breaker. If it fails to stay in, indicating that the fault is still present, men are sent to the spot to investigate. The relays which detect faults and trip the breakers are in the feeder stations and TSCs and give a broad indication, within three zones, of where the fault has occurred.

The immediate response to an emergency is to isolate the section concerned completely. A minor electrical fault in a locomotive causing a small fire can have dangerous consequences if the fire brigade brings hoses into action while any of the catenary is live. In the 50Hz ac system even a de-energised contact wire can be at as much as 5,000V above earth by induction from the adjacent wire. During maintenance the de-energised wire is earthed, but in the first minute after an incident when personnel from other services such as fire, ambulance and police come to the spot the rule is complete isolation. Only later will the area affected be reduced as far as possible by using the isolators which have been mentioned already to allow power to be kept on all tracks as close to the incident as possible on each side, with the affected section isolated, earthed and under permit working conditions.

The Weaver Junction-Glasgow electrification was the first to use vacuum interrupters as circuit-breakers. When contacts separate inside a vacuum chamber the arc is of low energy and the separation need be only half an inch instead of 8 or 10in as in the conventional circuit-breaker with its contacts separating under oil to help arc extinction. The arc is also less destructive of contact material, so that the interrupters do not need regular servicing but are simply replaced as complete units at long intervals. This work can be done at major maintenance periods when the whole substation is shut down. There are no longer separate isolators for individual circuit-breakers as were required when the oil tanks had to be winched down and the contacts examined during routine maintenance. The devices are relatively silent in operation compared with the thud of an oil circuit-breaker when it opens, which is an advantage when they are installed near built-up areas. Some of the Class 87 locomotives were fitted with vacuum interrupters in place of air-blast circuit-breakers and they have since become generally adopted for motive power as well as substation use.

The link between the power system and the motive power is the pantograph. Conventionally a panto-graph is a four-sided framework but the prototype LMR locomotives and emus were fitted with a modi-fied version of the Continental Faiveley 'half panto-graph'. This was retained in Class 86, although some of these locomotives were fitted with a four-sided 'crossed arm' pantograph of British design, the

Fig 15 'Crossed arm' pantograph as fitted to Class 87 locomotives

  1 Collector head,
  2 Upper moving arms,
  3 Cross brace,
  4 Lower moving arms,
  5 Buffer stop,
  6 Tubular main shaft,
  7 Connecting rod,
  8 Operating cylinder,
  9 Balance springs,
 10 Hydraulic damper,
 11 Operating lever.

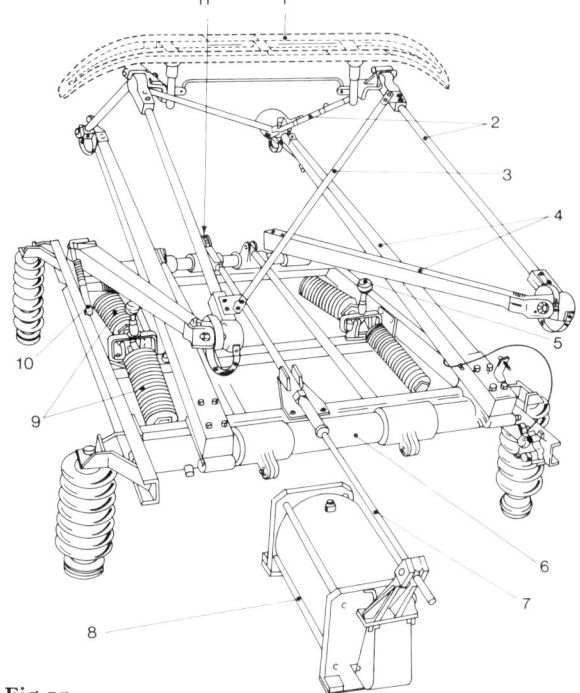

Fig 15

Below: A Birmingham-Euston express passing Weedon on 25 June 1975 is headed by 87.017./*John E. Oxley*

Far right: An up Freightliner is headed past Bushey by 87.024 on 30 June 1976./*Brian Morrison*

Below right: Parkside feeder station for the WCML electrification. The supply from the 'Grid' is taken from the fenced enclosure on the right to the building housing the vacuum interruptors. The supplies to the tracks are carried by the overhead gantries./*GEC Switchgear Ltd*

crossing of the lower arms reducing the overall length of the pantograph when it is lowered. This design, shown in Fig 15, was fitted in all Class 87 locomotives. The frame, carrying the pan head with carbon collector strips which bear against the contact wire, is raised by the four springs. They are brought into action by admitting air to the air motor, the spring-loaded piston pushing forward on the pull-down rod so that a slotted link at its end moves clear of a pin on the operating lever attached to the main shaft, the whole operation taking 10–15 sec. Contact pressure on the wire is 20lb/sq in.

The pantograph is lowered by exhausting air from the cylinder. The piston is pushed back by its spring, moving the pull-down rod with it. The slotted link on the rod engages with the drive pin in the operating lever and the pantograph is pulled down on to its buffer stops and held. While the pantograph is raised, air from the supply to the motor is piped to a gallery in the head. This is normally sealed by the carbon

collector strips. Loss of a carbon or damage to the head exhausts air from the motor and the pantograph is lowered. Lowering takes 5–7sec.

Up to 1977 the Class 87 locomotives were the stars of the West Coast Route. Towards the end of that year a still newer generation of motive power made its appearance when the first power cars for the prototype electric Advanced Passenger Train (APT-P) began trial running, hauled at first by other motive power to test mechanical characteristics and their new high-speed pantographs. By this time the prophecy of the end of the tap-changer was ten years old, but it was coming closer to fulfilment. The contract for the APT power equipment was placed with the Swedish firm ASEA, which had been building thyristor locomotives for Sweden and other countries since 1965. The APT circuit comprises two mixed (diode/thyristor) bridges which are advanced to full voltage in sequence as described in Chapter 9. The thyristors are of flat capsule form and clamped between channels carrying an oil coolant so that they are cooled on both faces.

Below: 'Discrepancy switches' for remote control of power supplies on the supervisory panel at Raynes Park, SR./*GEC*

Right: Double cantilevers support overlapping spans of the catenary at a site on the West Coast main line. The booster transformer on the pole on the left 'draws' return traction current out of the rails and channels it into a return conductor to prevent interference with nearby telecommunications circuits./*BICC*

Below right: Typical WCML simple catenary. The return conductors are supported by brackets near the top of the masts on the opposite side to the cantilevers./*BR*

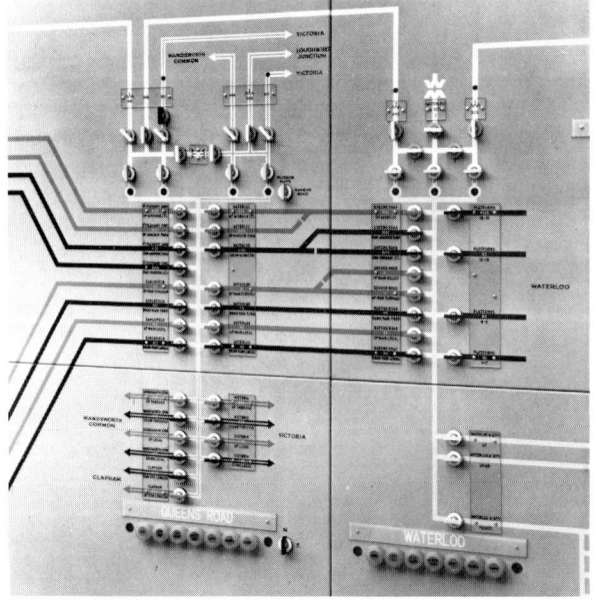

Diodes are of similar form but clamped to both sides of a central coolant channel.

The traction motors are separately excited under thyristor control. This arrangement was chosen as the most effective method of controlling the field strength to values lower than are normally practicable with series motors, thus achieving high tractive efforts at high speeds. The motors have compensating windings to maintain good commutation in these conditions. Separate excitation also ensures the earliest possible correction of slipping at high speeds when the adhesion is lower than 15%, which was the value assumed during acceleration up to 70mile/h (112km/h) in the design calculations. The only items of mechanical switchgear in the power circuits are the motor contactors and the reverser.

The distinctive feature of the power car installation is that the four 750kW (1,000hp) motors are arranged longitudinally inside the vehicle, each driving one axle through a transfer gearbox, cardan shaft, and a right-angle gearbox with quill shaft drive, the box being fully suspended on the bogie frame.

The main braking system is hydrokinetic, energy being converted into heat in a water/glycol mixture by a similar action to that of an engine dynamometer. Braking effort is controlled by regulating the pressure rise through the brake. The fluid is pumped by the brake itself into a reservoir and the heat is subsequently dissipated in fan-cooled radiators. A light-duty hydraulic brake is blended in automatically at speeds below 50mile/h (80km/h) where the hydrokinetic system is less effective.

With a top speed of 150mile/h (250km/h) over existing track in view, the coach bodies are tilted inwards by up to 9° on curves to compensate for the fact that the cant of the permanent way itself would not provide a comfortable ride at speeds much in excess of 100mile/h (160km/h). Of greater significance to the future of rail traffic in general has been the development of a wheel profile and articulation system which enables wheelsets to steer round curves and to run centrally on straight track without flange contact at any time in normal operation.

The original proposal for forming the APT was for one or two power cars to be marshalled between two rakes of coaches. Each rake would then have had to have its own catering services, for although there is a corridor through the power cars it would normally be used only by train staff. Trial running with an eight-car formation of this kind (two power cars between two rakes of three trailers) was scheduled to begin between Glasgow and Preston in the summer of 1979, but at the time of writing it is probable that production electric APTs will have a power car with driving cab heading a train of 10 trailers.

The large-diameter tubular axle of an APT vehicle, designed to accommodate the hydrokinetic brake, provided the basis for an experiment which could have a profound effect on the future of electric traction. In 1975 an experimental three-phase motor in which the axle formed the rotor was demonstrated by BR Research at Derby. Inside the axle, and concentric with it, was a fixed stator with a three-phase winding, occupying the place where the turbine blades would be if the axle were fitted for hydrokinetic braking. The three-phase supply was converted from a dc input by a transistor inverter which manipulated frequency and voltage in such a way that the torque/speed curve of the motor was similar to that of a conventional traction machine. The versatility of electronics has brought within reach the goal of an induction motor for traction which does not suffer from the relatively low torque and efficiency at low speed of the conventional induction motor operating at a fixed frequency. Unlike earlier three-phase motors used for traction, it does not have sliprings and brushes because there is no need to connect resistance in the rotor circuit at starting, the voltage being controlled by the electronics. The principle also avoids the problem of supplying three-phase power through the catenary system, which hitherto has required two contact wires per track. In fact it is immaterial whether the supply is single-phase from an overhead wire or dc from a third rail.

An interesting aspect of the development is that a traction motor has been incorporated with a driving axle, as in the early traction motors with axle-mounted armatures and no transmission gears. In this form a 250hp motor eminently suitable for emu stock could be produced within an acceptable axleload, but three-phase motors with inverter supply could equally well be built with larger outputs for geared drives in locomotives.

We have been looking some way into the future. The pattern for the next generation of emu stock for ac lines was set in 1975 when the British Railways Board decided that after completion of orders in hand, new ac emus should have thyristor control. First, of the family are the 16 three-car 25kV ac units of Class 314 for the Clyderail services operated by British Railways for the Greater Glasgow Passenger Transport Executive. In general design the car bodies are similar to the Class 313 units for the Great Northern Inner Suburban electrification (Chapter 12) and the formation is similar in that the centre vehicle carries the pantograph and transformer while the end vehicles are motorcoaches with all axles motored. In this case, however, the motorcoaches carry the thyristor converters instead of a resistance control equipment. Any change in the preset level of accelerating current is detected by dc current transformers and their output is used to adjust the firing angle of the thyristors as necessary. The accelerating current is adjusted to maintain a constant rate of acceleration irrespective of train weight by means of load cells acting on the phase angle control circuits.

The Clyderail network was due to be extended in 1979 by the reopening and electrification of the line between Rutherglen and Kelvinhaugh, linking the systems south and north of the Clyde.

Below: Versions of the Class 312 emu went to the London Midland and Eastern Regions. Unit No 312.115 of the 312/1 series (equipped for dual-voltage operation) passes Stratford on a Liverpool Street-Colchester working on 29 July 1976/*Kevin Lane*

12
Suburban Areas Electrify

Electrification of the main line from Kings Cross was a long-term proposal in the British Railways Modernisation Plan of 1955 but when electric trains eventually operated from the terminus it was in the second stage of a two-part scheme covering inner and outer suburban services.

Stage 1 of the scheme, introduced on 8 November 1976, covered electrification from Welwyn Garden City on the main line and from Hertford North on the Hertford Loop to Moorgate via Drayton Park. It was primarily a 25kV ac electrification, but the $2\frac{1}{2}$ miles from Drayton Park to Moorgate had formed part of the Northern City Line of London Transport (Moorgate to Finsbury Park) and had been electrified on the LT 630V third- and fourth-rail system. This underground section was taken over by the Eastern Region, but the tunnel clearances were insufficient for a 25kV overhead system and so the line was converted to 750V dc with third-rail, retaining the fouth rail to reinforce the return current path. The rolling stock for the Welwyn-Hertford North-Moorgate services therefore had to operate on both systems of electrification.

Previously Moorgate services had travelled over the LT 'Widened Lines' via Farringdon and Barbican to which there were connections at Kings Cross. Trains to Moorgate took the line which diverged outside the terminus on the eastern side of the main lines and ran through the York Road platform before diving underground. Down trains emerged from the tunnel to call at Platform 14 in Kings Cross Suburban on the opposite side of the main line station. Both connections were removed during the remodelling of the approaches to Kings Cross in 1976/7.

The Class 313 units built for this electrification were the first dual-system stock on British Railways. Some Continental railways had already met similar situations and several classes of ac/dc locomotives were fitted with duplicate control equipments, one with a tap-changer and the other with resistances. A more convenient solution was to use a conventional dc control system on both forms of input, supplying it with dc at the appropriate voltage via a transformer and

rectifiers when running on ac, and with dc direct from the track supply on dc sections. This was the arrangement chosen for Class 313.

Basically the centre vehicle of the three-car 313 unit – the rectifier trailer – can be regarded as a travelling rectifier substation, collecting current from a pantograph on the roof and by means of a rectifier and transformer on the underframe supplying 750V dc to a conventional dc control system with resistances and series/parallel motor connections in each motorcoach. This is the arrangement while running on ac. When the unit is on the dc underground section each motorcoach takes power independently from its own pick-up shoes running on the live rail.

The changeover from overhead ac to third-rail dc is made at Drayton Park. The overhead extends through the station to the tunnel mouth, while the third rail is extended from the tunnel through the station so that the two systems overlap. A train approaching Drayton Park from Finsbury Park passes over an apc (automatic power control) magnet mounted on the sleeper ends. This trips the circuit-breaker of the train, which coasts into the station. When at rest the driver operates a mode selection switch which lowers and locks the pantograph and makes electrical connection from the pick-up shoes, now in contact with the third-rail, to the traction circuit. Should the driver not lower the pantograph a warning is sounded in the cab when the power controller is opened, but the switching makes it impossible for both supplies to be connected to the equipment simultaneously.

When the changeover switch is operated to run on dc, the connections to the power cables which interconnect the two motorcoaches for ac operation, (when both are supplied from the rectifier trailer), are broken automatically. This complies with the regulation which forbids the use on underground lines of power buslines running through a train. The dc shoegear is not retractable. It is of similar form to the 'beamless' shoegear now used in Southern stock (Chapter 10) and its minimum height when clear of the live rail is restricted by a height limiting beam. Resistance notching and series/parallel switching of the four 110hp motors in each motorcoach are controlled by a camshaft driven by an air/oil engine which also has Southern antecedents, being derived from the type first used in the CIG stock (Chapter 7). The camshaft itself is similar to the one used in the prototype high-density stock (4-PEP, Class 445) built in 1972 and operated experimentally on the Southern Region, but whereas the prototype camshafts employed an electronic logic system for certain positioning functions, the Class 313 equipment returned to electromechanical logic because the electronic system had shown no overall advantage. There are 18 control steps for motoring.

When one recalls all that was said and written about energy losses in starting resistances during the early years of ac traction in this country it may seem surprising to find resistance control in use during ac operation in stock of such recent date. The resistances in the 313 units however, are used also for rheostatic braking and heat is recovered from them for heating the motorcoaches. The motorcoach heating module has a fan and a heating element as in the trailer but the thermostat only switches on the element if insufficient

heat to maintain the set temperature is available from the resistances.

The same camshaft controls acceleration and rheostatic braking. For braking, the motors act as self-excited generators with the resistances connected across their armatures. Current now flows through the armatures in the opposite direction to when motoring, and if the fields were still in series with them the reversal of flow in the field windings would quickly wipe out the magnetic flux and stop the regenerative action. The circuit is therefore rearranged as a 'figure of eight' with the armatures of motors 1 and 2 sending current through the field windings of motors 3 and 4 and vice versa. The current direction in the fields is now the same as when motoring so that regeneration is maintained, and load sharing between the motors is improved.

Rheostatic braking is controlled by the camshaft by switching out resistance in 14 steps. It is effective from the full speed of 75mile/h down to 12–16mile/h after which air braking with disc brakes effects the final stop. Control switchgear and resistances are housed in one main equipment case under the motorcoach. Air is blown through the central resistance

section by an axial-flow fan driven by a two-speed induction motor which runs at 2,900rev/min when resistances are in circuit and at 975rev/min at all other times. The supply for the fan motor comes from a motor-alternator with a 415V three-phase output which is carried under one motorcoach of the unit. This source also provides low-voltage dc for other auxiliaries through a transformer/rectifier.

A three-car 313 unit provides 232 seats, all second class. Trains are formed of two units when required. Arriving in an area which had seen the last BR locomotive-hauled suburban non-corridor compartment stock and various elderly types of dmus, they quickly earned approval for comfort and smooth riding. The coaches have air secondary suspension, the bodies being supported on the bogie frames by air springs which allow for rotational and lateral movements in the same way as the coil springs of a flexicoil suspension (Chapter 11). Tractive forces are transmitted through rubber-bushed traction links connected with a central pivot which thus has freedom to 'float' with the movements of the body relative to the bogie. Air spring pressure is measured and converted into an electrical signal which adjusts the notching current to maintain a uniform rate of acceleration in all conditions of vehicle loading. The notching relay is static, consisting of electronic components mounted on printed circuit boards, and the circuits for blending in the rheostatic brake with the air brakes are of similar form. The trains accelerate at 0.79m/sec^2 and have a braking rate of 0.92m/sec^2. Maximum speed is 75mile/h but is automatically restricted to 30mile/h on the underground section.

The GN suburban scheme was completed in February 1978 when outer suburban electric trains began running between Kings Cross, Hitchin and Royston. The link from Langley Junction, south of Stevenage on the main line, to Hertford North was electrified at the same time but not used for electric passenger services although a dmu service was put on from Hertford North to Stevenage, Hitchin and Huntingdon. While this further stage of electrification was in progress massive civil engineering works had been undertaken to improve and rationalise the approach to Kings Cross and the terminus itself. The catenary into the terminus was energised in August 1977 when crew training began on the new emu outer suburban stock of Class 312.

Left: The 312s for the Kings Cross outer suburban electrification were turned out in the main line blue and grey livery. Unit No 312.009 speeds out of Hadley Wood Tunnel with a semi-fast to Kings Cross./*B. Denton*

Power-operated sliding doors had been tried out in peak hour and off-peak conditions during trial running of the Class 445 prototype stock in the Southern Region and it was decided to use a similar system in Class 313. In this stock, however, opening was initiated by the passengers by pushing the leaves of the door apart (in theory after the train had come to rest) after which power took over. Commuters in the early days discovered that they could beat the unforgiving minute by forcing the doors apart while the train was still moving and modifications were necessary to make the locking positive. Experts in ergonomics and human engineering debated whether it would not have been preferable to stick to the pushbutton system used in the Class 445 vehicles.

Class 312, of which there were various versions to suit different Regions, was an up-date of Class 310. The same system of low-tension tap-changing with individual contactors was retained, also the natural cooling of rectifier and transformer, but the insulating washers were of boron nitride instead of beryllium oxide and the number of diodes was reduced from 48 to 16. A similar rectifier had been supplied for Glasgow suburban stock of Classes 303 and 311 since 1968. The 312 unit formation consists of battery driving trailer, motorcoach (four 300hp motors), trailer, and driving trailer composite. All seating is in open saloons and there is inter-vehicle communication throughout the unit. In Class 310 units there is no gangway connection between the two intermediate vehicles.

Class 312 units for the Kings Cross outer suburban services accelerate at 0.4m/sec^2 and have a top speed of 90mile/h, these characteristics being suited to their relatively long inter-station runs and to operation on fast tracks shared with HSTs and other long distance trains. In the Kings Cross 312s, and in those built for services of the West Midland PTE worked by the LMR, the transformers have a single primary winding for 25kV although provision was made for fitting a four-section primary and automatic voltage selection equipment for 25kV/6.25kV operation if necessary. Units for service on the main line from Liverpool Street were supplied with dual-voltage equipment as changeover at Shenfield was still in operation when they were delivered. Air-blast circuit-breakers, the louvres in the motorcoach side walls through which air is drawn for the self-ventilated traction motors, and the hinged 'slam' doors are visible reminders that this stock was the product of design policies that were soon to be modified.

The Kings Cross suburban electrification attracted international interest and was visited by railwaymen from many parts of the world while the work on the electrification itself and the remodelling of the Kings Cross approaches was in progress. A particular object of interest both then and since has been the electric maintenance depot at Hornsey where on a site of some 20 acres alongside the East Coast main line there is a complex of technical and administrative services concerned with maintaining the electric traction fixed equipment, cleaning and servicing the rolling stock and controlling power supplies. In equipment and organisation the depot represents the results of 20 years experience of suburban and main line electrification.

Multiple-unit stock based at the depot for servicing when I visited Hornsey while writing this book comprised 64 Class 313 units and 26 of Class 312. The depot also had two battery locomotives which had been Class 501 motorcoaches on the LMR London area third-rail electrification until they became surplus to requirements. One was on loan to Cricklewood for work on the St Pancras-Bedford electrification at the time of my visit.

It was interesting to note the emphasis on cleaning rolling stock, particularly necessary at a time when so many commuters are motorists in their leisure hours and probably compulsive weekend car cleaners. At Hornsey cleaning is regarded as part of the maintenance cycle. The washing plant at the depot was dealing with 28 Class 313 units and 10 Class 312s between peak hours every day, while overnight 26 Class 313s and six 312s passed through. After external washing, units enter the shed where five of the six roads have platforms alongside to facilitate internal cleaning. Something like 85% of the stock has its floors washed and polished and seats dusted every day of the week. A simplified external washing procedure and internal cleaning also take place at certain stabling points. One or two units arriving at Hornsey each day will be due for 'heavy cleaning', which takes place every six weeks and involves replacing the removable seat covers and backs, washing and polishing roofs, bodysides and associated fittings.

The philosophy of maintenance at the depot is based on the fact that the rolling stock has been designed for first-line servicing by replacement of faulty components. Units come in for examinations at intervals of 14 days, defective parts are identified and sent away to a repair depot, and replacements are fitted from the depot stores, which hold some 7,000 items. The operating department is given a 14-day forecast of when units will be required for servicing, the first seven days being a firm programme and the next seven provisional. Diagrams are changed as necessary so that units are available at the depot on the morning of their examination day. The depot carries out all examinations except the yearly and two yearly between the peak business hours and normally has ten units to work on every day. Inevitably some defects occur

while a unit is in service. A driver reports any difficulties to Hornsey by telephone from his next terminal point. The traction control desk at the depot is manned 24 hours a day, seven days a week, and the supervisor can call on a small team of trouble shooters for dealing with incidents of this kind.

The basic 14-day examination schedule specifies 53 operations ranging from an inspection of all underframe equipment, including brake pads, to checking that the ladders for detraining passengers in emergency are in good condition. Pantographs receive a detailed check at this examination and the pan head is changed if any of the three carbons are badly damaged, burned or worn below a minimum depth of 1/16in at any point above the clips that hold them. At the end of three 14-day periods the 42-day examination adds 12 more items, among them a detailed check of traction motors and auxiliary machines, with interior cleaning and replacement of brushes if necessary. At this stage, also, tyres are gauged. The depot has an advanced type of wheel profiling lathe which will reprofile all the tyres of an emu vehicle in less than five hours without removing the wheels. The machine works to the 'half-worn' profile which was established during the development of the APT and has proved as effective in maximising time between profiling for other classes of stock as for specialised high-speed vehicles.

The maintenance cycle continues with two more 14-day inspections before a more detailed examination at 84 days, and so on up to a two-yearly examination, after which units are due for a visit to the main works.

Brake pads are examined every 14 days. Distances run between renewals have rocketed compared with cast iron brake blocks. Pads on 312 units when I visited Hornsey had a life of 25,500km on motorcoaches and 55,700km on trailers, compared with 3,200km and 18,000km for cast iron blocks on an equivalent service. At the same period, while rheostatic braking on Class 313s was being recalibrated, motorcoaches of that series were running 19,300km and trailers 45,000km between renewals and it was estimated that with the rheostatic brake back in service there would be an improvement by a factor of four. Hornsey's 313s are intensively used, running 260,000 miles in a four-week period. A typical diagram extends over 22 hours, starting with a Kings Cross-Welwyn Garden City trip at 02.25 and finishing at Hornsey at 00.29. Return trips from Moorgate to Hertford North and to Welwyn Garden City alternate, often with turnround times as short as 5min.

In the stores at Hornsey I saw conventional traction control equipment alongside the printed circuit boards of accelerating relays and wheel slip-and-slide detection systems. At that time the components on the boards were identifiable as resistors, capacitors, transistors and diodes but one could already imagine the day when boards will carry only anonymous 'packages' containing integrated circuits of increasing degrees of complexity until each package becomes a system in itself.

Hornsey undertook driver training in the run-up to electrification and was still running courses when I was there, for drivers from the Scottish Region. In an energy conscious age, emphasis is placed on coasting after reaching line speed for as long as this speed can be maintained, but using judgment in balancing economy with the need to keep to the timetable. The falling gradients towards Kings Cross help matters by enabling a train which passes Potters Bar at 90mile/h to coast the rest of the way into Kings Cross in the time allowed by the timetable.

Feeder stations for the GN overhead suburban system electrification, are at Wood Green and Welwyn Garden City. At Welwyn there is an adjacent CEGB supply point, but although there is a similar point at Hornsey it was not possible to site the railway feeder station close to it and so power is fed over an oil-filled cable to Wood Green. In the underground section a railway 11kV ring main with connections at two points, to the local electricity authority's 11kV system supplies rectifier substations at Drayton Park and Moorgate. Power supplies are controlled and monitored from the Electric Control Centre at Hornsey by an electronic scanning system similar to that installed for the Weaver Junction-Glasgow section of the LMR electrification. Another feature in common with Weaver Junction-Glasgow was the adoption of the Mk IIIA simple catenary overhead system in which the contact wire is allowed a sag of 100mm (about 4in) in mid-span. Experience with earlier sections of the LMR electrification had shown that a level contact wire tended to form a series of 'humps' ahead of the pantograph which spoiled current collection at high-speed. A similar lift of a 'sagged' wire resulted in a level contact surface and good collection up to about 110mile/h. The older catenary south of Crewe has been modified to impart a similar sag by lengthening the droppers between the main and auxiliary cables of the suspension.

A modification of Mk IIIA catenary known as Mk IIIB was adopted for the next 25kV electrification in the London suburban area – St Pancras-Bedford, authorised in November 1976. The essential differences between the two types are in the tensions of the catenary and contact wires. In Mk IIIA the catenary is under mechanical tension of 1,140kg whereas the contact wire is under the lower tension of 910kg. In Mk IIIB both catenary and contact wire are under the same tension of 1,140kg, an arrangement which is considered to make for better current collection. In Mk IIIA catenary the contact wire is allowed to wear down to 50% of its original mass before replacement but in IIIB it is replaced when wear has reached 33%. The copper is recoverable and a valuable material. With this consideration in mind, more frequent renewals in the interest of good current collection are not seen as a disadvantage.

The St Pancras-Bedford electrification, scheduled for completion in 1982, covers 53 route-miles, including the section from Kentish Town to Moorgate over the LT 'Widened Lines'. By increasing lateral clearances in the tunnel between Kentish and Kings Cross underground (Widened Lines) station, it is possible to use 25kV throughout. A long-established travel pattern will change. Hitherto services between Midland line stations and Moorgate have run in peak hours only, generally confined to three up trains in the morning and three down in the evening. They were not heavily patronised at one period and it was sometimes more comfortable to join a down City train in the evening at Kings Cross Widened Lines station than to scramble for a seat in a dmu at St Pancras in competition with the rush hour crowds arriving from Kings Cross and St Pancras tube station. The problem was to find the Widened Lines station, of which few Londoners seemed to have heard if asked the way to it, and the directions they gave usually landed one up in the booking hall of Kings Cross & St Pancras. But it was worth persisting, and the reward in the days of which I speak was not simply a seat but haulage by a locomotive. This was before British Rail had introduced its Spotters' Friend numbering system with the Class indicated by the first two digits, and we lumped all the City trains locomotives together as 'Type 2s', but some may have been Class 24s of glamorous memory. There was also a brief appearance on this service of the Co-Bos, and the story that because of their length they scraped the sides of the tunnel between Kentish Town and Kings Cross at one of the curves.

In the future the service between Midland stations and Moorgate will assume new importance. Kings Cross Widened Lines station will be developed as the principal interchange point for the LT tube system, with direct subways from its platforms to the Piccadilly and Victoria Lines. The subway connection with the tube at St Pancras main line station is not well laid out for handling rush hour crowds. In the electrification timetable Moorgate will take the main suburban service throughout the day, with about 12 trains between St Albans and Moorgate in the peak and three trains an hour to Moorgate off-peak, two starting from Luton and one from Bedford. Four limited stop trains will run from Bedford to St Pancras in the peak hour and off-peak there will be an hourly train from Bedford to St Pancras calling at all stations to Radlett. Colour-light signalling over the whole route and extending north of Bedford to Sharnbrook will be controlled from a power box at West Hampstead.

The Midland line electric services will be operated by a fleet of 48 four-car emus with a maximum speed of 90mile/h and providing first and second class accommodation. In general arrangement they will be a development of Class 313 but equipped for ac operation only. Without the constraint of providing for ac/dc operation which entailed using resistances in Class 313, the traction motors in the new Class 317 will be thyristor-controlled.

Below: First of the 4-PEP derivatives, a Class 313 unit pauses at Hadley Wood with a Moorgate-Welwyn Garden City service on 24 March 1978./*L. Bertram*

13
LT and LRT

Many years ago a railway signal engineer foresaw the day when 'the signals will drive the trains'. Today the forecast has been brought close to reality on the Victoria Line of London Transport. Experiments with automatic train operation were begun by London Transport as long ago as April 1962, when trials took place between Acton and South Ealing. A passenger train with prototype equipment went into service between two District Line stations a year later, and in April 1964 London Transport inaugurated a complete service of automatic trains between Hainault and Woodford. The system used was the one later installed on the Victoria Line, opened throughout between Walthamstow Central and Brixton in 1971.

Automatic acceleration is a familiar aspect of emu working, and once the process has been initiated the train will attain balancing speed without further action. In the simplest possible arrangement it would then only be necessary to switch off power at a selected point before the next station and thereafter control braking to a standstill. The Victoria Line system performs these and other control functions in two ways. Certain 'safety' information is conveyed to the train continuously by inductive pick-up of the currents in the signalling track circuits, which are in the form of pulses occurring at various rates per minute according to the instruction to be given. Other instructions, such as to stop between stations, begin coasting, and regulate speed down to a standstill by braking, are given by audio-frequency currents applied to the track at specific points called 'command spots'.

Automatic driving cannot take place unless one of the safety codes is being picked up from the track. A code of 420 pulses/min allows a train to start from a station and accelerate to full speed after the driver (or 'train attendant') has pressed two pushbuttons simultaneously to show that doors are closed and it is safe to depart. While the train is in motion the code may change to 180 pulses/min, which initiates coasting and controls the brakes so that speed does not exceed 22mile/h. If a signal is at 'danger' a command spot a suitable distance ahead will be energised and the brak-ing increased to bring the train to a standstill. When the signal clears the track code changes to 270 pulses/min, which restarts the train automatically. While this pulse rate is maintained the train is restricted to 22mile/h, alternately motoring and coasting as necessary. Restoration of the 420 code allows acceleration to full speed.

Stopping in a station is controlled by a sequence of 'spots', the first switching off the motors so that the train coasts and the remainder transmitting frequencies proportional to the speed at which the train should be travelling at each point in order to stop accurately in the platform. Actual speed is compared with the 'command' speed and the braking adjusted accordingly.

Fully automatic working is now known as automatic train control (atc) – a term and initials formerly applied to a signalling practice. The London Transport system is not full atc because the driver controls the doors and the length of the stop at stations (the 'start and accelerate' code is not effective until he has pressed his pushbuttons). Strictly speaking it is a combination of two atc sub-systems – atp (automatic train protection, ie the control frequencies continuously present in the track) and ato (automatic train operation, ie the functions of the 'command spots').

Since the new trains for the extension of the Metropolitan Line electrification to Amersham in 1960, London Transport has been using 300V traction motors connected in series pairs. The practice is continued in the 1973 tube stock, (which actually appeared in 1976). From the new trains for the Victoria Line onwards, all LT stock has been equipped with rheostatic braking, and in the 1973 stock motorcoaches the resistors are forced-ventilated by a motor-blower combined with the motor-alternator auxiliary supply set. A six-car train of this stock consists of two three-car units with their cars semi-permanently coupled. The unit formation of motorcoach, trailer, and non-driving motorcoaches provides 8 motored axles out of 12, or two-thirds motored axles per train compared with half in other recent tube stock. The traction equipment has

Above: Prototype Metrocar for the Tyne and Wear Metro on the test track at Middle Engine Lane in 1978./*I. S. Carr*

been redesigned to use a single camshaft in place of the two carried by earlier motorcoaches with rheostatic braking. There are three weak-field steps, which are used in starting as well as at the top of the speed range. The train starts in weakest field with all resistance in series and full-field is only attained on the fourth of the 20 motoring notches – a procedure known as 'soft notch' starting. It sounds a refinement, but in a service with large numbers of standing passengers often dependent on each other for maintaining the perpendicular the smooth start is probably appreciated.

London Transport began work with chopper control in 1965 and has operated two four-car trains with this type of equipment on the Woodford-Hainault branch to test the effect on signalling equipment. New prototype chopper equipments being commissioned in 1978 incorporated rheostatic/regenerative braking with automatic changeover between the two modes so that energy can be returned to the line whenever conditions permit. In LT conditions chopper control is only considered economic if associated with energy saving by regeneration. It has other advantages, however, such as fewer moving parts, quicker response to different conditions of loading, and improved line current regulation because the large peaks associated with resistance control are absent. In the latest LT equipments the chopper occupies most of the car underframe and the chopper case itself is force-ventilated. The capsule type thyristors are cooled on both faces by being mounted between heat sinks.

Offsetting the advantages of the regenerative chopper are the constraints imposed on timetabling to ensure that trains are in proximity to each other to absorb regenerated power, and extra switchgear required for a modified system of substation inter-connection. For these reasons the LTE is also studying energy storage by flywheel as a long-term possibility and is developing a scheme based in principle on the flywheel booster circuit of the three original Southern Co-Co locomotives. It is estimated that a 25% energy saving could be achieved with accelerating and braking characteristics distinctly better than with other methods of control. There are problems at present, however, in high noise level and the very high reliability requirements set by the Department of the Environment if flywheels revolving at some 10,000rev/min are to be installed in passenger carrying vehicles.

City railway operations such as those of London Transport have long been described as 'rapid transit'. More recently the term 'light rapid transit' (lrt) has come into use to describe systems in which the vehicles are often of the articulated tramcar style long familiar on the Continent, and run on reserved tracks above ground in outer areas but enter tunnel sections with underground stations in city centres. The first example of such a system in Great Britain is on Tyneside.

Two British Rail electrified services had been based on Newcastle Central station. One was the North Tyne Loop via the coast to West Monkseaton and back to Newcastle via South Gosforth and Jesmond; the other was the line south of the river through Gateshead to South Shields. The last electric trains ran in 1967 but services were maintained to West Monkseaton and to South Shields by diesel multiple-units.

A detailed study of the North Tyne Loop was undertaken by the Tyneside PTE, this being the busier of the two lines and also the one with the largest deficit. Various alternatives were examined, including conversion of much of the Loop into a bus way. The conclusion was reached, however, that the transport needs of the area would be best met by developing an integrated rail/road system with Light Rapid Transit over the existing suburban rail routes north and south of the Tyne as its backbone. A grant was obtained under the terms of the 1968 Act and in 1972 the Tyneside Metropolitan Railway Bill was presented to Parliament, receiving the Royal Assent in the following year. This was the beginning of the Tyne and Wear Metro, so named because the PTE had become the Tyne and Wear PTE upon local government re-organisation in 1974.

The rail operations of the Metro were not planned simply to run over former BR tracks. Newcastle Central station may have been appropriately named in the past, but the city has spread northwards away from the River Tyne so that the station is now at one end of it, and the BR rail routes lie to the east of the central area. The Metro has therefore built two lines totalling 6.4km (4 miles) in tunnel under the centre of the city. The North-South line leaves the BR lines immediately north of Jesmond station and passes under the central city area in twin tunnels with new underground stations at Jesmond, Haymarket, Monument, Central Station and Gateshead. The line makes a short but impressive reappearance between two tunnel sections to cross the Tyne on a bridge with a span of 164.5m (540ft), the longest span on the river and a noteworthy addition to the panorama of bridges seen by the traveller arriving at Newcastle by rail from the South. After Gateshead underground station the line finally surfaces at Old Fold and joins the former South Tyne electrified line to South Shields, but after Tyne Dock it follows a new alignment to South Shields via Chichester (the first syllable here rhymes with 'pie'), which is the focus of the local bus system. It has been Metro policy to bring public transport where it is needed today. Another example is at Byker where a high-density housing area has developed away from the old station and a new alignment has been followed to provide it and the adjacent shopping area with a conveniently sited station.

The West-East line starts underground in a new terminal at St James and runs via Monument (interchange with the North-South line) and a new underground station at Manors before surfacing to cross the Ouseburn valley on a new viaduct to Byker. The North Tyne Loop is joined west of Walkergate BR station, the route continuing round the coast, through South Gosforth and southward to join the North-South underground line at Jesmond. The whole system comprises 12.8 route-km (8 route-miles) of new construction and 41 route-km (25 route-miles) of existing railway, but where existing tracks are used the Metro and BR services operate as separate systems. The two administrations collaborated in various engineering works to preserve separation, and common user of tracks is confined to a section with a minimal BR freight service where part of the former Ponteland branch from South Gosforth has been rebuilt to serve the Regent Centre Interchange and new development extending to Kenton Bank Foot. Regent Centre is one of several Interchanges laid out for easy exchange between road travel by public or private transport and rail. Bus services will be rerouted to serve the Interchanges and surrounding areas, bringing a useful reduction of road traffic in the city centre, and BR/Metro exchange stations will enable many travellers to reach their destinations without using surface road transport.

In planning the Metro consideration was given to using a third rail supply at about 750V, but local climatic and other conditions would have made a protected rail necessary and this would have brought clearance problems. Moreover, the Chief Inspecting Officer of Railways ruled that an unprotected third rail is only permissible as an extension to an existing system, and the Tyneside lines which had used third rail were no longer electrified. Finally the 1,500V dc system with overhead supply was chosen after a detailed study of the electrical requirements of the whole project and cost comparisons with overhead supplies at 1,000 and 750V dc. The eight substations required at 1,500V are just over half the number that would have been necessary at 750V and there was a considerable saving in capital costs. Comparing energy consumption at 1,000 and 1,500V on a typical station-to-station section it was shown that there was a saving of 9% with the higher voltage and, of course, there was the practical advantage of using a standard system.

Traction and passenger substations in the central area are fed by two 11kV ring main circuits supplied from a Metro primary substation fed at 33kV from the North Eastern Electricity Board bulk supply point at South Gosforth. In the outer area careful study of the local power supply situation enabled the traction substations to be sited close enough to supply points for them to be fed direct. The feeder cables are of cross-link polythene with copper conductors and a copper tape screen. This form of solid dielectric cable can operate at higher temperatures than cables of similar cross-section of older types and does not have the same problem of voids forming with expansion and contraction under changing load conditions. In this respect its qualities are similar to those of oil-filled cables, but without the complication of reservoirs and pressure-monitoring arrangements.

The six outer area substations are designed to have a capacity of 2MW, and South Gosforth, Byker and

Old Fold have 4.5MW installations. There is provision at South Gosforth for a further 1.5MW. The electrical system was planned as a whole, supplies for services at the underground stations and 415V signalling supplies being incorporated in the traction substation installations. The whole scheme was tested by computer. Comparative studies have shown the cost to be below that of what is believed to be the cheapest comparable existing supply system.

The remote supervisory control system at South Gosforth is computer based. The power network for traction and other services is shown in outline on a panel diagram, which is normally dark but signals a change of state, such as a circuit-breaker trip, with a flashing light at the appropriate position. Controls are transmitted from a keyboard on the operator's desk, and he can call up a fully detailed diagram of any substation area for presentation on a visual display unit. This shows all the switchgear, isolators, etc which may have to be operated from the control room or by staff on the spot under the operator's instructions in dealing with an incident.

The catenary and contact wire in the overhead system are both of copper, providing the required conductivity with a contact wire of the same cross-section as in BR 25kV electrification, with which many of the fittings are common. Special efforts were made to design a system that would be unobtrusive. Simple catenary with cantilever supports is used on open-line sections. Through stations the contact wires are supported directly from span-wires on poles at 40m (131ft) spacing. Where, as in these places and through the underground tunnels, there is no catenary, there are two contact wires over each track so that the copper cross-section remains the same.

Porcelain insulators, perhaps the most obtrusive items of lineside cantilevers, have been replaced by a new type of glass fibre rod insulator only 90mm (3½in) in overall diameter and 380mm (15in) long, with a cover of irradiated silicone rubber protecting the rod and its end fittings. This insulator has withstood severe impact tests and the rubber has a self-sealing quality which gives maximum protection of the rod against all kinds of damage.

The policy in equipping the whole system has been to use proven items wherever possible. In designing rolling stock for the first transport service of its kind in this country, some features were based on Continental

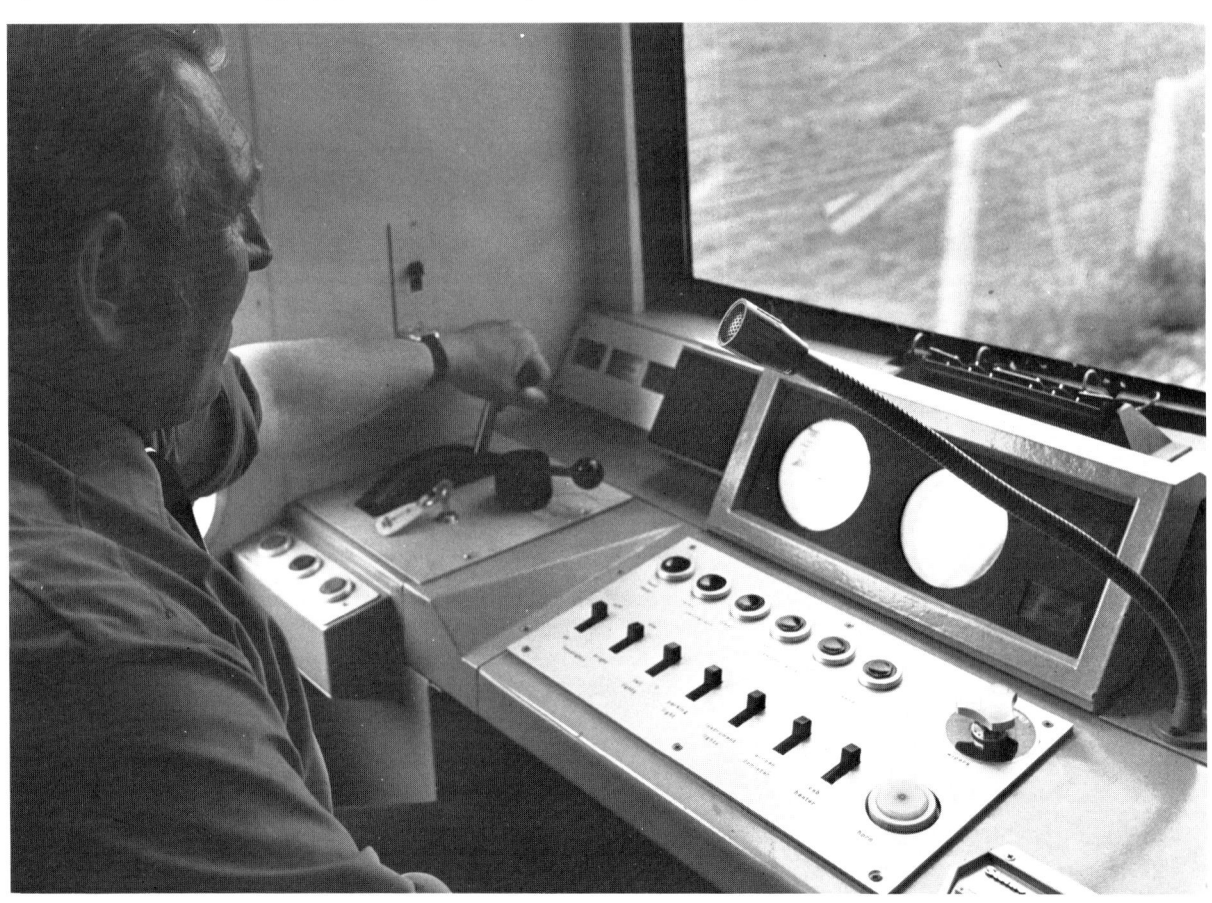

practice and experience. The Metro vehicle is an articulated car 27.8m (91.2ft) long overall carried on three bogies, each outer bogie being powered by one 185kW (248hp) motor driving both axles. The motors are mounted longitudinally and each drives both axles of its bogie through right-angle gearboxes bolted to each end of the motor frame. Transmission is by quill drives through couplings incorporating rubber rings fitted between discs on the quill shafts and on the axles.

Seats are provided in the car for 84 passengers; over 200 can be carried in crush load conditions but normal peak-hour loads average about 160 per car. The cars can operate singly or in sets of up to three under multiple-unit control from the leading vehicle. Ample provision has been made in the design for short-distance urban travel requirements, with space for prams, push-chairs and luggage in the wide bays at the entrances and over the articulation bogie. Noise levels are low, the vehicles having air secondary suspension, chevron rubber primary suspension between bogie frames and axleboxes, and resilient wheels. The plug type doors are positively sealed all round when closed and leave maximum free space inside the car. Doors are released by the driver and can then be opened by passenger pushbuttons. They are closed by the driver.

With the type of traction motor installed in the cars the required operating characteristic is obtained with the two machines in each vehicle permanently in series during motoring. The three continuous running steps are full-field, inter-field, and weak-field, and there is the usual shunting notch with all resistance in series. The motors have compensating windings to maintain good commutation in conditions of low-field strength and operate at 48% and 25% of full-field in the intermediate and weak-field notches respectively. Both these running notches are preceded by an introductory step of field weakening.

For rheostatic braking the motors are connected in a conventional figure-of-eight circuit with the fields cross-connected for self-excitation (Chapter 11). Notching is by a camshaft operated by an air/oil engine similar to the type fitted in Southern Region stock since the Kent Coast electrification and described in Chapter 7. There are separate resistance banks for acceleration and braking, with the accelerating resistors and a small section of braking resistance under one half of the vehicle, the rest of the braking

bank being under the other. This distribution helps to equalise the return of waste heat from the resistances to the interior of the car when the temperature requires it. Air is blown over the resistances by fans running on the 415V three-phase auxiliary system and can be ducted into the car mixed with cold air to produce the required temperature under the control of thermostats. When waste heat recovery is not required, the circuit can be reversed and air drawn out of the car and discharged underneath it.

Maximum service speed is 80km/h (50mile/h). Resistance notching is controlled by a static relay to give an initial acceleration of $1m/sec^2$ up to about 40km/h, which is maintained by load weighing control. Maximum service braking produces a retardation of $1.3m/sec^2$; use of the magnetic track brakes increases this value to over $2.3m/sec^2$.

Many features of the stock are in line with current main line practice which is described elsewhere in this book and others are likely to be seen more widely in future, such as the combination of power and braking control in one handle, which is moved forward to accelerate and backwards to brake the train. Four service braking rates plus emergency braking can be selected. Disc brakes are fitted to all axles but during service braking only the rheostatic brake acts on the motor bogie axles down to a speed of 15–20km/h (9–12mile/h). Below that speed the two disc brakes on each motor bogie operate in addition to the four discs on the centre bogie which are operative throughout. For an emergency application the rheostatic brake is cut out and air braking is applied to all axles, supplemented by two magnetic track brakes on each bogie which are energised from a battery to make them independent of the air supply. A futher safety feature is that the air brakes are applied by springs, the air pressure acting against them and being reduced to increase the braking effort so that loss of air supply would result in a full application. This arrangement also enable the discs to act as a parking brake.

Wheel slip and slide control is based on measurement of axle speeds by probes in proximity to toothed wheels on the axles acting in conjuction with electronic counting and comparator circuits. Wheel slide during braking is detected by a 'rate of change of speed' circuit and by comparison of axle speeds which in case of deviation from normal conditions releases the air brakes and halts camshaft progression on the half-car affected until the slide stops.

Scharfenberg and BSI automatic couplers were evaluated on the Metro's test track in the prototype vehicles and the somewhat simpler BSI type was found to be adequate for Metro requirements. Pantographs are of British manufacture.

With the development of track/train communication,

Left: Driving position in a Metrocar. The driver's hand is on the controller, which is pushed forward to accelerate and pulled back to brake the train.
/*Crown copyright, Department of Industry*

motive power can no longer be considered in complete isolation from the system on which it runs. The Metro trains carry Vetag positive train identification (PTI) equipment for passing information to a trackside unit via a tuned loop mounted between the rails. The driver can set up various information in coded form, including train number and destination. A passive transponder is carried on the vehicle and when interrogated transmits the information, which is used to operate platform indicators, to select routes through the route relay interlocking equipment, and to provide train descriptions on the control centre mimic diagram. The PTE had already been operating a two-way uhf radio link with buses and this will be duplicated for communication between the Metro control centre and the trains, and between control and operations

supervisors, station supervisors and maintenance staff. The trains are equipped for public address from the driver's cab and by means of the radio link the control centre can speak direct to passengers. The system is arranged so that conversations on the radio link are as secure as on an ordinary telephone, being inaudible except to the two correspondents.

Ordinary lineside signalling is by automatic two-aspect colour-lights and all lines on which passenger trains operate are track-circuited. Level crossings are without gates or barriers but protection by flashing lights is planned. The crossings at Howdon-on-Tyne and Coxlodge are at station locations. Here the platforms are 'staggered' on each side of the road and the road is not closed to road traffic until a train has come to rest at a platform, when the warnings are initiated

automatically. Train stops will give protection if a signal is passed at danger and the track brakes can stop the train very quickly.

Closed circuit television is used for station surveillance and for showing drivers at stations when the train doors are clear and can be closed. The driver's position is on the left, so that he could not see the doors in use at island platforms underground or at certain open-air stations without leaving his seat. Cameras on the platforms are therefore linked with monitors on the left-hand side of the track where they can be clearly seen from the driving position.

On the Continent tramways had been put underground in cities such as Frankfurt in the 1960s, but we had dispensed with our tramways by the time the Tyne and Wear scheme was planned. The task has been to convert an under-used suburban railway into a system of a kind that will make this country familiar with benefits that Continental cities have enjoyed for many years. Whatever opinions may be held about past attitudes to light rail city transport, history did at least create a situation which enabled the Tyne and Wear Metro to start with a clean sheet and access to technical advances which were not available to the pioneers of LRT.

Below: The first production Metrocar at South Gosforth car sheds after delivery./*Tyne and Wear Transport*

Index